STUDIES IN GEOGRAPHY IN HUNGARY, 16

Research Institute of Geography
Hungarian Academy of Sciences, Budapest

Chief editor:
  M. PÉCSI

Editorial board:
  L. GÓCZÁN, Z. KERESZTESI, ZS. KERESZTESI,
  Á. KERTÉSZ, D. LÓCZY, S. MAROSI, P. POLYÁNSZKY

ENVIRONMENTAL MANAGEMENT

BRITISH AND HUNGARIAN CASE STUDIES

ENVIRONMENTAL MANAGEMENT

BRITISH AND HUNGARIAN CASE STUDIES

Edited by

PAUL A. COMPTON
The Queen's University of Belfast

MÁRTON PÉCSI
Research Institute of Geography
Hungarian Academy of Sciences, Budapest

AKADÉMIAI KIADÓ, BUDAPEST 1984

Translated by
  Gy. BORA
  E. DARÓCZI
  L. GÖŐZ
  D. LÓCZY
  O. TOMSCHEY

Revised by
  P. A. COMPTON
  D. LÓCZY

Technical board:
  L. BASSA, ZS. KERESZTESI, M. KRETZOI,
  M. MOLNÁR, I. POÓR, E. TARPAY, K. TORNALLYAY

ISBN 963 05 3696 X

Printed in Hungary

84 004999

AUTHORS' LIST

Gy. BORA
   Department of Economic and Regional Geography
   Karl Marx University of Economics - Budapest

E. DARÓCZI
   Geographical Research Institute of the Hungarian
   Academy of Sciences - Budapest

L. GÓCZÁN
   Geographical Research Institute of the Hungarian
   Academy of Sciences - Budapest

L. GÖŐZ
   Teachers' Training College - Nyíregyháza

A. HOARE
   University of Bristol - Bristol

P.T. KIVELL
   University of Keele - Keele

D. KULCSÁR
   Department of Economic and Regional Geography
   Karl Marx University of Economics - Budapest

D. LÓCZY
   Geographical Research Institute of the Hungarian
   Academy of Sciences - Budapest

C.C. PARK
   University of Lancaster - Bailrigg, Lancaster

M. PÉCSI
   Geographical Research Institute of the Hungarian
   Academy of Sciences - Budapest

F. PROBÁLD
   Department of Geography
   Eötvös Loránd University - Budapest

T. O'RIORDAN
   University of East Anglia - Norwich

R. SIDAWAY
   Countryside Commission - Cheltenham

D.J. SPOONER
   University of Hull - Hull

D. SYMES
   University of Hull - Hull

P.T. WHEELER
   University of Nottingham - Nottingham

CONTENTS

PREFACE

Man's activities throughout the world are placing the environment under increasing pressure. In many areas it is pressure on the natural environment that is the principal concern. The threat of starvation is pushing back the last remaining wildernesses with the resulting destruction of natural ecosystems as man searches for new land to cultivate; while the newly industrialising countries may be profligate in their use of natural resources as they strive for development. By contrast, in technologically advanced nations the concern is just as likely to be about pressure on the man-made environment as on the natural environment, and dereliction and the encroachment of industry and urban sprawl on agricultural land may be regarded as much a threat as the pollution of the atmosphere and of surface water bodies. Given such widespread pressures, the need to manage the environment in a rational manner so as to conserve it for the use and appreciation of future generations is a manifest task for today.

The management of the environment is essentially an interdisciplinary task, requiring an understanding of both natural and human forces. A balance must be struck between the requirements of man on the one hand and the requirements of the environment on the other, and a fuller appreciation is required by man of his dependence on the environment for his economic well-being and standard of living. The management of the environment is an area in which geographers have a valuable contribution to make given the interdisciplinary nature of their subject, which transcends the traditional boundary between the natural and social sciences. Geographers are equipped with an understanding of the nature of both physical and socio-economic processes but more importantly of the interactions between the two. As a consequence they are less likely to emphasise one set of processes at the expense of another and are more able to see the task of environmental management in its complex totality.

The management of the environment is a topic of some urgency and given the important work which geographers have already

undertaken in the field it was selected as the theme of the
Third British-Hungarian Geographical Seminar held in the United
Kingdom between September 16 and 25 1982. The seminar took the
form of an exchange of views about environmental management in
Hungary and the United Kingdom and the papers presented at the
formal session conducted in the School of Environmental Sciences,
University of East Anglia, Norwich, comprise the subject of
this publication.

Hungary and the United Kingdom are two very contrasting
countries, with divergent histories, economic structures and
ideologies. Two examples will suffice to illustrate the depth
of these differences; Hungary for instance is still investing
heavily in its manufacturing base whereas Britain has entered
the post-industrial era and is rapidly de-industrialising.
Moreover, Hungary is socialist in organisation and ideology and
relies on economic planning, whereas the United Kingdom operates a mixed economy involving both private and state ownership
in which commercial considerations are generally paramount.
Such fundamentally different characteristics obviously have an
important bearing on the question of environmental management.
Yet the members of the seminar found that they were speaking
the same scientific language, were expressing the same general
opinion and held essentially the same set of values with regard to the environment. The differences in outlook that did
emerge were largely ones of emphasis and not of principle.

In both countries there is a concern about the management
of the industrial and urban environment but whereas in Hungary
the main threat is seen as urban expansion on to good agricultural land, in Britain there is much concern about the problems
of industrial dereliction. The management and conservation of
recreational areas is another common theme and it is clear that
similar problems now face the management of the Norfolk Broads
in Britain and Lake Balaton in Hungary. The conflict of interests surrounding the use of water in general is paralleled
in both countries as is the need to develop and manage alternative, renewable energy sources. On the other hand, the stress
placed on the evaluation of land in Hungary for the purpose of

rational planning in agriculture is not to be found in Britain largely because of the different ways in which farming is organised in the two countries. Similarly, the concern with the environmental management of Britain's coalfields is not echoed in Hungary because of differences in geological endowment.

A volume such as this cannot, however, present a comprehensive view of environmental management in Hungary and the United Kingdom. Nor has this been the intention. Rather the volume presents what is hoped to be a representative sample of the type of research work that is currently being undertaken by geographers in the two countries. The reader is asked to treat each contribution as a study in its own right, and not to seek a closely woven framework into which each paper neatly fits. The aim has been to inform the reader of the comparative positions in Hungary and the United Kingdom through the presentation of a series of case studies.

Drs Paul COMPTON and Malcolm MOSELEY organised the seminar on behalf of the Institute of British Geographers. They are indebted to the British Council whose generous financial support made the seminar possible; to Professor John CLARKE, Professor Ian SIMMONS and Dr. D. POCOCK /Department of Geography, University of Durham/ who entertained the Hungarian party in Durham; to Drs Neville DOUGLAS, Noel MITCHEL, Stephen ROYLE and Bernard SMITH /Department of Geography, The Queen's University of Belfast/ who led excursions in Northern Ireland to the Mourne Mountains, the Ards Peninsula, the City of Belfast and the Giant's Causeway; to Professor W. KIRK and the Queen's University of Belfast for hospitality; to Keith GRIME /Department of Geography, Salford University/ for his expert guidance around Merseyside and Manchester; to Professor Tim O'RIORDAN /School of Environmental Sciences, University of East Anglia/ who demonstrated the problems of the Norfolk Broads in the field: to the School of Environmental Sciences, University of East Anglia for the use of their facilities; to the Great Britain - East Europe Centre for hospitality in London.

The Editors

GEOGRAPHICAL STUDIES OF THE ENVIRONMENT IN HUNGARY

M. PÉCSI

1. ENVIRONMENTAL MANAGEMENT AND THE CONCEPT OF AN INTEGRATED GEOGRAPHICAL ENVIRONMENT

During the last decade we have emphasized in several papers the need for further development of the theoretical and practical relationships between landscape evolution and the qualitative assessment of the total geographical environment /Pécsi 1972, 1973, 1974, 1975, 1980/. Considering the needs that land use and regional planning have for geographical information, stress has been laid upon the elaboration and application of a regional assessment approach within the framework of an integrated environment.

According to our concept the landscape is both a natural historical and social historical category. The region as a subject of investigation and as the geographical environment of man may be considered as an integrated system that can be subdivided into four subsystems /Fig. 1/.

As a first step, the potentialities of environmental subsystems and of their component parts must be examined separately, taking into account the functional relationships between them. Such investigation is undertaken by a wide range of specialists including geographers.

"Physical space" is defined here as the assemblage of the component parts of a landscape unit. By physical potential we mean the sum total of all possibilities for cultivation, recreation, and habitation. These in turn provide the preconditions for social development and for the social reproduction of re-

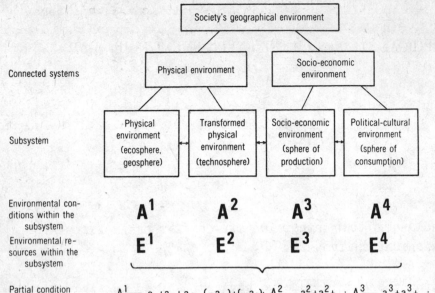

Fig. 1. The outline of the integrated /or total/ geographical
environment of society /Pécsi 1979b/

sources. A rational utilization of the physical or ecological
potential of the environment enables the accumulation of economic, technical and other potentials which in turn affect the
historical development of a region. These latter potentials may
themselves become environmental potentials or their effects may
be felt through some of the environmental potentials.

Environmental potential, including geographical environmental potential, integrates all capacities and possibilities
for cultivation, economic production, political organization
and so on.[1] The factors that constitute the four sub-systems
of environmental potential embody these qualities.

---

[1]Most recently Beale, J.G. has introduced a similar concept
with his "Total Environment" idea. /The Manager and the Environment, Pergamon Press, Oxford, 1980/.

A complex evaluation of the physical factors and of man's productive and non-productive activities in a region reveals the environmental potential of that region. The potentials of the geographical environment undergo change both in time and space depending on the level of social organization, standard of living and scientific and technological standards.

An integrated evaluation of the environmental potential of a region is only possible via a several-staged interdiscipli- nary problem-orientated approach. According to earlier research experience, the economic utilization of space by society does not always make full use of the potentials of an environment. Very often only the dominating partial potentials of a region are utilized through various economic activities, and research has focused on the study of these dominant environmental fac- tors with the aim of improving agricultural land use.

The above research trends and targets are described in the various monographs of the series Landscapes of Hungary /Pécsi and Marosi 1981/. This series is constantly being enriched with new concepts and material reflecting· the dynamism and changing relationship between science and practical demand.

2. ENVIRONMENTAL GEOMORPHOLOGY

Concurrently with regional landscape and environmental re- search involving multifactoral analysis, special investigations concerning the assessment of individual landscape components have also gained prominence within our scientific discipline. Environmental /engineering/ geomorphology /Pécsi 1970, 1974a; Pécsi and Scheuer 1979/, for example, is concerned with the engineering and constructional aspects of the evaluation of re- lief quality. This aspect of applied geomorphological research assesses the existing dynamic equilibrium, i.e. the "perma- nence" stability or instability of relief, for civil engineer- ing purposes.

The topography of the Earth's surface play a major part in most of the socioeconomic activities of mankind. The economic- technical activity of our era causes changes of ever increas- ing dimensions in the geographical environment, firstly, in the

7

relief itself. The mode and consequences of intervention call for the solution of many-sided and complicated scientific and practical problems.

Where the physical environment as a whole is neglected because of the incomplete evaluation of ecological factors /geological, lithological and geomorphological features etc./, it is possible that both building structures and the natural environment will be heavily damaged /i.e. in natural disasters/ though the buildings themselves were constructed safely from the technical point of view.

In many respects, the geomorphological elements of the built environment and its processes form a process-response system. This system is open and is capable of self-regulation, i. e. the active dynamic forces are impelled towards a steady state. The steady state is generally incomplete and exists only in certain places and at certain times; moreover the forces may act against each other as well. A geomorphological-lithological steady state does not mean static immobility but rather dynamic equilibrium.[2]

It is very significant that anthropogenic activity plays an increasing role in changing the dynamic environmental and geomorphological equilibrium. In other words, man's technical-economic activities have an impact on the environment which locally upsets this equilibrium.

Taken in combination the natural factors maintaining the relief equilibrium are generally stable, so that any change in or artificial transformation of an individual factor does not have a significant impact on the environment itself. Nevertheless, there are surfaces where a sudden change in one of the factors maintaining the equilibrium or some artificial intervention upsets the equilibrium in question, and the surface

---

[2]Thus, it is an important task in applied geomorphology to recognize the dynamic equilibrium of the relief and the temporal duration of this dynamic equilibrium. The state of equilibrium may be stable, periodic or, just episodic depending on the nature of the active forces /Pécsi 1975/.

becomes mobile or the environmnet unstable. In certain cases the establishment of relief equilibrium becomes impossible or needs expensive technical intervention.[3]

In certain regions, however, due to the intensification of land utilization, the development of a dynamic equilibrium for both the land surface and the environment as a whole is controlled by the combined effects of natural processes and the ever more complex activities of man in the spheres of production and consumption. In an integrated environmental system /Pécsi 1979b, 1980/ numerous and different equilibria exist within and between sub-systems, while disequilibria may also develop.

It should be emphasized that the geographical environment and, within that, relief and land forms should be considered and evaluated together with the land use and productive activities of man. It is in this way that stress can be placed upon the tasks in hand and the comprehensive relationships of the problem.

3. APPLIED RESEARCH AND ENVIRONMENTAL MANAGEMENT

Multidisciplinary applied environmental research, combining mining and earth sciences with the economic sciences, is carried out in Hungary within the framework of a national research project entitled "Comprehensive research and evaluation of the natural resources of Hungary". This activity is directed by the Hungarian Academy of Sciences with the assistance of

---

[3] A special goal of engineering geomorphology is to determine the areas where the dynamic equilibrium remains stable for a long period of time. Furthermore, there are surfaces /and lithological formations/ whose dynamic equilibrium remains stable only for shorter periods of time; such surfaces are periodically stable. During further development, such terrain is subjected to repetitive episodes of disequilibria. Change in surfaces in temporary dynamic equilibrium may be slow but in certain cases may be seasonal or episodic. At the time of disequilibrium the relief form is in a mobile state but may become stable after a certain period of time; such a surface is in an unstable state and is subject to the hazard of movement.

eleven institutions from different ministries, and is co-ordinated by the Institute of Geography of the Hungarian Academy
of Sciences.

3.1. Assessing the main components of the physical environment

After elaborating the main principles and research aspects
of the integrated geographical environment a plan was prepared
for the thematic mapping of environmental quality. Not only has
a register of the environmental map series been finalized, but
many thematic maps for the representation and qualification of
the total environment have also been prepared /Katona, Keresztesi and Rétvári 1978; Pécsi and Marosi, 1981; Pécsi and Rétvári 1980, etc./[4]

Among the thematic maps presenting an integrated assessment of the physical environment an experimental map series was
prepared in an attempt to establish a typology and regionalization of landscapes with a view to planning a more rational utilization of the land /Pécsi 1980/. According to the concept and
method of assessing the potential of the main ecological factors,[5] 10 categories have been established ranging from 9, the
highest, to 0, the lowest value.

We would like to outline briefly our method of assessment
using relief as an example. As a first step, the relief forms
depicted on a general relief map of the country /scale 1:
100,000/ have been classified into different types, for in-

---

[4]The three main groups of maps are: 1. analytical maps; 2. maps
presenting an integrated assessment of the environment depicting several environmental factors depending on the purpose of
investigation; 3. prognostic maps. Including among the analytical maps are: maps of relief, lithology, mineral resources,
climate, hydrogeography, vegetation, soils, land use, the population's living conditions, settlement typology, mining, industry, transport, recreational areas and environmental pollution.

[5]1. Relief; 2. surface lithology; 3. mineral resources and
other raw materials; 4. dominant climatic factors; 5. water
conditions; 6. soils; 7. natural vegetation and cultivated
crops.

stance relief forms on plains, hills, mountains, plateaus, crests, ridges, slopes and valley floors. Forms are then listed according to their relative relief and degree of dissection. With regard to agricultural potential, values ranging from 9 to O are assigned to the relief forms and types. The highest value /9/ was allotted to undissected flood-free plain surfaces which are best suited for both agricultural land use and for building construction /Table I/. The various hill and mountain forms are assigned lower values depending on relative relief, slope angle, degree of dissection, and valley density. All the categories have been depicted on maps. Forms can also be re-evaluated and a further loss of value for an individual category is possible; for instance a denuded slope segment prone to sliding has a lower value than similar stable relief types. Increase of slope has a similar effect.

For such an exercise in relief classification it is necessary to have maps of orographic forms, relative relief, and slope categories. Geomorphological maps should also be consulted so that the dynamic processes acting on the present-day surface can be assessed - for instance, replacement of banks, soil erosion due to deflation and so on.

Other ecological aspects of the physical environment may be assessed by a similar method and approach as elaborated experimentally by L. Góczán /1981/, from ideas initiated by M. Pécsi /1979b/.

3.2. The comprehensive inventory of soils, soil parent material, and relief as part of the new land-value survey of Hungary

In order to protect cropland, prevent further decrease in agrarian area and promote a more rational land utilization in Hungary, a so-called land-law has been enacted.[6] The cadastral

---

[6] The first phase of the implementation of the new land-law was the publication of a new regulation about land evaluation by the Ministry of Food and Agriculture prepared with the aid of many experts. This regulation forms the basis for the new land cadastre to be completed by 1985.

Table I. Parameters for assessing topographic factors /selected examples only/

Relief forms and elements	Factor scores based on quanti- tative evaluation /ranging from 1-- 100/	Scale of values based on assess- ment /0-9/	Relief characteristics reducing the quantita- tive value of the to- pographic factor	Amount to be subtracted from the factor score value
A/ Lowland /200 m a.s.l./				
1. Low flood plain	80--50	7--4	a/ flood channel	-30
			b/ temporarily flooded or covered by in- land water	
			25% of the surface	-10
			26-50% " "	-20
			50% " "	
2. Flood free low- land area cover- ed by unconsolid- ated deposits /loess, sand/	90--70	8--6	a/ slightly dissected area with flat derasional valleys, small depres- sions in the loess due to suffosion	
			5-10% of the surface	-10
			b/ dissected area 10% of the surface taken up by forms listed in a/	-20
B/ Hill country /200- 350 m a.s.l./				
3. Interfluves of different di- mensions	70--40	6--3	width of the interfluve top 300-200 m	-10
			300-100 m	-20
			100 m	-30
4. Slopes	50--10	4--0	a/ slope angle 5-12%	-10
			12-25%	-20
			25-40%	-30
			40%	-40

value of cropland was regulated by a very old procedure created at the time of the Austro-Hungarian Monarchy. Though this cadastral evaluation, expressed in terms of the former currency, the gold "korona", has been modified several times, it does not reflect present socio-economic requirements.

The new land value cadastre is derived from a site's production value which means a combination of soil value, relief and climatic conditions. The soil value represents a fertility index determined from genetic soil type and parent material as given by Table of Soil Evaluation /Table II/. Soil value is further modified according to the relief and climatic conditions of the area in question /Tables III, IV/. In the preparation of the new land cadastre the soil profiles and ecological characteristics of sample areas are taken into consideration together with the results of analyses of soils and sediments undertaken by numerous experts and laboratories. The results of pedological and agro-ecological research are also used in this context. In addition these findings provide a longer term possibility for studying the relationships between soil fertility and Quaternary sediments, a topic dealt with in more detail in this volume by L. Góczán.

3.3. Estimation of agro-ecological potential and agro-ecological regionalization

Due to world population increase, the raising of food production has become a universal problem and the significance of agricultural produce has been considerably upgraded - cereals in fact have become of strategic-economic importance.

During the last two decades the output of many types of agricultural produce in Hungary had doubled. Given the present world economic situation there is now an appreciation of the importance of increasing production, up to the turn of the millennium, with the proviso the more rational utilization of the agro-ecological resources of the country and the optimal selection of sites for crop production is also taken into consideration.

Table II. Soil evaulation /selected examples only/

Type of soil	Maximum and minimum standard soil number	Classification of the varieties' properties of soil		Reduction from the maximum value of standard number
Raman's Brown forest soil		a/ Parent material		
		Loess		Ø
		Sandy loess, sand		5
		Marl and grey-white clay		15
		Red or brown clay		10
Typically developed on loessic and clay parent material	90--35	b/ Mechanical composition		
		Sand		5
		Sandy silt		3
		Silt		Ø
		Clayey silt		5
		clay		10
		c/ Depth of humus layer		
Rust-brown, developed on sand	60-25	Thin	30 cm	10
		Moderate	30-60 cm	5
		Deep	60 cm	Ø
		d/ Content of humus in upper cultivated layer		
		Low	1,5%, in sand 1%	8
		Moderate	1,5 - 3,0% in sand 1,0 - 1,5%	4
		High	3,0%, in sand 1,5%	Ø
		e/ Acidity		
		Alkaline	8 Y1	Ø
		Acidic	8 Y1	4
		f/ Relime		
		Relimed to the surface		Ø
		In accumulation horizon $CaCO_3$ 10%		3
		Non relimed		5
		g/ Stone or gravel content of cultivated layer		
		In cultivated layer stone or gravel can be found		6
		h/ Depth of fertile layer		
		Thin hindering plant growth 50 cm		40%
		Moderate hindering plant growth 50-100 cm		20%

Table III. Correction table for relief

Standard number of plain the soil	Slope category								
	0-5%	5-12%	12-17%	17-25% I.	17-25% II.	17-25% III.	25% I.	25% II.	25% III.
				Corrected numbers					
100	100	95	95	90	93	93	87	90	88
9	9	4	4	9	2	2	6	9	z
8	8	3	2	8	1	1	5	8	6
80	80	6	5	70	3	2	7	70	8
9	9	5	4	9	2	1	6	9	7
8	8	5	3	8	1	70	5	8	6

Note: I = S, SW; II = W, NW, E, SE; III = N, NE exposed slopes.

Table IV. Correction table for climate

Correction standard number of the soil	Climatic category				
	1	2	3	4	5
100	100	99	97	95	93
9	99	8	6	4	2
8	8	7	5	3	1
7	7	6	4	2	90
90	90	9	7	5	3
9	8	7	6	4	2
8	8	6	5	3	1
7	7	5	4	2	80

Note: 1 = most favourable; 5 = least favourable.

To carry out this survey, the Hungarian Academy of Sciences has organized a composite team of earth scientists and agricultural and biological experts. In briefly summing up the results of two years of analysis it can be said that, by retaining predominantly open land production, total agrarian production can be increased by about 80 per cent compared to present yields. Moreover, with an optimal crop rotation the yields from cereals, wine and certain fruits can be doubled by the end of the century. This national investigation has unambiguously proved that the ecological regions most suited for producing cereals are those where the soil-forming material consists of loess or loess-like sediments.

Detailed investigations to select the optimal habitat for each type of plant species have also been carried out at a county /local district/ scale since it is apparent that in this way yield increases of about 20 per cent can be achieved /Láng 1980/. Therefore it is a further aim of the research to carry out a microagro-ecological regionalization of Hungary, the details of which are presented in the papers by Góczán and Lóczy.

3.4. The fertility of sandy soils

Another important task of agro-ecological research has been the study of areas with poor or weak lithological properties. In Hungary, considerable areas of raw sandy soils, slightly humic sands and sandy dunes are to be found in the general neighbourhood of the loessic soils of excellent fertility, as well as intercalated between them. Among other things it is clear that an analysis of the relationship between the fertility of these sandy soils, and the mineral composition of the sands, their geomorpological forms and soil water budget can produce important practical information /Pécsi, Zentay and Gerei 1982/:

a. The relatively small amounts of clay in the humic sandy soils play an important role since the clay minerals strongly affect the water and nutrient budgets due to their high absorption capacity.

b. The fertility of sandy soils is determined not only by their genetic horizons but also by the physical, chemical and mineral characteristics of the underlying sediments.

3.5. The cadastral survey of surfaces endangered by mass movements

In the interests of good infrastructural design, particularly the lines of new roads, and to maintain existing facilities in safe operation, the Central Geological Office decided to map regions liable to surface movements. Mass slope movements were formerly registered and investigated where and when such movements caused tangible damage. Now, however, unstable surfaces must be pinpointed at the preliminary stages of planning, while mass movements should be classified according to type since the kinds of surface protection necessary can vary according to the type of land movement. In the context of this programme, the engineering geological and geomorphological aspects already elaborated by us have been successfully applied by a team of geomorphologists in close co-operation with specialists in soil mechanics /Fig. 2/. As a result of this co-operation a series of surface movement maps have been constructed at a scale of 1:10,000 and a summarizing map drawn at the same scale as well. Detailed mapping at the scale of 1:10,000, as well as prognostic evaluation, are in progress in urban fringe areas, mining districts and recreation zones endangered by surface movements /Pécsi and Juhász 1974; Pécsi, Scheuer and Schweitzer 1979; Szilárd 1978/.

South of Budapest, for a distance of about 180 km, the Danube has formed a loess bluff where landslides and other mass movements periodically occur /Pécsi 1979a; Pécsi and Scheuer 1979/.[7] One of the most notable landslides happened at Duna-

---

[7] Engineering-geomorphological research of the bluffs along the Danube has proved necessary because landslides and other mass movements have taken place during the last decade affecting certain industrial settlements and railway bridges. In order to elaborate engineering methods to provide protection against landslides, certain case studies were carried out by Hungarian loess researchers and specialists in soil mechanics. In the course of these studies, the lithological properties and the

17

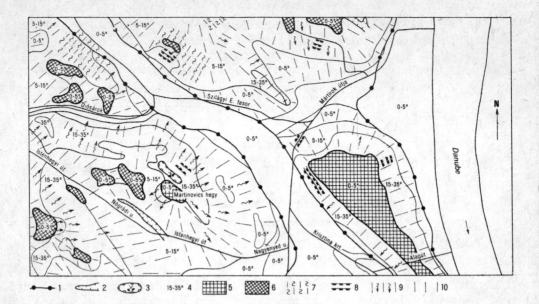

Fig. 2. Engineering geomorphological map of the Buda mountain
district of Budapest
1 = boundary of regional aggradation and degradation;
2 = erosional valley; 3 = excavated depression, disused
quarry; 4 = slope categories; 5 = plateau; 6 = hill
crest; 7 = slope with fossil landslides; 8 = recent
landslides; 9 = intensive slopewash; 10 = stable slope

földvár, which has been the subject of considerable research to
establish the reasons for its occurrence and to determine the
sliding plane together with the lithological and strength properties of the loess sequences /Figs. 3, 4/.

The slab landslide at Dunaföldvár was a form of movement
which differs from a slump and has the following characteristics:

a. the potential sliding plane had been preformed by the geomorphological and geological structure of the area;

b. the slab failure and its sliding plane developed on horizontal impermeable clays lying at the base level of erosion along
the bluffs in the form of a slightly inclined undercut;

---

7 /cont./ spatial distribution of the loess sequences were determined by processing data from numerous soil-mechanical
boreholes.

18

c. the aquifer overlying the impermeable layer acted as a lubricant;

d. the lower moistened strata of the loess sequence lost their compaction strength due to the pressure of the overlying sequence and when moisture content reached a critical value shear followed;

e. the collapsing slabs moved rotationally on the preformed sliding plane and horizontal displacement as a consequence was negligible.

The most important aspect of protection against slab failure is drainage of the free and confined ground waters.

The landslides at Dunaujváros occurred under geological-geomorphological and hydrogeological-hydrological conditions similar to those of Dunaföldvár. This slide is about 3 km long and, because it endangered part of the water supply installation of a new section of the town, large-scale precautions have been carried out along the Dunaújváros reach of the Danube; the engineering-geological and soil-mechanical investigations associated with this project required the sinking of many boreholes and shafts.

The essence of bank protection is to drain the water from the sandy aquifers of the river bluff by means of wells and subsurface channels. In addition, the bluff has been graded, reinforced and planted, and the surface drainage regulated. Due to these diversified protection measures, movement ceased about ten years ago and no displacement has been detected by subsequent geodetic measurements /Pécsi and Scheuer 1979/.

Finally it must be emphasized that loess is susceptible to collapse and the mobility of loess strata is closely connected to the geological, geomorphological and ecological characteristics of the environment. However, soil-mechanical investigation alone does not give enough information on the slide processes or on the periodicity and frequency of these movements. A more detailed knowledge of dynamic change within the loess sequence is supported by engineering-geomorphological observations, and by three-dimensional geomorphological-geological analysis of the strata concerned.

Fig. 3. Detail from the engineering geomorphological map of
the Dunaföldvár high bluff /Pécsi, Schweitzer and
Scheuer 1979/
A: mass movement forms: 1 = rupture front of landslides;
2 = earth mound of fossil landslide or slump; 3 = earth
mound of recent landslide or slump; 4 = steps or slices
of the landslide; 5 = depressions enclosed by earth
mounds of landslides; 6 = active mobile sliding slopes;
7 = slopes temporarily stable; 8 = steep high bluffs
prone to crumbling. B: Genetic surface forms: 9 = high
flood plain level terrace I/a; 10 = Early Holocene Danube channel; 11 = channels of smaller watercourses;
12 = Early Holocene meander spurs /terraces/ covered by

alluvial silt and clay; 13 = Early Holocene meander spur
terraces covered by alluvial and brown-sand; 14 = boggy,
watery areas with meadow clay; 15 = watercourses; 16 =
springs; 17 = lower boundary of the valley bottom; 18 =
erosional valley; 19 = flat loess ridges not affected by
erosion; 20 = derasional step; 21 = erosional-derasional
interfluve; 22 = derasional valley; 23 = erosional valley;
24 = thickness of loessy-silty slope deposit; 25 = stabil-
ized blown-sand surface; 26 = blown-sand dunes; 27 = wind-
furrows; 28 = deflational depressions. C: Slopes: 29 =
slopes threatened by surface erosion; 30 = slopes threatened by gully erosion; 31 = stable slopes. D: Anthropogenic
forms: 32 = artificial infilling

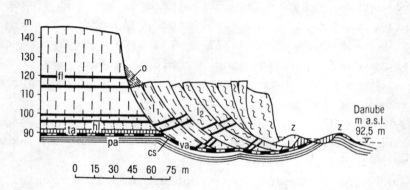

Fig.4. The Dunaföldvár river-bank landslide to the S of the
Danube's 1560 kilometre mark /Pécsi et al. 1979/
1 = loess sequence in primary position /autochtonous/;
l_1 = loess recently displaced by sliding; l_2 = waste of
earlier slides; hl = palepink sandy loess; O = talus;
z = earth mound and Pannonian clay upward from the Danube's streambed; fl = fossil soils; ta = dark-grey clayey
loam soil; pa = Pannonian clay; va = red clay; cs = sliding plane

REFERENCES

GÓCZÁN, L. /1981/: Assessing the ecological factors of the
    physical environment. Man and the biosphere Programme Sur-
    vey of 10 years activity in Hungary. Hungarian National
    Committee for UNESCO, MAB Programme, Budapest, 495-531.

KATONA, S.--KERESZTESI, Z.--RÉTVÁRI, L. /1978/: Új kutatási
    irányzat: A környezetminősités /A new research line: en-
    vironmental assessment/. - Területi Kutatások, 1, 30-36.

LÁNG, I.--CSETE, L.--HARNOS, Zs. /1983/: A magyar mezőgazdaság
    agroökológiai potenciálja az ezredfordulón /Agroecological
    potential of Hungarian agriculture at the end of second
    millenium/. - Mezőgazdasági Kiadó, Budapest, 265 p.

MAROSI, S.--SZILÁRD, J. /1973/: De l'évaluation physico-géo-
    graphique. - In La région. Problèmes théoriques et métho-
    dologiques. Ve Colloque Franco-hongrois de Géographie,
    Budapest, 7-13.

PÉCSI, M. /1970/: A mérnöki geomorfológia problematikája /Pro-
    blems of engineering geomorphology/. Summary in German. -
    Földr. Ért., 19, 369-380.

PÉCSI, M. /1973/: Geographical problems of environmental re-
    search. - Acta Geol. Acad. Sci. Hung., 19, 233-241.

PÉCSI, M. /1974a/: A környezetpotenciál integrált földtudomá-
    nyi értékelése /Integrated geonomical evaluation of the
    environmental potential/. - Geonómia és Bányászat, 7,
    193-198.

PÉCSI, M. /1974b/: Complex environmental studies. - Studies in
    Geography in Hungary, 11, Akadémiai Kiadó, Budapest, 59-65.

PÉCSI, M. /1975/: Geomorphology. /Mass movement on the Earth's
    surface./ - UNESCO 241. Internat. Post-graduate Course on
    the Principles and Method of Engineering Geology. Buda-
    pest, 241 p.

PÉCSI, M. /1979a/: Landslides at Dunaföldvár in 1970 and 1974.
    - Geographia Polonica, 41, 7-12.

PÉCSI, M. /1979b/: New aspect on interpreting and evaluating
    the geographical environment. Summary in English. - Földr.
    Közl., 27 /103/, 1-3, 17-27.

PÉCSI, M. /1980/: Qualification of physical environmental fac-
    tors on maps. - Symposium International sur la Carto-
    graphie de l'Environnement et de sa Dynamique. Caen 18-23
    juin 1979, France. - Univ. de Caen. Union Geogr. Inter-
    nat., 55-63.

PÉCSI, M.--JUHÁSZ, Á /1974/: Kataster der Rutschungsgebiete in
    Ungarn und ihre kartographische Darstellung. - Földr. Ért.,
    23, 2, 193-202.

PÉCSI, M.--MAROSI, S. /1981/: Survey of 10 years activity in
    Hungary. MAB 13. Project. Perception of environmental qual-
    ity. - Hung. Nat. Commit. for UNESCO MAB Programme, Buda-
    pest, 475-494.

PÉCSI, M.--SCHEUER, Gy. /1979/: Engineering geological problems
    of the Dunaújváros loess bluff. - Acta Geol., 22, 1-4,
    345-353.

PÉCSI, M.--RÉTVÁRI, L. /1980/: Maps of environmental qualifica-
    tion and related problems. - Földr. Közl. 28 /104/, 303-
    307.

PÉCSI, M.--SCHEUER, Gy.--SCHWEITZER, F. /1979/: Engineering
    geological and geomorphological investigation of land-
    slides in the loess bluff along the Danube in the Great
    Hungarian Plain. - Acta Geol., 22, 1-4, 324-343.

PÉCSI, M.--ZENTAY, T.--GEREI, L. /1982/: Engineering geology
    and the fertility of the sand soils of the southern Dan-
    ube-Tisza Interfluve. Quaternary Studies in Hungary. -
    Geogr. Research Inst. of Hung. Acad. of Sci., Budapest,
    255-270.

SZILÁRD, J. /1978/: Some aspects and present situation of en-
    gineering-geomorphological mapping in Hungary. Interna-
    tional Conference on Geomorphologic Mapping, Budapest 25-
    28 Oct. 1977. - Geogr. Research Inst. of Hung. Acad. of
    Sci. Budapest, 167-173.

ENVIRONMENTAL PLANNING AND THE URBAN FRINGE IN GREAT BRITAIN

R. SIDAWAY and D. SYMES

Urbanisation and the loss of agricultural land are close correlates of economic development. In a modern industrial or post-industrial economy, population growth is almost inevitably translated into an expansion of urban land uses; but even without the impetus of population growth, trends towards higher living standards imply an increasing demand for urban space. Urban growth and the extension of the urban fringe are thus irresistible forces.

A consistent definition of the urban fringe has proved elusive. Part of the problem lies in the choice of the term which suggests a regular geographical band of general occurrence, whereas definitions tend to stress its transitional nature. For example,

> ".... a zone of transition in land use, social and demographic characteristics laying between a/ the continuously built-up urban and suburban areas of the central city and b/ the rural hinterland". /Pryor 1968/.[1]

In its particular application, the term urban fringe may vary from a narrow contact zone - perhaps no more than a few hundred metres wide - especially where land use characteristics alone are being considered, to a much broader band, many kilometres in depth, over which urban influcences of a sociodemographic nature may be identified. In Britain, because of the fragmentation of urban land use on the edge of the city and also because of a long-standing academic interest in the social geography of the urban fringe, the latter condition is more widely assumed.

There is, however, a broad consensus concerning the general land-use characteristics of the urban fringe: namely a zone of mixed, non-conforming land uses where agricultural land has been infiltrated by urban housing, new industry and a wide range of urban services whose space-use requirements or other characteristics make them either uneconomic or incompatible with the predominant land uses in more densely built-up areas of the city. But the emphasis of most writing confuses the problematic nature of the transition zone with an assumption that it exists as a concentric band around most towns. Yet around the majority of urban settlements in Britain, including some of the larger cities, there is no transition zone. Where there is, it does not extend as a continuous belt.

Concern about the visual appearance of the urban fringe and the incongruity of non-complementary land uses may obscure the important functional role that the urban fringe can play in enhancing the quality of urban life. At its worst the urban fringe becomes an untidy and unattractive "urban backyard" for unwanted but essential by-products of an urban civilisation. At its best it can afford the urban population an immediate and accessible opportunity for a "countryside experience". For the urban fringe to be an essential and valuable complement to the built-up area, without undue prejudice to the pre-existing agricultural uses, requires both perceptive strategic planning and sensitive land management schemes. In Britain the task confronting environmental planners is as much one of remedial action, making good the blight caused by previous generations, as of a preventive nature to ensure that similar problems are not being created in our own lifetime.

In the first part of this paper we review some of the major issues relating to the development of the urban fringe in Britain and outline the nature of planning policies intended to resolve those issues; in the second part, we focus attention upon the more heavily urbanised areas of England - the Metropolitan Counties - and, through case studies, attempt to demonstrate the scale of the problem and the nature of the solutions that are possible.

I. ISSUES AND POLICIES

Urbanisation[2]

Judged by almost any criterion, Britain /and more especially England and Wales/ is one of the most highly urbanised
countries in the world. Four out of every five Britons live in
towns; the overall population density /229 persons/km^2/ makes
Britain the fourth most densely settled country in Europe; and
in 1970 almost 12% of Britain's land surface was occupied by
urban uses. Although variations in the system of collecting
land-use data make precise comparisons difficult, it is clear
from Table I that among developed western countries only Bel-
gium can claim a higher degree of urbanisation.

But just as important, in the context of the present discussion, is the long established urban status of Britain. Already in 1851 half the population lived in towns; during the
following 50 years the proportion rose over 75% since when the
ratio of urban to rural population has remained relatively stable. Even so, in the present century, improved transport systems allowed the growth of low-density suburbs to stretch the
elastic-sided city, leading to a doubling of the urban area between 1900 and 1960. Many of the environmental problems of the
urban fringe, certainly in the coalfield-based industrial regions of northern England, date from a period of unplanned
growth in mining and manufacturing activities in the 19th and
early 20th centuries.

The most recent census points to a continuing decentralisation of Britain's population. Between 1971 and 1981, the national population increased by only 0.5%. This historically
low growth rate conceals strongly divergent internal trends
with significant population losses being recorded by all the
Metropolitan Counties /-7%/ and by cities over 175,000 /-5%/
and a compensating growth of population in the smaller towns
and rural areas.

Table I. Urbanisation in the West

	Area km^2	Population /1979/ '000s	Density P/km^2	Urban land as % of national space /1970/	Annual rate of expansion of urban land /1960-70/ %	Area of land transferred to urban use /1960-70/ m2/capita
Belgium	30,513	9,651	322	28.0	2.4	188.3
Denmark	43,069	4,938	119	10.8	1.9	182.6
Federal Republic of Germany	248,577	60,651	247	8.7	1.9	61.3
Finland	337,032	4,718	14	3.3	n.a.	175.7
France	547,026	52,656	98	4.2	n.a.	123.1
Norway	324,219	3,874	13	4.9	0.2	40.3
The Netherlands	40,844	13,046	344	9.2	2.9	72.9
Sweden	449,964	8,209	18	n.a.	n.a.	141.0
United Kingdom	244,046	55,506	229	12.0	1.3	65.5
Japan	372,313	111,940	311	4.9	6.0	87.2
USA	9,363,123	2o3,235	24	3.9	1.1	180.1

Source: Demographic Yearbook 1980; OECD Land Use Policies and Agriculture 1976

Agricultural production[3]

Not surprisingly in a nation which imports almost half of its food requirements, much of the argument surrounding urban fringe development concerns the loss of agricultural production, which may be due to transfer of land to urban use or interference from urban pressure /e.g. trespass, vandalism, theft of crops/. The former situation can be minimised by effective development control.[x] Although rates of land transfer from non-urban to urban uses and the amounts of transferred land per capita are substantially lower in Britain than in the other western countries /Table I/, a fierce debate has surrounded the actual amounts of land lost to agricultural production and the long-term significance of existing trends. Coleman, basing her argument upon analysis of land use changes in South East England and noting that urban development not only involves transfers of land from agricultural to urban uses but also contributes to a growing stock of waste land, claims that at current rates the supply of agricultural land could be exhausted within 200 years. Best offers a more sanguine view and asserts that recent rates of land take from agriculture, running at 12-19,000 ha per annum, or anticipated lower rates in the future, are unlikely to give serious cause for concern in the immediate future; moreover, he points out that higher rates of land loss are sustained on the upland fringes - mainly to forestry - than on the urban fringe.

Much of the comfort to be derived from Best's assertion is due to recent trends affecting productivity in British agriculture which in the early 1970s had been increasing at roughly 2.5% per annum. Yet interpolation of future trends is surrounded by controversy. Some authorities indicate that pres-

---

[x] In Britain, the physical planning system comprises structure /strategic/ plans prepared at county level, more detailed local and subject plans covering districts or parts of districts, and development control, principally at district level in accordance with structure plan policies. Implementation is responsive i.e. it depends upon suitable proposals being submitted by a developer, in which case a planning permission is given.

ent rates may not be sustainable over the long-term both for technical reasons and also because recent productivity increases have been largely based upon an increasing consumption of energy /e.g. mechanisation and chemicalisation/.

Even if we accept that agricultural land losses have been contained by stringent planning policies, there remains the problem of declining productivity on residual agricultural land within the urban fringe. In other words, productivity increases in British agriculture in general have to account not only for actual land losses but also for declining productivity from urban fringe farms, especially in view of the disproportionate share of good agricultural land within the urban fringe. Agriculture in this zone is characterised by low input: low output systems of production. Several contributory factors have been identified: 1. the fragmentation of farms leading to a predominance of smaller, less viable size classes; 2. high land prices which preclude purchase of vacant land for amalgamation; 3. uncertainty over the future status of farmland which inhibits long-term capital investment necessary to exploit opportunities for increasing productivity; 4. acquisition of farmland by speculators which is then left unused or underemployed in "farming to quit"; and 5. direct costs to farming attributable to the proximity of urban populations in terms of trespass, vandalism, theft, stock worrying, rubbish dumping etc. Moreover, attempts to increase output through intensive indoor feeding of pigs and poultry, thereby insulating the system of production from interference by urban populations, are increasingly likely to be the subject of planning controls designed to protect the suburban population from nuisance caused by smell and/or pollution of water courses.

On the other hand, the disadvantages of farming on the urban fringe may have been overstated and insufficient attention paid to the benefits of a location these in terms of opportunities for direct selling /farm shops, pick-your-own, producer-retailer milk distribution/ and the development of ancillary enterprises /caravan sites, riding stables, dog kennels, shooting clubs etc./. But, in general, while the urban fringe farmer adapts to changing conditions, the economic and social

structures of urban fringe agriculture contribute to the problems of degraded land use and landscape through poorly maintained field boundaries and farm buildings /often repaired if
not actually built with cheap, second-hand materials abundantly
available in the urban fringe, poor grassland management - especially associated with horse-culture - and waste land.

Recreational opportunity[4]

Within the last decade, increasing attention has been focused upon opportunities for the provision of recreational a-
menities, based on the premise that the urban fringe affords
the nearest countryside accessible to millions of urban dwellers and is of especial value to the deprived inner-city populations. The post-war period has seen substantial growth in
personal mobility with a majority of households gaining access
to a car. This has resulted in a sharp increase in countryside
recreation, mainly in the form of day visits and partly chan-
neled towards more vulnerable upland environments in National
Parks and Areas of Outstanding Natural Beauty. From 1970 onwards, Country Parks were established closer to urban centres,
often within the urban fringe itself, to divert pressure away
from more vulnerable environments. Awareness of the urban fringe
as a recreational environment was heightened in the aftermath
of the 1974 energy crisis when it was thought likely that future countryside visits would involve an increasing proportion
of shorter distance trips.

In part, the premise of an accessible countryside experience in the urban fringe was falsified on a number of accounts:
1. recreational provision is unevenly distributed and public
open space /as opposed to private property/ is comparatively
rare; 2. it is not easily accessible to urban populations, except those living in the outer suburbs or with private transport; 3. local access has been severely dislocated by development and by modern farming practices so that the pattern of
footpaths and bridleways is usually one of disconnected frag-
ments rather than continuous or circular routeways; and 4. the
unconformity of land uses and the frequently blighted landscape
is the very antithesis of the "real countryside".

Policy constraints[5]

Effective policies for dealing with urban fringe problems have been inhibited both by a negative philosophy towards rural areas in general and by the fragmentation of responsibility within the urban fringe in particular. Much of the sterility of rural planning in Britain stems from recommendations by the Scott Committee /1942/ that both farming and forestry should have prescriptive rights over rural land use and be excluded from direct development control. The separation of a locally administred physical planning system for most land uses from a centrally administered financial incentive system for agriculture and forestry severely constrains planning opportunities within the urban fringe in Britain, compared to those countries /e.g. the Netherlands/ where the processes are integrated.

The concept of the Green Belt, first implemented by the Greater London Council in the 1930s, became the most important policy instrument, especially after 1955. Today 15,000 km^2 of urban fringe land /about 11% of the area of England and Wales/ is protected by Green Belt designation. The aims were defined by central government in 1955 as: 1. to check the further sprawl of built-up areas; 2. to prevent neighbouring towns from merging with each other; and 3. to preserve the special character of towns. On those terms, Green Belts have proved remarkably successful. Indiscriminate sprawl has been arrested within the designated area by denying new industrial and residential development but generally permitting certain urban-related recreation uses /sports fields, golf courses etc./. Thus in 1974 Hall was able to state: "Physically, the urban areas have been contained: losses of rural land to urban land have been restricted in quantity and compact in form." But the Green Belt has not been able to prevent the corrosion of urban fringe landscapes; nor has the concept given rise to specific policies for environmental improvement there.

It is important to distinguish between negative policies of development control in the Green Belt and schemes for positive management within the urban fringe. A first step towards more positive attitudes may lie in the identification, in structure plans, of priority areas which distinguish, for example, between "agricultural priority areas" and "amenity corridors". A range of uses is accommodated within each category, the emphasis being on agriculture and low-key recreation in the former; landscape conservation and recreation provision take priority over, but do not exclude, agriculture in the latter.

Although the system of structure planning has begun to define development priorities, implementation of specific projects faces a number of constraints: 1. the predominance of private land ownership, often severely fragmented; 2. a general opposition of residential property-owning interests to any form of new development; 3. weak political support for urban fringe investment; 4. the high cost of land held by speculators for its "hope value" precluding its public acquisition for recreation; and 5. the multiplicity of agencies representing different institutional interests and the fragmented local authority responsibility. Although local government reorganisation in 1974 went some way towards easing the friction between local authorities of equal status but frequently different political attitudes towards development, the present local authorities remain insufficiently integrated to coordinate effective policies for the urban fringe.

Large-scale regional leisure projects in the urban fringe, with autonomous management /such as the Lea Valley Regional Park/ have had their advocates but are certain to remain the exceptions. Smaller, single-uses recreational projects /e.g. Country Parks/ will remain limited in number by financial constraints. The main opportunity for the extension of recreational provision, protection of agricultural land and landscape improvement, at least in southern England, would seem to lie in low-key, small-scale management schemes. In this context, the Countryside Commission, with its managerial experience and, more importantly, its powers for limited grant-aid, has proved an important catalyst. It has already pioneered a number of experimental projects both within the London urban fringe and in the northern Metropolitan Counties. In these northern counties, the legacy of derelict land requires a larger scale of operation; an important example is "Operation Groundwork" being carried out in the Metropolitan County of Merseyside /see below/.

To date the approach to management problems in the urban fringe appears to be shaped largely by pragmatism and the literature similarly reveals a high level of empiricism. There has been little attempt to build a theoretical model; nor has much attention been paid to the variety of structural form embraced by the term. A general stereotype, closely related to the traditional concentric models of urban growth, thus prevails though its applicability may refer only to parts of the urban fringe in general and to the Greater London area in particular. A fundamental distinction exists between the popular image of the dynamic urban fringe of the metropolitan South East, where land use changes are mainly related to the expansion of residential and urban service functions into rural areas, and the situation found in parts of northern urban fringes where the land-use problem is heightened by a conflict between declining mining and industrial activities and expanding residential and service areas. Here the ebb tide of industrialisation has uncovered extreme problems of blighted landscapes. It is upon such areas that the rest of this paper concentrates.

II. THE METROPOLITAN COUNTIES[6]

The urban fringe reaches its maximum extent and presents the greatest environmental problems in the context of the largest cities. Despite recent inner-city decline and resulting depopulation /Table II/ Greater London and the 6 Metropolitan Counties still account for more than one third of the population of England and Wales. Notwithstanding their urban status, the 6 contain important transitional areas of open land much of it still in agricultural use /Table III/. But also included is a disproportionate share of the country's derelict land. Much of this may be attributed to past and present mining activity for coal, the quarrying of building stone and the working of sand gravel deposits.

Table II. Population of the conurbations

	Area ha	Population density /1981/ /p/ha/	Population /'000s/ 1961	1971	1981	% change 1971-81
Greater London	157,946	42.4	7,992	7,452	6,696	-lo.2
Tyne and Wear	54,006	21.2	1,244	1,212	1,143	- 5.7
West Midlands	89,943	29.4	2,732	2,793	2,645	- .5.3
Greater Manchester	128,674	2o.2	2,720	2,729	2,595	- 4.9
Merseyside	66,202	23.2	1,718	1,657	1,513	- 8.7
South Yorkshire	156,049	8.3	1,303	1,323	1,302	- 1.6
West Yorkshire	203,912	10.0	2,005	2,068	2,038	- 1.5
Total	855,732	23.0	19,715	19,233	17,921	- 6.8
England and Wales	15,120,709	3.2	46,105	48,750	49,011	+ 0.5
Gtr. London and MCs as % England and Wales	5.7	-	42.8	39.5	36.6	-

Source: Census of Population, 1981.

West Yorkshire and the conurbation core[7]

West Yorkshire is the largest of the Metropolitan Counties in area and one of the least densely populated. Urban development is intrinsically bound up with the rapid expansion of the wool textile industry in the Aire and Calder valleys during the 19th century and development of the contiguous northern parts of the Yorkshire coalfield. Present urban form is the result of a coalescence of several independent settlements creating an open-textured, polycentric conurbation, in part conrolled by local topography. No one focal centre dominates the conurbation;

Table III. Metropolitan counties - open land

	Area	Agriculture		Woodland		Derelict		Of which mining related
	ha	ha	%	ha	%	ha	%	%
Tyne and Wear	54,006	18,550	34.4	2,200	4.1	1,277	2.4	41.4
West Midlands	89,943	19,996	22.3	n.a.	-	1,519	1.7	45.9
Greater Manchester	128,674	45.604	35.4	2,400	1.8	3,186	2.4	50.4
Merseyside	65,202	20,346	31.2	3,000	4.6	457	0.8	60.8
South Yorkshire	156,049	83,631	53.6	10,3000	6.6	1,374	0.9	82.8
West Yorkshire	203,912	112,166	55.0	10,000	4.9	2,578	1.3	46.6

Source: Ministry of Agriculture, Fisheries and Food, Agricultural Statistics 1979;
Elson: The Urban Fringe 1979.

instead the central area is formed of a ring of several towns. Complete coalescence of these main towns has been restrained by wedges of green land found mainly along the watersheds. At the core of the ring of towns is an extensive, if fragmented, area of open land exhibiting features of urban fringe conflict in extremis /Fig. 1/.

By contrast, much of the outer periphery of the area reveals a subdued urban fringe landscape with comparatively little derelict or degraded land /Fig. 2/. Along the western perimeter in particular, pressures have been damped down by the Pennine hills, an area of comparatively difficult terrain and of generally high landscape value. Urban fringe characteristics, at least in their most serious form, are largely confined to the south eastern sector of the Metropolitan County and to the conurbation core. Much of the pressure for urban fringe development appears to have been turned inwards towards the conurbation core, where locational values, both for urban service functions and new manufacturing and distributing activities have been enhanced by the east-west arterial spine of the M62.

The conurbation core presents the most serious challenge to environmental planning. It is an area of particularly acute land-use conflict between competing pressures from farming, mineral extraction, urban services and informal recreational activities. Much of it presents a severely degraded and polluted landscape /Fig. 3/. In the past it has been deployed as the "backyard" of the conurbation, accommodating "hazard industries" which need to be kept clear of residential areas and, more importantly, the bulk of the Metropolitan County's massive waste-disposal problem. The vital wedges of open, mainly agricultural, land are mostly designated as Green Belt implaying restrictions upon future urban development, though this presumption does not necessarily extend to the activities of central government agencies /e.g. road building and the National Coal Board/.

Whereas the population on the outer fringes of the Metropolitan County have easy access to the countryside - its boundary abuts onto the Yorkshire Dales National Park to the north-

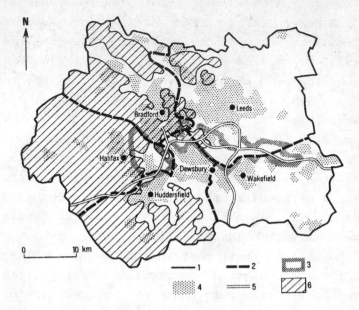

Fig. 1. The West Yorkshire Metropolitan County
1 = Metropolitan County boundary; 2 = district boundary; 3 = conurbation core; 4 = main urban areas; 5 =
motorways; 6 = land over 150 metres

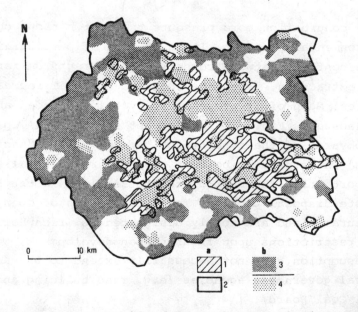

Fig. 2. West Yorkshire MC: landscape characteristics
a = landscape character; 1 = fringe urban; 2 = degraded; b = landscape quality; 3 = good; 4 = main urban
areas

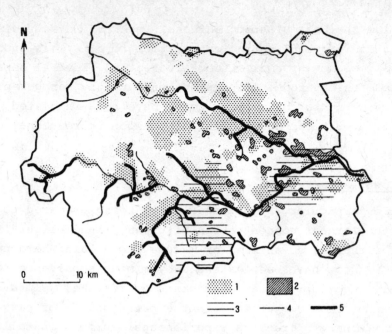

Fig. 3. West Yorkshire MC: derelict land and environmental
pollution
1 = main urban areas; 2 = derelict and despoiled land;
3 = athmospheric pollution; 4 = rivers; 5 = rivers
/grossly polluted sections/

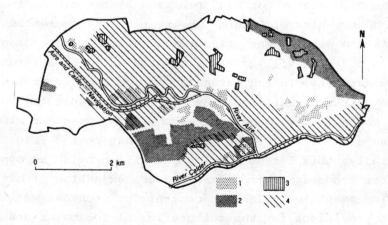

Fig. 4. The Lower Aire Valley: environmental assets and constraints
1 = areas of open water; 2 = grades 1 and 2 agricultural land; 3 = woodland; 4 = areas of derelict, disused, active and future mining activity /undifferent-
iated/

west and the Peak District National Park to the southwest - the
population surrounding the conurbation core is less endowed
with access to informal outdoor recreation. Several separate
schemes for environmental improvement and the management of
open land in the conurbation core, have been initiated, all as-
sociatied with the development of outdoor recreational opportunities.

The Lower Aire Valley[8]

In particular, a Subject Plan is being prepared to deal
with the largest concentration of urban fringe blight in the
Lower Aire Valley, an area of mature floodplain where natural
water meadows have been extended by mining subsidence to form
locally important wetlands. Pockets of fertile, well drained
farmland are interspersed with the paraphenalia of past and
present mining operations /spoil heaps, surface installations/,
a fragmented pattern of urban settlement, polluted waterways
and wetland areas /Fig. 4/. Here two interrelated issues pre-
vail: 1. competition for land between the activities of farming, opencast mining and the need for nature conservation in an
area already seriously disturbed by deep-mining activity; and
2. competing claims for land released by the mining industry
between agriculture, nature conservation and recreation.

Future development pressures upon landscape and environment in the area will continue to come principally from coalmining activity, in the extension of spoil heaps from underground workings, which threaten to encroach upon the more valuable wetland areas, and from a continuing opencast mining
programme involving 219 ha over a 10 year period /Fig. 5/. Pa-
radoxially, this latter development will provide an opportunity for landscape improvement and the expansion of outdoor recreation amenities. Planning consent for opencast workings includes provisions for the restoration of footpaths and reclamation of the land on completion. The present programme will
serve to eliminate large areas of long-standing derelict or

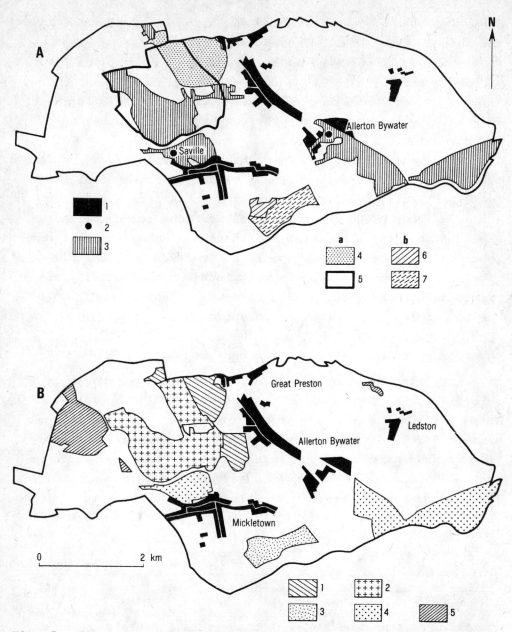

Fig. 5. The Lower Aire Valley
A: mineral workings: 1 = settlements; 2 = operational
pit; 3 = land associated with deep mining; a = opencast
land: 4 = active area; 5 = St. Aidans extension area;
b: sand and gravel workings: 6 = active area; 7 = future
permitted area. B: restoration schemes: 1 = areas under
active restoration; 2 = area covered by St. Aidans restoration scheme; 3 = progressive restoration /sand and
gravel/; 4 = no agreed restoration scheme to date; 5 =
areas recently restored

despoiled land[x] ensuring its return to a green landscape. In
the latter phases, the excavated void will be used to tip spoil
from underground workings and, in addition, a new 73 ha lake
will be created for use as a regional water recreation centre.
An area of sand and gravel extraction will provide a further
45 ha site suitable for competetive water sports, fishing or
power-boating.

A reclaimed landscape is inevitably devoid of mature features /trees, hedgerows etc./ and visual improvement of the
Lower Aire Valley will rely heavily upon skilful landscaping
and screening. Although the Plan cannot hope for complete re-
habilitation, its successful realisation will make a considerable contribution to landscape improvement and the the provision of recreational opportunity in an environmentally deprived area readily accessible to a significant proportion of
the population of the conurbation core.

Development of countryside management schemes

The principles and practice of countryside management
were originally developed in the upland areas of England and
Wales which had come under growing pressure from recreational
activities. Exceptionally large numbers of visitors in sensitive upland environments carried a serious threat of increasing conflict between farming, conservation and recreation. Upland Management Experiments were initiated in the Lake District
/1969-76/ and Snowdonia /1970-78/ to provide a framework for

---

[x]The Metropolitan County contains one of the largest concentrations of derelict and despoiled land in Britain: in 1974,
2860 ha were identified as derelict /"land so damaged by industrial or other development that it is incapable of beneficial use without treatment"/ and a further 4031 ha as despoiled /i.e. potentially derelict/. Central government makes
available 100% grant aid for approved land reclamation pro-
grammes but priority is given to those schemes where the reclaimed land is intended for industrial use. In the Lower Aire
Valley, where there are 545 ha of derelict and despoiled land,
the proposed schemes for environmental enhancement and recreational development are less likely to attract central government grant aid.

42

the implementation of small-scale projects aimed at conserving key landscape features, improving the landscape and enhancing local opportunities for informal recreation without unduly impeding farming practice. The success of these original schemes led to their indtroduction, in one form or another, in the remaining National Parks and in the potentially more challenging environments of the urban fringe - first in the Bollin Valley, an area of 26 km^2 on the southern edge of the Greater Manchester conurbation, in 1972 and subsequently in south Hertfordshire /130 km^2/ and in the Boroughs of Barnet and Havering /19 km^2/ in the Greater London Green Belt.

One of the earliest local authority schemes, Tong-Cockersdale in the more stable central area of the conurbation core of the West Yorkshire Metropolitan County, is jointly funded by the Metropolitan County /50%/ and the Bradford and Leeds Metropolitan Districts /25% each/ with substantial grant aid from the Countryside Commission. The scheme relies heavily upon local voluntary labour and employs one full-time Project Officer whose role is to secure improvements in the rural landscape and public access for informal recreation /e.g. picnic sites, footpaths and bridleways/. He enjoys considerable delegated responsibility from the local authority employers which enables him to respond quickly and practically to requests for assistance from local farmers and landowners, and so build up confidence in the project and achieve better public access.

The success of countryside management schemes lies in their ability to 1. bring together different interest groups in an identifiable task, to clarify objectives, realise some of the area's potential and effect changes in attitudes; 2. create an atmosphere of greater cooperation with farmers and landowners through a programme of small-scale practical improvements and thereby reduce conflicts; 3. produce more appropriate and cheaper results through simplified administration that would be achieved by the local authorities; and, 4. involve voluntary groups from the local community in securing a range of social and educational benefits.

The limitations of such schemes are more readily apparent in areas of major uncertainty and speculation over future land use - conditions which are inherent in the urban fringe. They require a stable planning environment as they have no statutory basis; not all interest groups or government organisations can be persuaded to take part; and not all community needs can be satisfied /e.g. major investments in sport and recreation/. However, they are often the only feasible solutions given high costs of alternatives involving land acquisition on the open market.

The most ambitious programme to date covers an area of 215 km^2 of urban fringe land on the eastern edge of Liverpool and surrounding the town of St. Helens; here good agricultural land and attractive rural landscape is interspersed with tracts of seriously degraded landscape arising from a 200 year history of deep mining and industrial activity. The foundation of the scheme lay in the Merseyside Metropolitan County Structure Plan and in a concern by central government to concentrate invest-ment in a major political initiative in Merseyside. "Operation Groundwork" was launched in 1981, for an initial 5 year period, at a time when resources for both public and private invest-ment were scarce. The significance of this project lies in its attempt to come to terms with the structural and financial lim-itations of countryside management by synchronising a major public investment in the restoration of derelict land with the establishment of a charitable Trust to harness private capital for environmental improvement. Initially, pump-priming funds will be available from the Countryside Commission and from lo-cal authorities but the aim is for the Trust to become increas-ingly self-sufficient. It will coordinate a number of individ-ual environmental improvement projects within the designated area, including landscape restoration schemes in areas left derelict by past mining and industrial activity and the pro-vision of informal recreation opportunities. Particular en-couragement is given to local industry and to local voluntary organisations to propose and assist in the carrying out of im-provement schemes. Certain projects will be carried out with the assistance of temporary employment schemes funded through the Manpower Services Commission. "Operation Groundwork" thus represents an important extension of the principles of partner-

ship between the public sector and private enterprise first
identified, within the framework of countryside management, in
the Upland Management Experiments. It also marks a significant
step forward in the concept of environmental planning in the
urban fringe.[x]

CONCLUSION

The case studies used in this paper to illustrate the problems of the urban fringe in Britain were deliberately chosen
to reinforce the distinction between the urban fringe viewed
as a geographical zone surrounding all towns and cities within
which certain urban-related functions may be expected to occur
and as a specific environmental condition demanding strong prescriptive action by the planning agencies.

Practically all urban settlements will generate some kind
of functional pressure upon the surrounding countryside and
changes to the patterns of land use are inevitable. To this extent the urban fringe may be interpreted as a problem for land
use planning rather than environmental planning. But there is
an important environmental role for the planning agencies to
restrain such pressures from encroaching upon particularly attractive areas of countryside or sensitive ecological sites.
In most cases the urban fringe should be adequately safeguarded
by the sensible application of planning controls and by the
use of existing policy instruments /e.g. Green Belts/.

Urban fringe functions may, however, be combined in such
a way - and with such intensity - as to create a serious environmental condition where the landscape is so abused, patterns of land use and land ownership become so fragmented and
and uncertainty over future land uses is so pervasive that
normal countryside functions, and especially those of agriculture and recreation, can no longer operate efficiently. Under
such conditions, defensive policies based upon planning con-

---

[x]Since this paper was presented the Government has announced
its intention to sponsor similar schemes, through the mechanism of environmental trusts, in the north west of England.

trol are inadequate and remedial action becomes necessary. The danger is that the environmental situation may be allowed to deteriorate so far that normal controls are ineffective and the planner is left with no option but to sacrifice the area. Severe environmental degradation is comparatively rare and where it does exist it is almost certainly not developed as a continuous spatial feature. Thus the urban fringe condition does not occur in a continuous zone around all towns and cities but is more likely to be limited to certain sections of the urban perimeter.

In this paper, we have differentiated between conditions of dynamic economic growth and the stresses of economic decline. Manifest in the growth condition are pressures of land speculation against current measures for the containment of urban expansion. Mineral extraction for aggregates, transportation and distribution systems, refuse and effluent disposal are typical examples of activities which consume and fragment agricultural land. The activities of speculators, keen to realise "green field" options compared to the higher costs of developing inner-city sites, add to the uncertainties.

The need for an outer membrane of city services is as great in regions of relative economic decline. The legacy of previous eras of industrial expansion, the neglect and decay of a scarred landscape is an added burden, while present day mining operations may aggravate the problems still further.

In either case, agriculture is the victim of uncertainty as it struggles with a variety of urban pressures in its attempts to adapt and compete with more productive rural areas. Recreation exerts little-market force and has to be content to follow, taking up the cheaper options. Effective environmental planning has, therefore, to combine a strategic planning of major changes in land use with the finer practical detail of countryside management, based upon the support of all sections of the community. The challenge to environmental planning is to accommodate and move with change in what is, almost by definition, an ever-changing zone. Environmental planning must respond to change by using the opportunities which change pre-

sents. The Lower Aire Valley illustrates the point well, where
open-cast coal working can be harnessed to deal with the problems of residual areas of derelict land and waste disposal and
at the same time provide the basis for a valuable new recreation opportunity. The continuing decentralisation of urban population suggests that the need for environmental planning is
likely to occur over a wider range of locations in Britain in
future.

REFERENCES

1. PRYOR, R. J.: Defining the rural-urban fringe. Social
   Forces 47, 1968, 2o2-215.

2. Urbanisation. Office of Population Censuses and Surveys.
   Census 1981, Preliminary Report England and Wales 1981.

   O.E.C.D. Land Use Policies and Agriculture 1976.

3. Agricultural Production.
   Advisory Council for Agriculture and Horticulture in England and Wales: Agriculture and the Countryside 1978.

   ALBARRE, G., MARSDEN, T.K. and SYMES, D.G.: Intensification de l'agriculture et amenagement du territoire en
   Grande-Bretagne: l'example du North Humberside. Revue Belge
   de Geographie lo4, 1980 3-12.

   BEST, R.H.: Land Use and Living Space 1981.

   Centre for Agricultural Strategy. Land for Agriculture, CAS
   Report No. 1, 1976.

   COLEMAN, A.: Land use planning: success or failure? Archi-
   tects Journal 19 Jan., 1977, 94-134.

   COLEMAN, A.: Is planning really necessary? Geographical
   Journal 142, 1976, 411-457.

   Countryside Review Committee: Food Production in the Countryside. C.R.C. Topic Paper, No. 3, 1978.

   LOW, N.: Farming and the inner Green Belt. Town Planning
   Review 44, 1973, 103-116.

Ministry of Agriculture, Fisheries and Food: Agriculture in the Urban Fringe: a Survey of the Slough/Hillingdon Area. ADAS Technical Report 30, 1973.

MUNTON, R.J.C.: Farming on the Urban Fringe, Chapter 10 /pp. 201-223/. In: Suburban Growth: Geographical Pressures at the Edge of the western City /ed. J.H. Johnson/, 1974.

THOMSON, K.J.: Farming in the Fringe. CCP 142, Countryside Commission, 1981.

4. Recreational Opportunity
Countryside Review Committee: Leisure and the Countryside. CRC Topic Paper, No. 2, 1977.

DAVIDSON, J.: Recreation and the Urban Fringe. The Planner 60, 1974, 889-893.

ELSON, M.: The Leisure Use of Green Belts and Urban Fringe. 1979.

FITTON, M.: The Urban Fringe and the less privileged. Countryside Recreation Review 1, 1976, 25-34.

HALL, A.: Management in the Urban Fringe. Countryside Recreation Review 1, 1976, 8-13.

TRAVIS, A.S. and VEAL, A.J. /eds/: Recreation and the Urban Fringe. Conference Proceedings, 1976.

5. Policy Constraints
BLACKSELL, M and GILG, A.: The Countryside: Planning and Change. 1981.

Countryside Commission: Countryside Management in the Urban Fringe. CCP 136, 1981.

Countryside Commission: The Bolin Valley: A Study of Land Management in the Urban Fringe. CCP 97, 1976.

Countryside Review Committee: The Countryside - Problems and Policies 1976.

DAVIDSON, J. and WIBBERLEY, G.: Planning and the Rural Environment. 1977.

ELSON, M. /ed./: Perspectives on Green Belt Local Plans. Oxford Polytechnic Department of Town Planning Working Paper, No. 38, 1979.

HALL, P.: The containment of urban England. Geographical Journal 14o, 1974, 386-417.

STEELEY, G.: Low-key solutions: the contribution of country-side management, the Hertfordshire experience, pp. 83-89. In: Making the Most of Limited Resources - Practical Lessons in Countryside Recreation, Conference Report, 1980.

6. The Metropolitan Counties
ELSON, M.: The Urban Fringe: Open Land Policies and Pro-grammes in the Metropolitan Counties. Countryside Commission Working Paper 14, 1979.

7. West Yorkshire and the Conurbation Core
West Yorkshire Metropolitan County Council: Structure Plan Report of Survey, Vols 1 and 2, 1977.

8. West Yorkshire County Council: Lower Aire Valley Environ-mental Subject Plan /Phase 1/, Draft Report of Survey 1981.

THE PROTECTION OF AGRICULTURAL LAND ON THE URBAN FRINGE: THE CASE OF VESZPRÉM CITY

E. DARÓCZI

IMPORTANCE OF LAND PROTECTION

The demographic explosion, radical changes in the quantitative and qualitative aspects of production, degradation of the conditions of biological existence and most directly the energy crisis have amplified the concern for vulnerable, exhaustible natural resources all over the world. Among these agricultural land deserves particular protection for providing the vital conditions for renewing vegetation - food, fibre, energy. It is also a finite resource, and substitution is only possible to a limited extent.

As for Hungary, long standing efforts to make rational use of existing natural resources, to develop an economic structure which squares with national endowments as well as the strategic importance of food have recently focussed attention on land protection. The need had already been formulated in the Land Protection Act of 1961 but important advances were only made following the 11th Congress of the Hungarian Socialist Workers' Party in 1975 which stated in a programme declaration: "Land in the Hungarian People's Republic - irrespective of the form of ownership - represents national wealth." /19, p. 2o1/ and /17/

Delay in acting cannot be justified but can be partly explained by an undervaluation of productive land stemming from the socio-economic policies predominant in Hungary until late 1970s, which favoured industry and urban development at the expense of agriculture and rural settlements. The relative abundance of land also delayed recognization of the damage caused by wasteful land management. In spite of a significant loss of cultivated areas, and important changes in land use structure /5, 12, 18/, land supply can still be regarded as favourable.

In 1981, 70.9% of the total national territory was used for agricultural cultivation. In Europe, Hungary ranks second to Denmark with regard to the proportion of intensive farming: out of the total area of the country, 50.4% is arable land, 3.7% gardens, 3.0% orchards and vineyards and 13.8% is meadows and pastures /31, p. 148/. Population density is only 1.6 person per one hectare of the agricultural area.

Only a small part of the land is of excellent quality, however, and most is of mediocre fertility while about one third is poor soil requiring amelioration. Nevertheless, due to the mutually reinforcing effects of relatively advantageous relief and climatic conditions and high farming standards, Hungarian agriculture has successfully raised yields and quality /6, 10/.

The economic importance of this sector is shown by the fact that in 1981, one quarter of the total value of exports and one third of exports in convertible currency were made up of agricultural and food industrial products /31, p. 197/. According to certain estimates, it will be possible in the long run to export one third of Hungary's total food production /6/.

The results achieved are particularly valuable considering the fact that traditionally, agriculture has been the least profitable productive sector /11/. After correcting the serious agro-political mistakes of the 1950s, important steps were taken to strengthen the self-management of cooperative farms and to widen their range of activities. But even so, agriculture still has a disadvantageous position in the system of state taxation and subsidies due to the extensive application of fixed and maximum prices for socio-political consideration and for the purpose of maintaining export marketability. An over-centralization of food foreign trade plays a negative role, too /10, 23, 30/.

At the same time, there has been a growing demand for urban land resulting from vigorous population growth in cities and towns and from the concentration of production and servicing activities in central places. There are several reasons for this. In-migrants have settled mainly on the urban peripheries in new housing estates of medium and high rise dwellings, while the need of town dwellers for green areas and daily and weekly recreation has been increasing. Furthermore, the low cost of the acquisition and use of industrial, commercial, institutional areas has not encouraged investors to economize on land. Master planners consider primarily safety and health protection factors when deciding on the location of incompatible urban uses. Their hands are much more bound by compulsory "minimal distances", immediate cost factors and the likelihood of rapid realization than the requirements of rationally compact /not crowded!/ urban planning and the need for the reconstruction of derelict and untidy "urban" plots.

Up to 1923 the expansion of agricultural land through deforestation and drainage projects surpassed any contraction due to urbanization. Since World War II, however, agricultural areas have been rapidly decreasing: up till now 500,000 ha have been lost to production /12/. Following the introduction of the Land Protection Act, the decrease in the cultivated area slowed down temporarily, but the process again intensified during the 1970s /18/. There is an urgent need for amplifying and improving legislation concerning the protection of land harried by the expansion of the built up as well as green leisure areas /4/ and which at the same time is not being protected by economic interest.

LEGAL FRAMEWORK OF LAND PROTECTION

The economic benefit of the environment- including land - usually shows up only in the long run and is not necessarily restricted to its owner/user. Due to the lack of direct and strong economic interest by farmers and due to strict restrictions concerning the market in land as a means of production, legislation plays an outstanding role in land protection in Hungary.

The Land Protection Act of 1961 contains provision for agricultural land use, soil protection, increasing fertility and land conversion. The Act is actuated by a progressive spirit but for long it served mainly as a guiding principle. Since its introduction several detailed amendments have been made but the first comprehensive enacting clauses appeared only in 1977. It is quite symptomatic that sanctions against land conversion from agricultural to urban uses were made much more rigorous in 1977 and again in 1981. One cannot yet speak of coordinated, comprehensive legislation embracing all aspects of the protection, use, ownership and marketing of land, including regulations for both agricultural and urban use, but preparations are being made to elaborate a new, integrated Land Code and Urban Development Act and the related issues are widely debated at expert meetings and in professional publications.

From among the various land control regulations, only those will be touched upon below which are directly connected with settlement development namely, legislation concerning the expansion of areas to be urbanized and land conversion.

The administrative areas of all Hungarian settlements are divided into inner and outer areas and some have garden zones, too. Districts are made according to specific functions. Consequently, compelling and forbidding regulations concerning land use /cultivation, construction/ and the modes of property acquisition and alienation vary by locality in inner or outer areas or in the garden zone, not to speak of land prices which differ considerably also. As for the inner areas, the purchase or expropriation price is defined by the market value of construction sites in personal ownership but in outer areas the bargaining has to be based on the agricultural value of the land.

The inner area is designed for settlement /urban/ development. It is managed by the local council which fixes its boundaries and decides upon its use. Modifications are made when the master plan is being prepared and later continuously as the realization of the plan advances, usually in five year periods.

The outer area, pragmatically, is the land between inner area/s/ and the administrative borders of a settlement. Its function depends on local endowments and needs, i.e. large-scale farming and silviculture, wildlife, industry, infrastructure, tourism, recreation and special state use.

The garden zone - traditionally orchards and vineyards - is a part of the outer area and is usually found in hilly areas where large-scale farming is not economical. In order to maintain farming, these areas are designated for individual ownership. The primary function of the garden zone is production - however small the land should be, it has to be cultivated - but it also serves recreational, hobby purposes.

The personal right to agricultural land was recognized in 1967 with the introduction of the new economic mechanism. Subsequently, garden zones were delimited by expert committees created in each of the 19 counties of Hungary.

Land for agricultural use is defined in the Land Protection Act as arable land, vineyards, gardens, orchards, grassland, reeds and fishponds located in the outer areas and garden zones of settlements /the capital, cities, towns and villages/ and any other uncultivated land which justifies restoration. Land control regulations are enforced in inner areas as well if there is a land of more than 1,500 m^2 suitable for agriculture.

Land for non-agricultural use is located in the inner areas of settlements together with land withdrawn from agricultural use and land for which such a permission was given.

Both the expansion of inner areas and land conversion from agricultural to other uses are subject to previous permission. According to the regulations introduced in 1977, land offices were given powers that replaced their earlier advisory role, and only with their permission should appropriation of agricultural land be ordered and investments started.

Applications should be submitted to the lowest level /town and non-urban district/ land offices who have the power to make decisions for land up to 3 ha in extent. Between 3-10 ha the consent of the county land office is required, while above 10 ha the consent of the Ministry for Agriculture and Food is needed. Town and district land offices cannot refuse permission if a higher ranked institution has consented. Unfortunately, this may impede land protection because applicants with high level connections may wangle extra favours.

This obligation also relates to areas which are designated for building in master plans. Thus at present, the right of control over urban sprawl lies with the land offices.

Regulations stipulated in the National Building Code, according to which

"Land use categories - excepting agricultural and silvicultural land - are to be designated so that first of all those lands should be used which are inadequate for agricultural production or which are of poor quality. Designations should be limited to the smallest possible areas satisfying the needs." /32, p. 9/ only give principle guidelines but do not stimulate the planner to manage the area of a settlement in a rational, thrifty way.

The fact that inner areas have been under-utilized for urban purposes is reflected by the legal measures taken in 1977 /enacting clauses of the Land Protection Act/ and in 1980 /instructions of the minister for Building and Urban Development/ in which a revision of inner area boundaries of all Hungarian settlements was ordered. The aim was to provide increased protection to those lands which are cultivated by large scale farms and the urbanization of which is not expected within five years, by transferring them from inner back to outer areas.

Where land is converted from agricultural to other uses an indemnity is usually levied, irrespective of the compensation paid for the acquisition of the ownership or the use of the land. This is an essential feature of the 1977 amendment to the Land Protection Act laying great stress on the importance of land control by rendering location on cultivated land more expensive.

In Hungary, land is grouped into eight quality classes within each agricultural land use, the best land being first class. According to the regulations of 1977, indemnity was only to be paid for the conversion of lands in classes 1 to 5 and the rates of taxes were graduated moderately depending upon the quality of land. For example, the rate of indemnity on first class arable land was double that on the fifth class. The taxable property value until the new land value system under preparation is introduced, is the net income of land as established at the end of the last century and revision in 1909. Regulations valid from 1982 stipulate that an indemnity shall be paid for the conversion of land in all eight quality classes, while the tax rates have been significantly increased as follows: in class 5: tax rates increased 3 1/4 times, in class 4: 3.6 times, in class 3: 3 5/6 times, in class 2: 4 times while in the first class 4 1/8 times.

An indemnity is not levied if the interested party recultivates the land to a value equivalent to the sum otherwise charged, or if the investment concerned serves soil protection or irrigation. It is important for urban development that conversion of agricultural land in inner areas into public parks is tax-free, while the indemnity is reduced by one half if land conversion is for the purpose of housing. Where conversion without permission takes place, the usual indemnity is tripled.

Until 1982, such indemnities were paid into the development funds of count councils which decided on their use within regular budgetary planning. These most concerned, namely the tax-payers, the former farmers and those who knew the local situation best, i.e. the local councils and land offices, had no means of influencing the way in which this money was used.

According to the present regulations, only half the receipts from such indemnities are paid into the development funds of county councils with the other half going towards the creation of a Land Protection Fund which may also have other financial resources. It would, however, be preferable if all indemnities as well as all taxes and fees related to land use went into this Fund which would thereby ensure that all secondary revenues derived from the land be used for its amelioration and reclamation /22/. The Land Protection Fund is used for the reclamation of derelict and fallow lands, and subsidies from it are allocated by county councils upon application from state and cooperative organizations.

During 1980 and 1981, the total sum of indemnities levied in County Veszprém came to 12,800,000 and 9,500,000 forints respectively, i.e. an average of 1.1% of the development fund of the County Council. In 1980, 93 permissions were given for the withdrawal of 355 ha land from agricultural use. Besides claims for afforestation /12 cases making up 147 ha/, 19 other cases comprising 68 ha were tax-free. No application was refused.

In 1981, 106 permissions were given on 1,136 ha, while 19 applications for afforestation on 753 ha and 12 cases on 90 ha were tax-free. 5 applications relating to 189 ha were refused /47, 51/.

Also in County Veszprém alone, the size of the Land Protection Fund was estimated at six million forints for the year 1982 which are assessed to be sufficient to cover the reclamation costs of 500-600 ha of land /39/.

Although the above regulations stand for urban fringes as well, no specific measures were taken.

It is expected that legislation introduced in 1982, will encourage the re-utilization of agricultural alnd and will curb any decrease, particularly that of arable land on good quality soils.

In 1981, agricultural land decreased by 19,022 ha /-0.3%/ in Hungary and at the same time 7,418 ha of forest, reed or unused areas were recultivated. The area of land withdrawn from agricultural use increased by 18,010 ha, from which 2,157 ha were withdrawn without permission. Out of the above increase, 30.5% was taken from arable land, 30.6% from gardens and 21.4% from forests. 21.4% of the newly withdrawn land was land on quite good quality soils. The proportion of classes 1-3 land among withdrawn arable land was even higher at 32.6% /48/.

The effects of the latest measures cannot yet be evaluated. Lasting results, however, will only be achieved if the societal interest in maintaining cultivation and in protecting land is given direct expression in the financial interests of agricultural employers, the farmers themselves, as well as urb-

an land users. This should also be promoted by increased state
subsidies differentiated by regions and products.

Nevertheless, the above restrictive and incentive measures
- which stand for urban fringes as well - can only be effective
if they are based on reasonable land values /22/. A new evaluation system for productive land is already under preparation.
Parallel to this, the evaluation of urban areas will also be of
supreme importance because at present rational urban land use
is not backed by any principled system of norms /45/, even
though this is an important factor which also influences the
extent to which the non-agricultural use of land can be limited.

VESZPRÉM CITY. A GENERAL DESCRIPTION

The city is situated in Transdanubia, between the Bakony
Mountains and Lake Balaton /Maps 1, 2/ on a low plateau surface
dissected into seven hills by a series of narrow valleys. North-
South fractures are dominant to which variety is added by an
incised meander of the River Séd.

The past development of this historical city was determined by the coincidence of various central functions, the most
important of which were royal quarters, county seat, religious
and military centre, city character from the turn of the 18th-
19th centuries, crown and church estates, handicrafts, and
trade. During the 20th century, the royal character and handi-
craft functions have disappeared while the role of the church
has diminished significantly, but the other functions have been
transformed and strengthened and the city has also obtained important new roles.

During the past decades, productive, administrative, educational, scientific and tourist activities have become predominant. The city was already surrounded by large industrial
centres /mainly the chemical industry/ when significant industrialization was begun in Veszprém during the 1960s. But in
spite of her function as an administrative centre, only 15 of
the 39 state and cooperative industrial plants located in the
city have their headquarters there /29/. This is disadvanta-

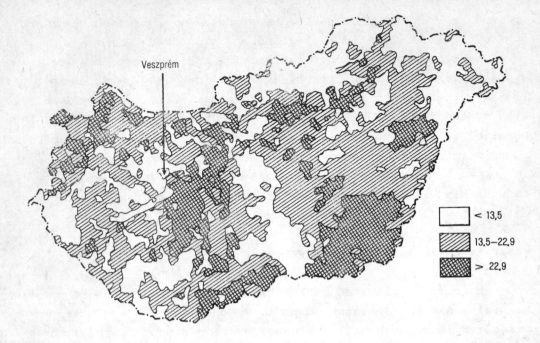

Map 1. The net income of productive land /gold crowns per hec-
        tare/. After /6, p. 186/

geous from the aspect of urban development because it is much
more difficult for local organizations to cooperate   with and
influence enterprises which are located locally but controlled
from a distance; furthermore, locally managed institutes and
factories care much more about settlement development.

        The historically developed radial road network has only
recently changed, in spite of extensive urban sprawl. The relatively even concentric development could continue for so long
because the railway was at some distance from the centre to
the north and large industries have only recently been located
in peripheral areas, close to the railway /Map 3/, /29/.

        During the last two decades, population increase in Veszp-
rém has been extremely dynamic in comparison with average urban population growth in Hungary. Within the present administrative boundaries, the number of inhabitants has grown from
22,000 in 1941 to 38,000 in 1970 and to 57,000 by 1982, and
such an unprecedented development has rendered all master plans

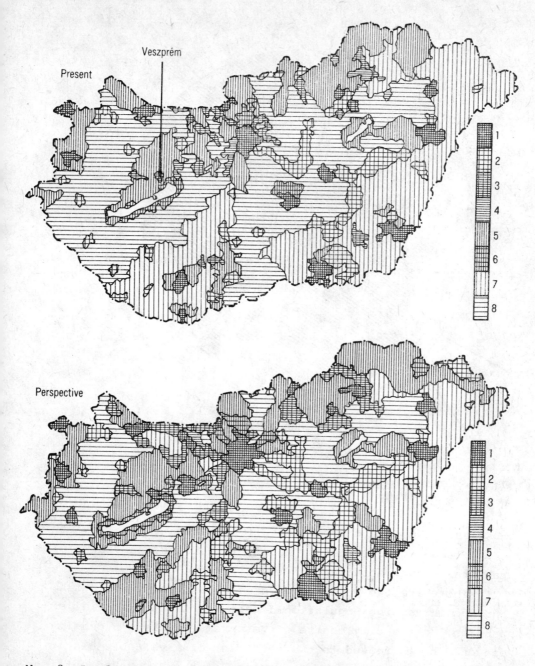

Map 2. Land use zoning in Hungary. Source: /23/
1 = urban zone; 2 = urban-like zone; 3 = built-up zone;
4 = natural zone with built-up areas; 5 = natural zone;
6 = built-up zone requiring environmental development;
7 = agricultural zone; 8 = agricultural zone with built-
up areas

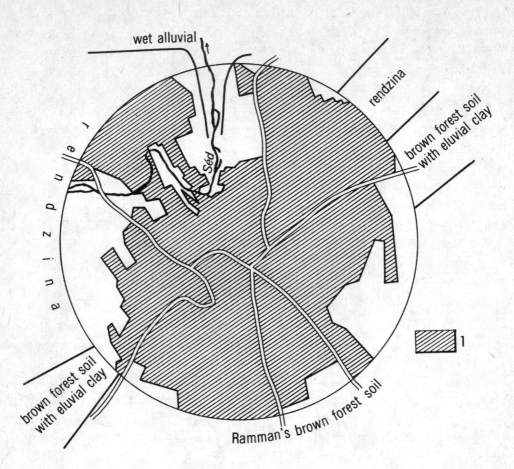

Map 3. Soils around Veszprém City. Source: /36, 38/
        1 = built-up area

obsolescent before they could be implemented fully. The constant race to tackle needs, mainly in housing, has transformed
the traditional structure of the city.

There are two possible ways of urban growth, either
through increasing population density or through spatial expansion. In the city centre of Veszprém, population density
can only be increased to the detriment of a valuable historic
core or at the expense of the valley of the River Séd outside
those limited area requiring slum clearance /33/. Moreover,
the construction of the necessary public utilities would be

very expensive in some parts of the city due to the dolomite sub-surface, while proper sewage disposal is of paramount importance as the city is supplied from karst water in its immediate neighbourhood.

In order to speed up housing construction and for technical and other reasons, new residential districts, as in most Hungarian towns, have been built on the peripheries since the 1960s, as a result of which the urban area of Veszprém has expanded in a North-South direction.

Increased inner city and transit traffic has overstreched the only East-West main road to such an extent that acute traffic congestion in the centre now forms a constant obstacle to the normal functioning of the city.

Traffic surveys made during 1964 established an average travel speed of 22-23 km/h while 1,160 vehicles per hour used the main road in the city centre, in each direction. Another problem to be solved was the diversion of freight traffic, because a weight limit imposed on the viaduct, a particular feature of the city, could not be lifted /40/.

The construction of a ring road has become a major issue and besides improving communications, has also been given an important role in planning the spatial expansion of the city as well.

The latest master plan for Veszprém City was approved by the local council in November 1982, following several years of preparation. The plan could not disregarded land protection requirements, and had to take into consideration the quality of land on the urban fringe where the existence of soils of excellent fertility is very precious in a region where good land is not abundant /see Maps 1 and 3/, /36/.

1. To the south and south-east of the centre, along about 40% of an imaginary circle drawn around the built up area, there is a contiguous zone of Ramann's brown forest soil, the best land of the urban region with second and third class arable land as well. This area is located between the city and Lake Balaton, and is very attractive for developers,

not only because of a privileged geographical situation but also because construction is relatively easy and cheap.

2. At each end of the above mentioned area, along about 5-5% of the circle there are brown forest soils with eluvial clay, which are second in terms of quality.

3. On an extensive area to the west and less prominently to the east of the city /along about 25 and 5% of the imaginary circle/, poor rendzina soils are found.

4. Finally, to the north of the city centre, beyond the railway, along the remaining 20% of the invisible ring, as well as in the valley of the River Séd, wet alluvial soils are predominant.

About two-fifths of the last two sections are covered, in effect, by bare dolomite /33/.

Urban expansion in the direction of poor soils is limited by industry, the railway and last but not least by military use, and given there constraints it follows that it is the best quality land that is under the greatest pressure, and is most directly threatened.

CONFLICTS BETWEEN AGRICULTURAL AND URBAN LAND USE

At the beginning of the 1970s, the present economic difficulties and slow down in the dynamism of demographic processes were not perceptible. The policy-makers of Veszprém county and the City had ambitious expectations: the number of inhabitants in Veszprém City would reach 100,000 by the turn of the century, the city would develop into an important industrial centre and would attract a good part of the tourism along Lake Balaton. Financial means were strongly concentrated for the development of the county seat. Several housing estates were built and some spectacular projects realized to increase the prestige of the city but no mature strategic plan was elaborated to coordinate these developments. Deficiencies in technical and social infrastructure caused intolerable tensions. A solution to these problems was sought through a new master plan for the city /45/. Plan investigations had already started in 1974. Various and sometimes conflicting standpoints and interest were expressed during the planning process, and the plan finally approved reflects a compromise reached after consultation and debate as well as highlighting the modified socio-economic circumstances and priorities.

The limits of urban expansion have been determined in the master plan by defining the size of the inner area. Earlier aspirations for the city are expressed in the facts that the village of Kádárta was annexed to Veszprém in 1973 while the inner area of the city was enlarged from 920 ha to 2,246 ha in 1976. Later, with regard to the changed economic situation and in the interest of land protection 257 ha were transferred back to the outer area on the north and south sides of the city. Thus at present, most of the areas planned to be urbanized are delimited by the ring road. The original plan, according to which the inner area would have extended beyond the south arc of the road by 600 ha was refused by the Ministry for Agriculture and Food, and permission was only given for the withdrawal of 65 ha of agricultural land for housing purposes. But for the moment it seems that even this smaller area will not be developed for some time.

Frequent modifications of inner areas and delayed registration of changes have led to several misunderstandings and legal cases. The owners whose lands are to be appropriated are interested in receiving the market prices of construction sites while those who have to pay, are keen to assert that the land concerned has been in agricultural use.

Gross losses of agricultural land within the total administrative area of Veszprém City are shown in Table I, broken down by purpose of conversion, for the period 1972-1981. /All data set out here and below are estimated figures./

In spite of considerable decreases, one third of the present, reduced inner area /1,989 ha/ was still used for agriculture in 1982, while the proportion of forests was 5% and the remaining 62% represented other uses. But a large part of this withdrawn area was not or could not be used by the city

Table I. Withdrawal of agricultural lands for other uses in Veszprém City[x] between 1972-1981 /in ha/

Use Year	Build-ing in-dustry	Manu-fac-turing	Roads and re-lated uses	Ware-hous-ing	Commun-al es-tablish-ments: dumps, purifica-tion plant, energy,sup-ply etc,	Hous-ing, ga-rages	Servicing repair, clean-ing etc.	medical cultur-al etc.	Parks	"Urban" total	Mining	Forest-ry	Other state uses	Others total	Total
	1	2	3	4	5	6	7	8	9	1-9	10	11	12	10-12	1-12
1972-73	-	3.84	0.37	-	0.08	7.32	-	-	-	11.61	16.19	20.o9	-	36.28	47.89
1974-75	11.90	51.33	10.70	21.56	5.88	7.65	-	2.76	11.50	123-28	-	23.04	-	23-o4	146.32
1976-77	15.14	-	6.79	3.18	0.05	86.39	3.19	-	-	114.74	-	140.52	0.25	140.77	255.51
1978-79	-	3.70	0.43	-	1.61	1.36	-	-	-	7.10	-	18.24	-	18.24	25.33
1980-81	-	7.21	10.91	-	3.33	4.98	-	-	-	26.43	-	-	420.38	420.38	446.82
Total ha	27.04	66.08	29.20	27.74	10.95	107.70	3.19	2.76	11.50	283.16	16.19	201.89	420.63	638.71	921.87
%	9.6	23.3	10.3	8.7	3.9	38.0	1.1	1.0	4.1	100.00	-	-	-	-	-
%	2.9	7.2	3.2	2.7	1.2	11.7	0.3	0.3	1.2	30.7	1.8	21.9	45.6	69.3	100.00

[x]The administrative area of Veszprém City amounts to 7.945 hectares

Source: Sebestyén, E. /48/

and consisted of derelict sand and gravel workings, industrial
sites and military use. This fact has been used for argumenting
against inner area expansion: let the reserves within the boundaries be used first. But developers alleged technical difficulties, environmental constraints and costs as reasons. The conflict has been "resolved" with the passing of time: the pace of
urban growth has diminished, the period of large new industrial
investments is over, urban construction and qualitative improvements have gained ground, and at the same time, rigorous land
protection regulations have been introduced.

In 1980-81, most of the agricultural land converted for
urban uses /26.43 ha, see Table I/ was located in the inner
area of Veszprém City. Indemnities were levied for all conver-
sions, occasionally very large sums, amounting to 100,000-
150,000 forints per hectare. And this financial burden was mul-
tipled as of 1982 /50/. The local council is particularly affected, and in spite of the allowances is unable to cover indemnity payments for the withdrawal of agricultural land for
housing from its regular budget, while new residents can only
be charged with these expenditures within the limits of construction site market prices /34/.

The largest consumer of good land in the city is the local
Public Road Management which is responsible for the construction and maintenance of the ring road. The construction started in 1977 connecting with road reconstruction carried out in
1974-76. Its total length will be 16 km, out of which 11.8 km
were open by the end of 1982 /40/. So far 55 ha of land have
been appropriated for the purposes of the finished section,
mainly productive land, most of it prior to 1978 when indemnity
payments were first enforced /41/.

Up to now, about 6,000,000 forints /41/ have been spent
on the acquisition of land. Most of this sum has been for the
appropriation or purchase prices even so it amounts to almost
3% of the total investment in the finished road-section.

The proportion of land costs is expected to increase, not
only because of the enforcement and augmentation of indemnities
but also because state owned lands were exchanged free of

charge up to 1978, since then money can be charged for the transfer of the use of land. Veszprém City Council has not exercised the right with Public Road Management although Veszprém State Farm has done so. Furthermore, extra expenses are caused by the tardiness of the land office /41/.

Most of the agricultural land in Veszprém City is owned by Dózsa Agricultural Cooperative, and conversion to urban uses therefore mainly affect their land. The total area of the cooperative is 6,000 ha. There are 800 cooperative members and 1,200 effective workers - including employees - out of which 900 persons are engaged in industrial activities /44/.

The president of the cooperative "successfully speculated" in land: as soon as it became possible in 1968, the cooperative bought up all the state owned land which it had cultivated and later when some of the cooperative land was used for non-agricultural purposes, considerable sums had to be paid as compensation for expropriation. As a result, serious charges were brought against the cooperative and its president /44/; that agriculture should profited from the differences in land value was without precedent at that time.

From 1968 onwards, 200-300 ha of arable land belonging to the cooperative and around 600 ha of other land /forest included/ were expropriated for about 15,000,000 and 20,000,000 forints, respectively. During the same period, the cooperative invested 200,000,000 forints and the contribution of the compensation payments to this was therefore considerable. As a matter of fact, the cooperative naturally rids itself of its poor land with pleasure but at the same time is still keen to preserve a relatively low average land value in order not to loose state subsidies /43/.

In the view of the president, the most serious problem derived from the location of the cooperative on urban fringe is the various disfunctional operations carried out on cultivated land which disturb agricultural production. The ring road has disrupted some of the best land on which machine cultivation is now very difficult. The cooperative also has to tolerate the use of its land for the laying of pipe-lines etc.

Although the users have to pay compensation for damage caused, they can usually charge this to others and there is therefore no incentive to diminish such damages. Apart from personal persuation, the cooperative has no means of decreasing damages by the proper scheduling of outside work. It can come to terms with the City Council and local enterprises but it is very hard to influence institutions controlled from other counties, particularly from Budapest /44/.

CONCLUSIONS

The protection of irreplaceable agricultural land, an asset of increasing value, is a national cause. It would be best safeguarded by rendering agricultural production more profitable. In the present situation, it is very difficult to change the prevailing view that the loss of cultivated land is normal and inevitable /16, 18/. Improved legislation is needed but cannot replace economic regulators while the present legal frameworks provide more for the financial compensation of loss than in preventing it.

"It is most important, however, that instead of a simple money flow, that land be esteemed and respected. The Land Protection Act must become a matter of common knowledge like the red light in traffic control..." /44/.

Land protection should cover not only cultivated land but all land withdrawn from agriculture. This requires the elaboration of basic principles of rational urban land use. For the moment one must rest satisfied that the requirements of land protection are considered in master planning as constraints /2, 15/; the use of unreasonably large and particularly good quality agricultural land for urban use is now significantly more difficult than previously.

Finally, qualitative improvements are needed in the activities of institutions professionally dealing with land control. It is not necessary the case that a higher level decision-maker takes national interests more into account than a local one. It would therefore seem advisable to invest local authorities with more competence for the sake of the land.

REFERENCES

1. ANDORKA, R. /1982/: Az életmód területi különbségei az idő-mérleg-felvétel alapján /Spatial differences in the way of life based on time-budget surveys/. - Területi Statisztika, Vol. 32, No. 4, 344-358.

2. BARÁTH, E. /1981/: Az országos területrendezési tervkoncepció /The national strategic physical plan/. - Városépités, No. 2, 5-18.

3. BARTA, B. /1982/: Az urbanizációs folyamat társadalmi és környezeti vonatkozásai /Social and environmental aspects of urbanization process/. - Területi Statisztika, Vol. 32, No. 4, 313-329.

4. BERÉNYI, I. /1980/: Die geographischen Typen der Brache in Ungarn /Geographical types of fallow in Hungary/. - Erdkunde, Vol. 34, No. 1, 36-46.

5. BERÉNYI, I. /1980/: A területhasznositás átalakulásának főbb irányai az Alföldön /Main tendencies of land use transformation in the Great Hungarian Plain/. - Alföldi Tanulmányok, IV, 63-84.

6. BERNÁT, T. /ed./ /1981/: Magyarország gazdaságföldrajza /Economic geography of Hungary/. - Tankönyvkiadó, Budapest.

7. BUNYEVÁCZ, J. /1981/: A települési környezet epitésének, a-lakitásának környezetvédelmi szempontjai /Environmental aspects of building and shaping settlement environment/. - Városépités, No. 1, 12-15.

8. DARÓCZI, E. /1982/: Suburban land economy. A case study in Veszprém functional urban region. - In: Development of Rural Areas /Ed. by J. Kostrowicki and W. Stola/ Proceedings of the 4th Hungarian--Polish Seminar, Goldap, Poland, 20-30 May, 1980, 69-89.

9. EGRI, A. /1982/: Gondolatok "A jog szerepe termőföldjeink megóvásában" cimü tanulmányhoz /Comments to a study on "The role of legislation in land protection"/. - Tudomány és Mezőgazdaság, Vol. 20, No. 5, 28-31.

10. ENYEDI, Gy. /ed./ /1976/: Rural transformation in Hungary. Akadémiai Kiadó, Budapest.

11. ENYEDI, Gy. /1982/: Industrial activities in large scale farms. In: Development of rural areas /Ed. by J. Kostrowicki and W. Stola/ Proceedings of the 4th Hungarian--Polish Seminar, Gołdap, Poland, 20-30 May, 1980, 41-54.

12. HOFFER, I. /1982/: A nemzeti kincs megőrzése /Preserving the national wealth/. - Figyelő, Vol.26, February 3.

13. JANTNER, A. /1982/: A települési környezetvédelem koncepciója és követelményrendszere /The concept and the system of norms in settlement environment protection/. - Városépités, No. 1, 1-2.

14. KATONA, S. /1981/: A települések környezetre gyakorolt hatásának értékelése /Evaluation of settlement influence on environment/. - Földr. Ért., Vol. 30, No. 1, 123-132.

15. KÁLNOKI KIS, S. /1982/: A városfejlesztés-településfejlesztés új tendenciái /New tendencies in town and settlement development/. - Társadalmi Szemle, Vol. 37, No. 5, 63-71.

16. KORONCZAY, M. /1982/: A termőföld hasznositását elősegitő jogi eszközök /Legal means promoting the use of productive land/. - Állam és Igazgatás, Vol. 32, No. 5, 411-417.

17. LÁNG, I. /1982/: A hazai környezetvédelmi kutatások eredményei és további feladatai /Results and tasks of environmental research in Hungary/. - Magyar Tudomány, Vol. 27, No. 12, 894-903.

18. LUKÁCS, B. /1982/: A termőföld védelmének időszerü kérdései /Current issues in land protection/. - Geodézia és Kartográfia, Vol. 34, No. 6, 402-406.

19. A Magyar Szocialista Munkáspárt XI. Kongresszusa /The 11th Congress of the Hungarian Socialist Workers' Party/. - Kossuth Könyvkiadó, Budapest, 1975.

20. Mezőgazdasági és Élelmezésügyi Értesitő /Bulletin of the Ministry for Agriculture and Food/. XXXIII, 10, Budapest, April 30 1982, 526-596.

21. MOLNÁR, I. /1982/: Miért nem nő a mezőgazdaság nemzeti jövedelemhez való hozzájárulása? /Why does the contribution of agriculture not grow in national income?/ - Közgazdasági Szemle, Vol. 29, No. 2, 172-179.

22. NAGY, L. /1982/: A földtulajdon és a földhasználat szabályozásáról de lege ferenda /On the regulation of land ownership in land use de lege ferenda/. - Állam és Igazgatás, Vol. 32, No. 8, 686-695.

23. ROMÁNY, P. /1982/: A szocialista agrárátalakulás és a falu változása /Socialist agrarian transformation and changes in villages/. - Társadalmi Szemle, Vol. 37, No. 4, 39-52.

24. SÁRÁNDI, I. /1982/: A jog szerepe termőföldjeink megóvásában /The role of law in land protection/. - Tudomány és Mezőgazdaság, Vol. 20, No. 5, 24-27.

25. SOÓS, G. /1982/: A termőföld a mezőgazdasági termelésben /Productive land in agricultural use/. - Tudomány és Mezőgazdaság, Vol. 20, No. 5, 9-12.

26. STEFANOVITS, P. /1982/: A termőföld megismerése, használata és védelme /Knowing, using and protecting productive land/. - Tudomány és Mezőgazdaság, Vol. 20, No. 5, 3-8.

27. THIERY, A. /1981/: Királynék városa /Town of Queens/. - Szépirodalmi Könyvkiadó, Budapest.

28. TÓTH, J. /1981/: A településhálózat és a környezet kölcsönhatásának néhány elméleti és gyakorlati kérdése /Some theoretical and practical problems of the interrelationship between the settlement network and the environment/. - Földr. Ért., Vol. 30, Nos. 2-3, 267-292.

29. Veszprémi településcsoport általános rendezési terve /Master plan of Veszprém functional urban region/. - Városépitési Tudományos és Tervező Intézet, Budapest, 1982.

30. ZSUFFA, E. /1982/: A mezőgazdasági nagyüzemek differenciált fejlődése /Differentiated development of large-scale farms/. - Társadalmi Szemle, Vol. 37, No. 4, 3-19.

31. Statistical Pocket Book of Hungary, 198. - Statistical Publishing House, Budapest, 1982.

32. Országos Épitésügyi Szabályzat /National Building Code/. - Épitésügyi Tájékoztatási Központ, Budapest, 1974.

Private communications and unpublished materials from:
Veszprém City Council
    33. BALASSA, László
    34. TAKÁCS, Zoltánné

Veszprém County Land Office
    35. Dr. FÖLDY, János
    36. HOLCZHAUSER, Jenő
    37. Dr. PALATINUS, Sándor
    38. ZACHARIÁS, Márton

Veszprém County Council
    39. Dr. GÁNCS, Lajos

Public Road Management, Veszprém
    40. BORDÁCS, Szilveszter
    41. Dr. SZENTMIKLÓSSY, László

DÓZSA Agricultural Cooperative, Veszprém
    42. Dr. ORTUTAY, Gábor
    43. POSTA, László
    44. Dr. VARGA, Zoltán /President/

Institute for Town Planning and Architecture, Budapest
    45. KOSZORU, Lajos

Computer Centre of the Ministry for Agriculture and Food
    46. PINCZÉS, László

Data collection and unpublished materials from:
Veszprém County Land Office
    47. ERŐS, Tamás
    48. SEBESTYÉN, Emil
    49. TÁBORINÉ VÉGH, Judit

Veszprém Town and Non-Urban District Land Office
    50. BALOGH, Árpád

Veszprém County Council
    51. Dr. SEBESTYÉN, Béláné

ENVIRONMENTAL MANAGEMENT THROUGH DERELICT LAND RECLAMATION

P.T. KIVELL

INTRODUCTION[x]

As the pioneer urban-industrial society, Britain became one of the first nations to face a large scale problem of land dereliction and despoilation. Beaver[1] suggests that three significant stages can be identified: first the nineteenth century development of coal, iron, chemical and quarrying activities, second the period 1900-1940 when mechanisation increased the scale and affected the type of dereliction created, and third the period since 1945 when the growing size and power of machines further increased the scope of land dereliction but also offered new techniques of restoration. Apart from a few isolated examples little was done about this problem until the 1950s and 1960s when growing public concern about the quality of life, changing industrial patterns and a planning system of increasing sophistication all combined to focus attention upon land use and environmental issues. At about the same time a number of organisations, notably the Ministry of Housing and Local Government /now the Department of the Environment/, certain local authorities and the Civic Trust began to collect and publish information on the problems of derelict land and the challenging possibilities of reclamation.

---

[x] Part of the paper is based upon a project entitled "An evaluation of land reclamation policies in North Staffordshire." I would like to acknowledge the work on that project of my co-director, Dr. P. W. Buch, and research fellows Angela Bannell and Malcolm Fenn.

6*

Although a certain amount of derelict, or waste land
/loosely defined/ is an inevitable feature of a changing urban
society, at least as a transitional feature, it is clear that
in many parts of Britain derelict land is a severe problem. The
nature of this problem is fairly obvious and need not be described in detail, but in brief derelict land constitutes a/ a
waste of a potentially valuable resource, b/ a danger and a nuisance, c/ an eyesore and d/ a disincentive to future development. In general terms there is also an inevitable association
between derelict/waste land and economic decay. The dereliction stemming from mineral extraction and processing, although
itself a product of active industrial development, is now high-
lighted by the contraction or rationalisation of many traditional industries and the wasting tracts of land in the inner districts of our large cities bear witness to industrial change
and the declining development potential of these locations. For
the most part, both these forms of dereliction and the symptoms
rather than causes of a deeper economic malaise, but in certain
areas, including North Staffordshire which is discussed later
in more detail, derelict land has become so widespread and so
unattractive as to deter economic and social development and
thus become a prima facie cause of decline. Indeed it is probable that the amount of land becoming available, often in un-
fashionable locations, through the ageing of our large industrial cities, may well exceed the resources available for its
management.

THE SCALE OF THE PROBLEM

The Department of the Environment collects figures on derelict and restored land from local authorities, but changes in
the way in which these figures have been gathered /after 1974
only data on restored land was collected/ and changes in local
authority boundaries make long term comparisons difficult. The
last comprehensive survey, for which national figures are a-
vailable, was undertaken in 1974, and as Table I shows, it revealed a total of 43,000 ha of derelict[2] land in England. From

Table I. Derelict land in England by regions, 1974 /in ha/

Region	Spoil heaps	Excavations and pits	Military	Abandoned railways	Other	Total	Per cent of total
East Anglia	1	408	513	612	249	1,783	4.1
East Midlands	1,090	1,166	816	1,606	493	5,171	11,9
Northern	2,922	1,690	232	1,830	2,737	9,411	21.7
North West	2,083	1,203	1,205	1,338	2,186	8,015	18.5
South East	53	1,136	113	662	396	2.360	5.5
South West	4,307	843	141	940	184	6,415	14.8
West Midlands	1,373	672	518	776	1,328	4,67	1o.8
Yorkshire and Humberside	1,289	1,599	239	1,343	981	5,451	12.6
England Total	13,118	8,717	3,777	9,107	8,554	43,273	100.o
Per cent of	30.3	20.1	8.7	21.0	19.8	100	

Source: Table D1. Survey of Derelict and Despoiled Land in England 1974. Department of the Environment.

the categories listed, it will be seen that derelict land is
largely a by-product of mineral working and for this reason its
incidence is closely related to the historic pattern of Britain's industrial and urban development, with the traditional
coal-field and heavy industrial areas being particularly badly
affected /Fig. 1/. In relation to their size, it is the North
West and Northern regions which contain the most severe problems, with the South East, East Anglia and South West England
having the lowest rations. Outside of the traditional urban-industrial areas, however, some predominantly rural counties also
have substantial problems of dereliction, e. g. Cornwall /China
Clay/, Cumbria /Gypsum/Anhydrite/ and Derbyshire /Limestone/.

Yet this table represents simply the hard-core of inherited dereliction and the real scale of the problem is somewhat
larger. It will be shown in a later section that legislation
since 1947 has gone some way towards preventing new dereliction
as a result of mineral workings, but in 1974 there was still a

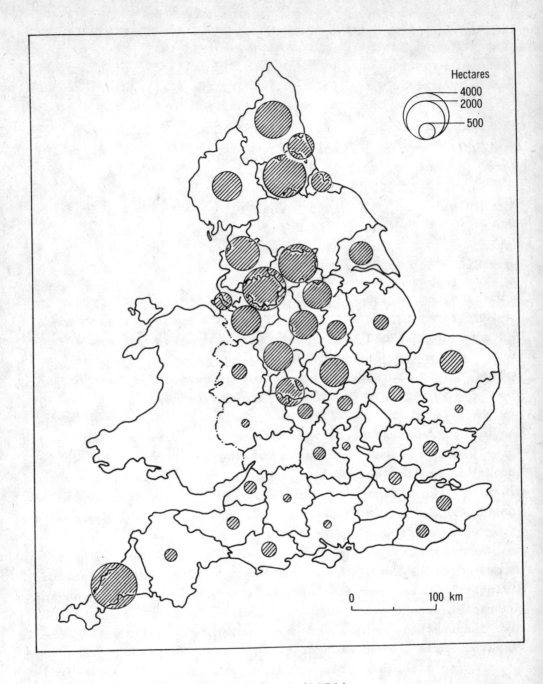

Fig. 1. Derelict land in England /1974/

total of 94,402 ha of land on which permission for mineral working had been granted. Approximately 75% of this had restoration
conditions attached, but 21,000 ha did not and must therefore
be considered as possible future derelict land. It can also be
argued that the definition of dereliction used in the collection of these figures is too narrow. Using broader definitions,
the Civic Trust[3] suggested that the borough of Wigan, for example, which in 1974 had 1045 ha of officially recorded derelict
land also possessed 1400 ha of "other wasteland" and that Merseyside with 529 derelict ha had an additional 2,300 ha of neglected wasteland.

Despite attempts to prevent further dereliction, the 1974
Department of the Environment study revealed an increase of
10, 309 ha since the previous /1972/ survey. Only a small proportion of this, however, stemmed from mineral extraction, the
vast majority /70%/ being due to the resurvey and reappraisal
of existing sites.

Lastly, that the scale of the problem is somewhat larger
than the official figures suggest is shown by the fact that a
derelict site has a blighting effect upon adjacent land by reducing its value, limiting the activities which it can support
and lowering its development potential. In West Yorkshire Casson[4] has estimated that land so affected may be equivalent in
area to that actually derelict.

DERELICT LAND, PREVENTION AND CURE

Since the institution of large scale land use planning in
the period after World War II, there has been a two pronged at-
tack on the problem of derelict land. The first part of this
programme has sought to prevent future dereliction from occurring whilst the second has been addressed to the substantial
stock of inherited derelict land.

The prevention of dereliction has been mainly aimed at the
mineral extraction industries which although essential to the
nation's economic wellbeing do represent one of man's most devastating impacts upon the environment. It was the 1947 Town

and Country Planning Act which first gave local authorities a powerful control over the way minerals were extracted and how the land was to be left, and there are now 13 separate pieces of legislation relating to mineral extraction and 9 more with general applicability. Mineral working is different from most other forms of development and presents planners with a particularly challenging task. There is little locational flexibility for it must take place where the minerals occur naturally. It also normally has a limited life, and it is one of the few forms of development which is intrinsically destructive.

Comprehensive legislation on land restoration after mineral extraction now exists and in some spheres, notably open cast coal mining, sand and gravel extraction and the ironstone industry where the 1951 Mineral Working Act imposed a restoration levy on each ton mined, considerable success has been achieved. Despite the legislation, however, statisfactory restoration is not always carried out. A government sponsored sample survey[5] of 12 counties in 1976 revealed that out of 1,777 mineral permissions granted since 1943 and covering 44,750 ha, 638 /36%/ had no or inadequate restoration conditions. Additionally, in 122 cases where work had been completed, adequate conditions existed but restoration had not been carried out. Many reasons can be suggested for the failure of restoration conditions. The one must commonly cited, although not actually supported by the evidence, is that the company ceases trading or goes into liquidation. Perhaps more serious is inadequate monitoring and enforcement of conditions by local authorities, coupled with lengthy legal proceedings and inadequate sanctions in cases of non-compliance. Other reasons include the possibility of reworking at some future data, a shortage of suitable filling material, the existance of user rights from before 1947 and the absence of a restoration fund.

In addition to legislation there are other means of preventing dereliction. At present between 85 and 100 million tonnes of mineral waste are dumped on the surface annually, but certain controls on this tipping do exist. Improved mining techniques, including backfilling and underground stowage are being encouraged, as are the constructive uses of such materials as colliery shale, slag and pulverised fuel ash but high transport costs and a failure to take into account the true social costs of tipping tend to limit progress.

The second major approach to the problem of derelict land concerns reclamation of the inherited stock, generally that created before 1947. Successive governments have committed themselves to the idea of using restored derelict land for such activities as industry, housing and schools in preference to taking agricultural land, and in 1970 the government of the day announced its aim of eradicating all derelict land is Assisted Areas by 1980[6]. In the event neither of these aims have been fully realised, but substantial progress has been made. In passing it should be noted that not all derelict land justifies restoration. Approximately 25% of the 43,273 ha of land recorded as derelict in 1974 was not thought to justify treatment, either because it would make unduly large demands on resources for the benefit obtained, or because it was located in remote rural areas.

It is difficult to assign responsibility for the reclamation of land which became derelict before restoration conditions became widespread in 1947. Initially it would seem logical to suggest that the cost should fall upon those who created the dereliction, but in practice this is often impossible, especially in cases where ownership of land has changed hands. The result is that central government, acting through the Department of the Environment, and local authorities have taken over the responsibility. The main way in which this work is that the Department of the Environment pays grants to local authorities in order to reclaim derelict land in their area. Many government and local authority departments are involved and a stylised summary of the process is shown in Figure 2.

Between 1945 and 1960 only small grants for reclamation were available, notably within National Parks and Assisted Areas, but pioneer work by local authorities in the West Midlands, Lancashire, Yorkshire and Durham showed what could be achieved. The 1966 Local Government Act extended grants of 50% of re-

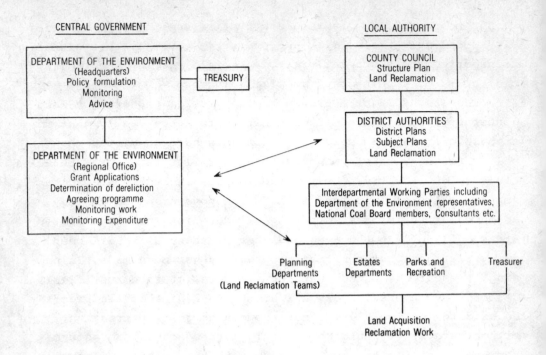

CENTRAL GOVERNMENT

LOCAL AUTHORITY

DEPARTMENT OF THE ENVIRONMENT
(Headquarters)
Policy formulation
Monitoring
Advice

TREASURY

COUNTY COUNCIL
Structure Plan
Land Reclamation

DEPARTMENT OF THE ENVIRONMENT
(Regional Office)
Grant Applications
Determination of dereliction
Agreeing programme
Monitoring work
Monitoring Expenditure

DISTRICT AUTHORITIES
District Plans
Subject Plans
Land Reclamation

Interdepartmental Working Parties including
Department of the Environment representatives,
National Coal Board members, Consultants etc.

Planning
Departments
(Land Reclamation Teams)

Estates
Departments

Parks and
Recreation

Treasurer

Land Acquisition
Reclamation Work

Fig. 2. Central government and local authority involvement
in land reclamation

clamation costs to all parts of the country; in 1970 the grant
was raised to 75% of approved reclamation expenditure in Assisted areas and in special Derelict Land Clearance Areas and
further raised to 100% in 1975. Finally Section 117 of the Local Government Planning and Land Act /1980/ extended grants to
private landowners and developers. As a result of improved grant
facilities the area of land restored increased dramatically, especially in the late 1960s and early 1970s, a period which has
been summarised by Wallwork.[7]

There is no doubt that the present period is witnessing a
change of direction in land reclamation policies. The 1982 Derelict Land Act serves to consolidate and slightly extend previous legislations but perhaps more importantly current government policy is encouraging private developers and private in-

vestment to become involved in the reclamation process. Future
grants for reclamation are likely to favour partnership schemes
whereby local authorities and private developers work jointly
to bring derelict land into use for housing or industrial use,
although some money will continue to be made available for local authority schemes leading to environmental improvement
through reclamation for public open space. One corollary of this
is that derelict land grants will be increasingly used to support the regeneration of the inner city.

The grants which are payable are not automatic, but must
be related to other local needs and priorities. They cover the
acquisition of land, survey and administrative costs, consultants' fees, actual reclamation works /but not for buildings,
roads or sewers/ and maintenance costs for three years. Grants
are not payable if the restored value of the land is thought
by a valeur to be greater than the acquisition and restoration
costs; in other words profitable reclamation for developments
such as housing and industry are not normally grant aided and
as is shown later this has had a significant effect upon the
afteruses to which restored land is put.

The total amount of grant available has fluctuated in recent years as Table II shows. From the mid-1960s to the early
1970s there was a strong upward trend, following by a trough
in 1976-77 as a response to public expenditure cuts. During the
late 1970s the amount available stabilised but House of Commons
Civil Supply Estimates suggest that the money allocated in the
early 1980s is actually running at a higher level again, thus
allaying the fears of those who thought that changes in the way
in which local government expenditure is financed would reduce
money for land reclamation.

Table II. Land reclamation and grants in England, 1967-78

Years	Area reclaimed ha	Grant aid s millions
1967-68	644	0.25
1968-69	855	0.44
1969-70	1,013	0.54
1970-71	1,475	1.40
1971-72	1,939	2.80
1972-73	2,169	5.10
1973-74	1,501	14.60
1974-75	1,323	11,70
1975-76	2,460	1o.75
1976-77	1,617	9.78
1977-78	2,640	13.40

Source: Land availability and the use of derelict land in the
West Midlands /1979/ JURE, University of Aston.

On a national scale approximately 60% of land reclaimed
during the late 1970's involved specific derelict land grants
but two other forms are also important. Local authorities also
reclaim land by making use of other sources of finance, for example housing or education grants, and a significant amount may
also be undertaken either by private developers without grant
/although note the changes in the 1980 Act/ or incidental to
such works as road construction.

The geographical pattern of land restoration accentuates
the roles of local authorities in the West Midlands, North and
North Western regions and is largely explained by two factors.
Firstly, in terms of economic geology this is where the main
stock of derelict land, resulting from coal mining, and clay
and limestone quarrying is to be found. In the South and East
of England these minerals are less common, while the main ones
which are extracted, especially ironstone and sand and gravel

are covered by restoration conditions. Secondly, derelict land restoration has always been seen as a part of the government's aid to the problem regions and the grant has therefore tended to favour those areas of heavy industrial decline.

A CASE STUDY OF NORTH STAFFORDSHIRE[8]

Since many of the important issues cannot be illustrated by examining land dereliction and reclamation at a national scale, a case study of North Staffordshire is included here. North Staffordshire's past and present economy has depended heavily upon coal mining, pottery and bricks and steel making, all of which have combined to create one of the most acute problems of dereliction in England. It is also true to say that over the past 15 years this district has carried out one of the most ambitious, and largely successful schemes of restoration to be seen anywhere, in fact a programme of environmental management on a grand scale.

Changes in the way in which official figures are presented make temporal comparisons difficult, but between 1965 and 1978 a total of 982 ha of derelict land were reclaimed by Stoke-on-Trent /810 ha/ and Newcastle-under-Lyme /172 ha/, the two major local authorities involved and a total of 6.9 millions was paid to them in reclamation grants. The most active period coincided with the culmination of Stoke-on-Trent's "crash programme" and the availability of enhanced levels of grant aid in 1972-74. Overall, 76% of the restoration between 1972 and 1978 took place with specific grant aid, and a decline in the rate of restoration since 1974 is a reflection not only of reduced grant levels after theat year but also of the completion of certain very large, high priority schemes and the increasing difficulties of land acquisition. The average cost of completed schemes works out at approximately 7,250 per ha /= 14,350/ha at 1981 prices/, but there is so much variation in individual sites that averages are misleading. There is no such thing as a "typical" site, but Table III gives an illustration of the costs which might be expected.

Table III. Crude estimates of reclamation costs per hectare

Land for public open space		Land for housing or industry	
Basic site preparation /demolition and earthworks/	5,000	Basic site preparation /demolition and earthworks/	5,000
Planting and path laying	2,500	Treatment of mine workings, filling' shafts etc.	30,000
		Roads and sewers	10,000
Total	7,500		45,000

Although general policy guidelines are laid down by the Department of the Environmnet, which also acts as the arbiter over grant awards, the different needs, policies and administrative organisations of individual local authorities result in considerable variations in reclamation practice. For these reasons, even adjacent local authorities such as Stoke and Newcastle have tackled their problems in slightly different ways. Within the general Department of the Environment framework, each has proceeded in a largely pragmatic fashion with relatively few clear statements of overall policy or priorities, but both have been concious of the dual need to improve their overall environment and to bring wasting, derelict land back into a positive use. The aims of reclamation have changed somewhat over time and there has been a discernible shift, especially in Stoke, away from the early schemes designed to achieve high visual impact for low cost, towards more balanced developments. The 1981 Staffordshire Structure Plan emphasises this trend by listing as a priority "the best use of all available resources, particularly regarding the increased use of reclaimed land for development".[9]

Whatever the overall guiding policy may be, however, in-dividual sites have been selected for reclamation on largely pragmatic grounds, taking into account the following reasons.

1. The pressing need for environmental improvement and the strongly expressed desire by residents of Stoke to improve the city's image. This was seen not simply in aesthetic terms, but as an economic necessity if new employers were to be attracted to the area.
2. The value for money represented by a particular site, with an understandable policy of undertaking first those sites which would achieve maximum improvement for modest cost.
3. The development potential of a site, bearing in mind its location and surface characteristics, and the likelihood of it being restored by other agencies.
4. The ownership of a site, with preference being given to those already owned by the local authority, or which could readily be acquired.
5. The physical nature of a site, although with modern tech-niques virtually any kind of dereliction can be overcome and it is cost, not engineering considerations which is the ultimate constraint.
6. The availability of grant aid which will vary according to the nature of the site and its proposed afteruse.

Given the wide variety of environmental, administrative ecological, economic, engineering and financial considerations, it will be understood that the programming of land reclamation is best done on a local, site-specific basis.

The final characteristics to be considered in this brief review is the use to which restored land is put. Again there are considerable variations from one area to another, and at different time periods, but Table IV summarises the situation in North Staffordshire.

Table IV. Afteruses of restored land in Stoke-on-Trent and
           Newcastle

	Stoke-on-Trent, ha	1970-80 %	Newcastle ha	1974-80 %
Public open space	5o1.9	86.9	6o.0	44,0
Industry	68.4	11.8	51.6	38.3
Housing	5.5	1.0	11.2	8.3
Agriculture	1.9	0.3	12.1	9.o

One of the most striking facts about this table is the
high proportion /over 75%/ of restored land which has been used
for public øpen space, compared with the relatively small areas
for industry and housing,[10] but the explanation for this is
fairly straightforward. When the reclamation programme began
open space provision took priority because in the congested urban environment of North Staffordshire it was a major need. It
also represented a relatively easy technical solution, was in
line with locally expressed pleas to improve the environment
and was expected to make an indirect contribution to other forms
of development by making the area more attractive. There is also the blunter explanation that grant aid favoured public open
space. These are powerful reasons for developing public open
space ant there is no denying that the programme has been largely successful. However, it is also important to note that with
the present achievement of a satisfactory level of open space
provision, together with increasing maintenance costs, the possibility of deterioration on present reclamation schemes, a
government committed to positive development and the involvement of the private sector, there is a growing need for local
authorities to promote other afteruses for the restored land.

CONCLUSION

In a small country like England there is a paramount need
to pay careful attention to management of the environment, including the efficient use, and re-use of land. As this paper
has shown, considerable restoration work has been undertaken
and major advances have been made in preventing new dereliction, especially that connected with mineral extraction, but a
threefold problems remains:

1. An existing backlog of derelict land amounting in 1974 to
   43,000 ha;
2. the creation of new dereliction from the continuing rationalisation of traditional industries such as coal, steel, the
   docks and the rail network;
3. the derelict, dormant, vacant or waste land, often consisting of very small sites, which is so widespread in the inner districts of most large industrial cities.

The availability of government grants has done much to encourage the reclamation of derelict land during the past 15
years, but it is clear that there is currently a change in the
direction of government thinking. In an attempt to promote development and the regeneration of older urban areas the government is likely to favour reclamation schemes which involve private developers a logside local authorities, and those which
result in housing or industrial development rather than public
open space. These are understandable and commendable aims, but
in pursuing them it is vitally important that the government
and local authorities should not lose sight of the fact that
reclamation for environmental improvement through the provision
of public open space and amenity land is still an entirely le-
gitimate planning goal.

NOTES AND REFERENCES

1. BEAVER S. H. /1969/: An appraisal of the problem. Proceedings of the Derelict Land Symposium, Leeds.

2. There is no statutory definition of derelict land, but the one used by government and local authority departments is "land so damaged by industrial or other development that it is incapable of beneficial use without treatment".

3. CANTELL, T. /1977/: Urban Wasteland. Civic Trust, London.

4. CASSON, J. /1969/: Dereliction, its nature and potential. Proceedings of the Derelict Land Symposium, Leeds.

5. DEPARTMENT OF THE ENVIRONMENT /1976/: Planning Control over Mineral Workings. H.M.S.O. London.

6. This aim was stated in 1970 by Anthony Crosland, Secretary of State for the Environment, and is quoted in WALLWORK, K. /1976/: The Extent and Development of Derelict Land in England in the 1970's. Royal Town Planning Institute, London.

7. WALLWORK, K. /1974/: Derelict Land. Ch. 7, David and Charles, Newton Abbot.

8. Fuller details are given in Derelict Land and Restored Derelict Land in N. Staffs. 1964-1980, Working Paper, No. 2 /1981/ - Department of Geography, University of Keele and Department of Geography and Sociology, North Staffordshire Polytechnic.

9. Staffordshire County Council /1981/: Staffordshire Structure Plan 1981. Draft Written Statement, Section 13.5.

1o. Although it should be noted that the table refers to land restored with grant aid it does not include approximately 12o hectares of effectively derelict land developed for housing by private builders without grant.

ENVIRONMENTAL MANAGEMENT IN THE LAKE BALATON REGION

Gy. BORA

The immediate area of Lake Balaton is a region suitaole for the study of the economic problems of the environment and environmental management. This paper attempts to answer the following questions: how would a reduction in environmental risk to this much frequented area influence land use, and what kinds of economic and social interests might thereby come into conflict with each other? The environmental protection problems of the Balaton area are also representative of the general problems facing shallow lakes.

1. THE MAIN CHARACTERISTICS OF THE BALATON RECREATIONAL AREA

The long but narrow feature of Lake Balaton is situated along the southern margin of the Transdanubian Mountains, and lies in a tectonic rift valley of Pleistocene age. It is not only Hungary's, but also Central Europe's, largest lake. To the north it is bounded by the Balaton Highlands and the Bakony mountains,where the summits reach a height of 300 to 400 metres above sea level, while to the east it is bordered by the Mező-föld loess plateau. The southern shore is generally a low-lying broken hilly region, although some points do reach an elevation of over 250 metres.

The main features of the lake are as follows:

Longitude	km:	78	Total length of water		
Average depth	m:	3.1	courses	km:	2420
Length of shore	km:	195			

Surface area	km^2:	596	Potential water resources/average annual runoff $\frac{10^6 m^3}{year}$	: 1000
Height above sea level	m:	104		
Average water quantity 10^6	m^3:	1900	Total amount of fertilizer used in the catchment area in equivalents	
Dimension of catchment area	km^2:	5775		
Average yearly precipitation	mm:	690	P_2O_5 $\frac{10^3 t}{year}$	: 70

As regards other characteristics, the Balaton is a shallow lake with a depth of under 3 metres. The rate of sedimentation is high: one part of the lake has been comletely silted up by river sediment, while the Bay of Keszthely has been damaged by sedimentation. As a consequence of its shallow depth, a part of the lake's sediment is ruffled by wave action, while the amount of suspended matter is also high.

A further characteristic of the Balaton is that although its catchment is extensive and encompasses 125 watercourses, only 33 of these are permanent watercourses flowing into the lake. The largest is the Zala river, which accounts for about 50 per cent of the water supply arriving from the catchment. The Sio canal has been closed by a lock gate where it leaves the lake and is the only river transporting water from the Balaton.

The water of the lake, except for small variations, has not been changed for a long time. The largest loss derives from evaporation, during the high temperatures of summer. This together with water flowing into the lake plus precipitation is just sufficient to maintain a stable water level, with any periodic excess being carried away by the Sio canal /the canal, as well as the lock, serve the additional function of water-level regulator/.

The catchment of Lake Balaton - 5180 km^2 - occupies about 5 per cent of the country's area with its greatest extention to the south and southwest of the lake shore. Mountainous regions form only a small part of it, and most is of a hilly character, well dissected by watercourses and with a high frequency of steep slopes that produce a considerable risk of erosion.

The agriculture of the catchment area is predominantly arable and the traditional practices of ploughing contribute to the risk of erosion. The planting and cultivation of grapes directly on the lake shore is also a source of erosional risk. As a consequence, a considerable quantity of alluvium arrives in the lake from the catchment area, mostly brought in by the Zala river, which traverses a region of above annual average precipitation. The regulation of that river during the last century means that most of this sediment is deposited in the Bay of Keszthely. In addition to the transportation of sediment, it is mainly via the Zala river that fertilizer eroded from the soil enters the lake.

2. FUNCTIONS AND ECONOMIC STRUCTURE

Over the centuries, the economy of the region has focused on agriculture and fishing in the lake and these activities have determined the settlement pattern of the area. Since the beginning of this century, however, recreation and tourism have become more important. At first the growth of this function was slow but, during the past three decades, expansion has been so dynamic that it has been designated by the decisions and resolutions of the different levels of authority as the most important function of the Balaton recreation area.[1] It is also an area that is now under stress and is so treated by the national long term tourism and recreational concept.

The recreation functions of the lake may be divided into a number of categories.

a. So-called "social-tourism" is associated with the buildings owned and maintained by trade unions, enterprises and different institutions for the purpose of organized recreation.

---

[1] The "Balaton recreation area" is an area designated by the authorities to which long term planning and environmental protection decisions and regulations apply. 49 settlements are to be found within the recreation area, of which only three - Keszthely, Balatonfüred and Siófok - possess the rank of town.

In 1980 accommodation amounted to 77,100 beds, or 62 per cent of the national total, while the number of guest nights reached 6.35 millions, or 57 per cent of the national total.

b. So-called "commercial tourist activities" are organized through local and national enterprises, and are centred on hotels, camp sites and rooms let out privately. The number of beds was 102,400 in 1980, that is 46.3 per cent of national capacity.

c. "Recreation of a private character" takes place in privately owned buildings such as weekend houses, and summer and second homes, where not only the guests, but also the owners, may pass their leisure and spend their summer holidays. There are about 32,000 buildings where the owners and their family members spend an average of 50 to 55 days annually.

In underlining the importance of the Balaton, we can mention that in 1980 approximately 30 per cent of Hungary's foreign currency revenue from tourism was derived from international tourist activity originating in the Balaton area.

3. THE CHANGING ENVIRONMENT OF THE BALATON REGION

During the last century, land use in the Balaton region underwent radical change. The last third of the 19th century was a period when the agriculture and land use of certain parts of the lake-shore were closely associated with the agriculture of the surrounding mezoregions. Consequently much of the north-eastern part of the region - like the Mezőföld - was devoted mainly to wheat and maize production and animal husbandry. Although part of the southern shore had a similar economy, much of the so-called Somogy region was given over to traditional livestock, mainly cattle-breeding, because the marshy and swampy surface there was naturally suited to pasture and meadow land. Along the norther shore, by contrast, land use was of a more disparate character, as arable land was available in limited quantity only. Because the Bakony Mountains and surrounding hill regions, including the volcanic areas of the Tapolca basin, occupied a littoral position and also because of the favourable sunshine and temperature characteristics, a high quality wine-producing viticulture evolved, on the volcanic and red stone covered surfaces. Otherwise most of the northern part was characterized by continuous forest cover.

Railway construction which linked the settlements of the southern lake shore initiated important changes, and from the turn of the century the development of recreation became increasingly associated with the belt extending between the railway-line and the lake-shore. Between the two world wars, guest houses and hotels were established in this zone and recreation areas often separated from the original settlements came to be formed there. Along the northern strip, by contrast, the configuration of the topography meant that the railway line closely hugged the lake shore almost everywhere. As a result intensively built-up recreation areas have formed only at the northwest corner of the lake between the railway line and the lake shore and elsewhere resort homes have been built on the lower slopes in a more dispersed fashion.

The fast development of recreation and tourism between the two world wars led to the rapid expansion of the built-up area along the shore-line. Banks and real estate firms divided the land into parcels which were then purchased from the landlords and local smaller-sized land owners at a considerably higher ground value. Although we have no exact data concerning the rise in ground values we can say that it was not as radical as during the 1960s and 1970s.

Industry is comparatively poorly developed in the Balaton area and the amount of land so utilized is rather low. On the northern shore, mainly in the Tapolca basin, basalt quarrying was once important but was largely discontinued at the end of 1960s for reasons of landscape protection. There is only one significant industrial concentration on the lake shore, a chemical plant in the region of Balatonfüzfő, which has been continually expanded since the 1930s. The three towns of Siófok, Balatonfüred and Keszthely also possess some smaller although nonetheless notable industrial plants.

After the Second World War particular emphasis was placed on the development of social tourism but since the 1960s more attention has been given to the creation of a large-scale tourist capacity with the provision of hotels and other establishments. This has resulted in more construction activity and for the sake of the preservation of the Balaton, the government compiled a regional plan, in which building regulations were underlined. The basic target of this plan was to protect areas for so-called collective recreation, e.g. for further hotels, enterprise resort hotels, beaches, parks, sports grounds, playgrounds etc. The plan generated world-wide interest, and the planner, moreover, won the Abercrombie prize. Because of the enormous needs for building land, this plan failed to assert itself. The plan assumed less growth than has actually occurred and because of the rise in incomes and growth of recreation, land use and the face of the lake-shore have been changed radically.

Infrastructure is most highly developed in the settlements of the region, but the supply of water and electricity is more widespread as is the public transport system. As a result of the growth in the recreation and tourist function, the settlement pattern of the area has undergone change, and now takes on a linear form, which follows the configuration of the lake. The functional structure of settlements has also been transformed, although the old settlements of rural character are still sharply segregated from the new recreation areas in most of the Balaton district.

Infrastructural provision has been expanded in the recreation area for a number of reasons. Firstly, it is designed to guarantee a satisfactory level of supply for the permanent population and for those productive activities which are not connected with tourism, for instance dwelling stock, education and much of the health service. Secondly, it also has to guarantee a level of supply, appropriate to the needs that the permanent population and the augmentated tourist population have in common, such as retailing, catering, postal and telephone services, electricity and water supply, the sewage network and treatment plants, filling stations, polyclinics, ambulances, amusements, cultural facilities and so on. Thirdly, there is

the infrastructure serving only the needs of tourism, for example the lakeside beaches.

As regards the actual infrastructural provision for the
permanent population of the recreation area the dwelling stock
has grown rapidly, especially in the three towns, as well as in
the other main settlements. On both shores, but mainly on the
southern shore, the possibility of augmenting ones income from
summer tourism was a great motivating factor behind the construction of private houses.

The number of resort and weekend houses is also extremely
high in the region. As a consequence of rising incomes, increased leisure time and the unsatisfied demands of both social
and commercial tourism the country has been passing through a
"weekend-house building boom" since the end of the 1960s, which
has had both positive and negative effects. The construction of
weekend homes has been very common in the Balaton recreation
area, as it offers the most concentrated water-side recreational possibilities in the country.

The above mentioned facts have resulted in the recreation
area becoming more extensively built-up than was either planned or would be regarded as rational, causing environmental and
land use problems. Land use itself has changed unfavourably,
while new constructions has not followed the original concepts
of the Balaton development plan.

In several places building has been overly dense or unregulated. Multi-storey homes are frequently found on small
plots of land; between the two world wars plots were generally
of 1200 to 1600 m^2 in area, but in the 1960s and 1970s this had
dropped to an average of 400 to 600 m^2. The shoreline is now
almost continuously built up, whereas it should have been used
for the construction of beaches, promenades and resort houses
serving the collective types of recreation activities. Moreover,
architectural style and building regulations have not been a-
dapted to the lake-shore's characteristics. Peripheral areas
have also been parcelled out, which has resulted in the construction of thousands of buildings unsuited to the region in
places with deficient infrastructural provision.

The main reasons for the creation of the above situation are to be found mostly in the lack of governmental regulation of the land market and the operation of market forces has produced a great inflation in prices over a comparatively short time space. The increasing demand for building plots has induced speculative prices, and as a consequence the market value of the majority of sites around the lake contains a speculative element over and above any reasonable increase.

The rapid increase in construction activity was followed only later by infrastructural provision. In the 1960s there were serious problems concerning water supply, and although this problem has now been largely solved by the development of new capacity, deficiencies in mains sewage and sewage treatment still remain and untreated or partly treated effluent is still discharged into the Balaton. One of the reasons for this is that the system for co-ordinating common and private interests in the provision of public utilities has evolved only slowly and in an unsatisfactory manner, while central funds cover only part of the needs and cannot be increased.

As far as the agriculture of the recreation area is concerned, suitable land has been overburdened with the infrastructure of settlements, recreation and tourism, because these functions provide a higher rent of income than that of agriculture. Even in marginal cases, recreation still provides the higher rent. Because of this the continuation of agricultural cultivation in cert   areas has become less advantageous, and the sale of plots or a switch over to tourist activities has been regarded as more beneficial.

During recent decades, the structure of agriculture in the recreation are has changed as the large-scale production of certain types of fruit, table grapes, together with vegetables, flowers and other kinds of ornamental plants have become more important. On the other hand, agriculture in the general catchment area has developed traditionally in a nonspecialized manner with wheat, maize, potatoes, fodder crops, fruits, vegetables, grapes and beef-cattle the main enterprises. At the same time, however, agriculture in this area has developed rapidly as mechanization and the use of chemicals have increased, contributing to the deterioration of water quality in the lake.

The catchment area influences the quality of the water in a number of ways. The methods of cultivation are one of the causes of soil erosion; the increasing use of fertilizers leads to more P and N nutrients getting into the lake and similarly with pesticides containing toxic components and the liquid wastes from large-scale animal husbandry.

4. THE EUTROPHICATION OF LAKE BALATON AND ITS CONSEQUENCES

Since the beginning of the 1970s, the progressive eutrophication of the Balaton has been observed, and has grown to dangerous proportions mainly in the southwestern part of the lake in the Keszthely Basin. There are a number of reasons for this phenomenon. The Zala river, with the largest discharge, drains this part of the catchment where erosion potential is highest. The river also introduces into the lake a substantial amount of chemical fertilizer leached from the soil. During the last century, the Zala river deposited the greater part of the alluvium forming the marshy area of the Little Balaton, but drainage for agricultural purposes means that the river now discharges directly into the lake, avoiding the marshland. In addition, a significant quantity of nutriments and agricultural chemicals is discharged by other streams into the lake, with the untreated liquid waste produced by large scale animal husbandry being particularly dangerous. To all this must be added the increase in human waste resulting from the large-scale building programme and general use of the lake shore. It is sufficient to refer to the fact that barely 15 per cent of homes are connected with the sewage disposal network, while a considerable part of the phosphorus originating from individual septic tanks infiltrates into the lake. Viticulture is also not without its problems because precipitation running off the steep slopes of the vineyards also releases nutriments and chemicals into the lake.

The origin of the pollutants entering Lake Balaton

	Communal	Industrial	Agricultural	Transportation
Localized origin	1. Direct sewage discharge into lake Balaton without or after treatment of varying efficiency 2. Direct sewage discharge into certain water-courses without or after treatment of varying efficiency 3. Waste water discharge into the ground, sewage irrigation, disposal of sewage sludge 4. Garbage disposal			

Regional origin			5. Fertilization:
			  – dung
			  – liquid waste
			  – fertilizer
			6. Plant protection
			7. Soil erosion
				8. Emissions from the air
				9. Solution from the bottom sediments

The relative distribution of primary nutrients causing eutrophication

	Organic matter	Nitrogen	Phosphorus
		per cent	
Origin:			
communal	20-25	15-20	15-20
industrial	10-15	4-10	4-8
agricultural	60-70	70-80	70-80
By source:			
localized sources	30-40	30-40	30-40
regional sources	60-70	60-70	60-70
By method of reaching the Balaton			
direct	10-20	8-12	8-10
from water courses	60-80	50-60	80-85
from groundwater	0-4	0-2	0-2
from the air	10-20	30-40	6-8

Source: based on estimates made by the Research Institute for Water Resources Development. /Vizgazdálkodási Tudományos Intézet./

The process of eutrophication involves the risk of the lake becoming unsuitable for recreation purposes within the foreseeable future, and there is a pressing need for the regulation of the amount of nutriments reaching the water body.

5. THE ENVIRONMENTAL PROTECTION POLICY FOR IMPROVING THE WATER QUALITY OF LAKE BALATON

The prospect of the eutrophication of the lake's water raises numerous problems. If water quality deteriorates so much from the effects of algae that it is not suitable for recreation, considerable macro-economic and social problems could arise. Firstly, being a significant natural asset, the lake itself could be in danger. Although it is not be explained in an economic sense, this unique feature of the natural environment of the country is undoubtedly worth protecting. Secondly, this is the only area of the country suitable for mass water-side recreation. Although Hungary is well-endowed with thermal water and watering places, these could not constitute a substitute for the Balaton. Moreover, significant capital investment would be needed for the establishment of new capacity. In other words, if the important recreation capacity and infrastructure of the Balaton area were unutilized, the macro-economic loss would be great.

If the quality of the Balaton for water-side recreation deteriorates substantially, more Hungarians would travel to the Black Sea coast in Bulgaria and Rumania, to the Adriatic resorts of Yugoslavia or to Greece, Italy and Spain which would mean extra foreign currency expenditure, including convertible currency. At the same time foreign exchange earnings from the Balaton would fall, thereby adding to the national economic burden.

In recognition of the dangers, a significant environmental protection strategy has been elaborated by the authorities to protect the Balaton, which involves arresting eutrophication and improving water quality. With regard to the scientific domain of the sixth five year plan, a co-ordinated research programme promoted by the government is under way, consisting of the following projects:

a. the elaboration of economic and environment protection regulations to bridge over conflicting economic, social and other interests in the Balaton area;

b. research into the biological processes going on in the lake, focused mainly on the processes of eutrophication;

c. research into the technical interventions needed to improve the water quality of the lake;

d. research into the public health situation around the lake;

e. long-range planning of the settlement network and the physical environment of the Balaton recreation area.

Among the scientific research programmes, two activities should be emphasized here. The first is the modelling of projects b, c and e, in collaboration with the International Institute for Applied Systems Analysis /IIASA/, Laxenburg, Austria. This work is centred on the Computer and Automation, and Biological Research Institutes of the Hungarian Academy of Sciences and the Research Institute for Water Resources Development. It is concerned with the eutrophication process, mainly the effect of phosphorus, and with modelling the optimum technical intervention. Besides this, various models are being prepared by the Ministry of Construction and Urban Development concerning the future development and optimization of tourism, including land use, pollution associated with tourism and investment requirements.

A second interesting and new research field is connected with the various interest groups and how these may conflict with each other. Project a above is under the guidance of the Karl Marx University of Economics and has a decidedly economic and sociologic character. Among others, such important questions as the recreation behaviour of tourists in the area and the public view of the Balaton problem are being raised. The most important field, however, is the examination of the different interest groups and the research is concentrating on a number of areas.

The most important functions of the Balaton are recreation and tourism, and it is necessary to investigate the conflicting interests arising from the deterioration of the water quality of the lake and the role of agriculture in increasing environmental risk. The amortization of investment in improving the water quality of the lake has to be examined. This requires substantial macroeconomic inputs, and the major investment and intervention to stop the eutrophication process has to be financed from central government funds. Serious social contradictions may arise from the fact that the national economy is obliged to allot considerable sums of money to this task, thereby diminishing the funds available for her important economic or social activities. The solution here may be to form a mechanism whereby the users of the lake, such as the institutions having resort homes on the waterside, are levied for part of the expense involved.

The formation of economic regulations that promote the elimination of infrastructural shortcomings, mainly the large deficiencies in sewage treatment, is also very necessary. Moreover, in order to relieve the pressure on the Balaton, the search for new water-side and thermal water recreation areas has to be made as well as the establishment of mechanisms for their development.

To date the most important measures taken by the government regarding environment management have been:

/i/ the re-establishment of the original filtering function of the Little Balaton, which is being achieved by the establishment of reed covered reservoirs that will use up much of the phosphorus transported by the Zala river;

/ii/ the extension of the sewage network, as well as sewage treatment capacity, mainly by constructing tertiary clarification plants;

/iii/ the prevention of the further enlargement of the area under vineyards;

/iv/ work is in progress to reduce the damage caused by agriculture, among other things the regulation of the water economy of large-scale farms;

/v/ penalties for those causing water-pollution in the Balaton catchment area have been established.

In 1979 the Government made two important decisions, one about the large-range tasks concerning the maintenance of the water quality of the lake and the other about the formulation of a new regional physical plan. An end to unregulated construction activity is envisaged, together with the re-establishment in some places of open collective recreational forms.

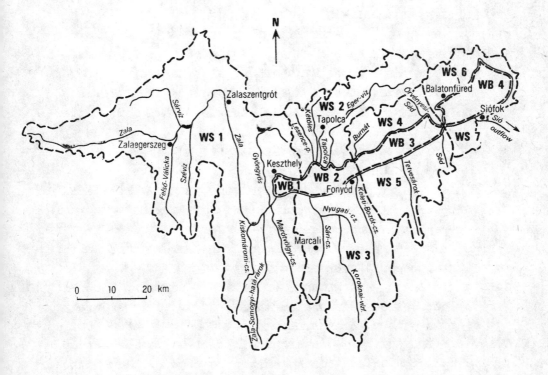

Fig. 1. Regionalization of the Balaton Basin
        WS = watershed; WB = waterbody

BIBLIOGRAPHY

ÁDÁM, L.--MAROSI, S. /eds./ /1975/: A Kisalföld és a Nyugat-
    magyarországi peremvidék /The Little Hungarian Plain and
    the West Hungarian border region/. - Akadémiai Kiadó, Bu-
    dapest, 605 p.

BARANYI, S. /1979/: A Balaton vizének megújulása. A tó környe-
    zetvédelmére ható tényezők /The renewal of the Balaton's
    water. Factors influencing the lake's environment protec-
    tion/. - Buvár, 11, 491-494.

BAUMOL, W.J.--OATES, W.E. /1975/: The theory of environmental
    policy; externalities, public outlays, and the quality of
    life. - Englewood Cliffs, Prentice Hall Inc., 272 p.

BENDEFFY, L. /1972/: Természeti és antropogén tényezők hatása
    a Balaton vizállására /Influence of physical and anthropo-
    gen factors to the water supply of the Balaton/. - Földr.
    Ért., Nos 2-3. 335-358.

BORA, Gy.--KULCSÁR, D.--RÉCZEY, G. /1979/: A balatoni környezet-
    védelmi modellrendszer beruházási alternativái és ezek köz-
    gazdasági aspektusai /Investment alternatives of the en-
    vironment protection modelling system of the Balaton and
    their economic aspects/. - Manuscript. Karl Marx Univer-
    sity of Economics, Department of Economic Geography and
    Regional Economics, Budapest, 118 p.

BOWER, B.T.--MAUSCH, S.P. /1976/: Regional residuals environ-
    mental quality management modelling /RREQMM/. Criteria for
    an optimal planning effort in the real world. - Journal of
    Environmental Management, 275-292.

California State Water Resources Control Board: Tahoe Basin
    studies report. Sacramento, 1974, 79 p.

DONIGIAN, A.S. Jr.--CRAWFORD, N.H. /1976/: Modeling nonpoint
    pollution from the land surface. - U.S. Environmental Pro-
    tection Agency, Athens, Georgia, 280 p.

DÁVID, L.--TELEGDI, L.--van STRATEN, G. /1979/: A watershed de-
    velopment approach to the eutrophication problem of Lake
    Balaton /A multiregional and multicriteria model/. -
    IIASA, Collaborative Paper CP-79-16, Laxenburg, 44 p.

EGERSZEGI, Gy. /1979/: A vizi környezetvédelem kérdései a Balatonon. Magyar Hidrológiai Társaság, Budapest /Questions of the water environment protection at the Balaton/. - Hungarian Hydrological Society, Budapest, Meeting of Keszthely, 17-18 May 1979. III. B. 1, 10 p.

ENTZ, B.--HERODEK, S. /1976/: A Balaton eutrofizálódása. Magyar Hidrológiai Társaság, Budapest /The eutrophication of the Balaton/. - Hungarian Hydrological Society, Budapest, Balaton Meeting, Keszthely, 30 Sept.-1 Oct. 1976, 12 p.

JOLÁNKAI, G.--SZÖLLŐSI NAGY, A. /1979/: A Keszthelyi-öböl foszforháztartásának matematikai modellje. Magyar Hidrológiai Társaság, Budapest /Mathematic model of the phosphorus cycle of the Bay of Keszthely/. - Hungarian Hydrological Society, Budapest, Meeting of Keszthely, 17-18 May 1979. III. A. 14 p.

JOLÁNKAI, G.--SZÖLLŐSI NAGY, A. /1978/: A simple eutrophication model for the Bay of Keszthely, Lake Balaton. - Paris, IIASA Publication 125, 138-150.

JOÓ, Ó. /1976/: A Zala szerepe a Balaton vizminőségében. Magyar Hidrológiai Társaság, Budapest /The role of the Zala river in the water-quality protection of the Balaton/. - Hungarian Hydrological Society, Budapest, Balaton Meeting, Keszthely 30 Sept.-1 Oct. 1976. 18 p.

KOLACSEK, A.--KOVÁCS, L. /1975/: Principes directeurs du développement de la région du Lac Balaton /Hongrie septentrionale/. - Paris, Éditions KS. 46-49. /Rapports et communications au 24e Congrès de l'AIEST 9-14 sept, 1974./

MAROSI, S.--SZILÁRD, J. /1975/: Balaton menti tájtipusok ökológiai jellemzése és értékelése /Ecological characterization of the Balaton-side landscape types/. - Földr. Ért., 4, 439-477.

O'MELIA, C.R. /1972/: An approach to the modeling of lakes. - Schweizerische Zeitschrift für Hydrologie, 1, 1-33.

PINTÉR, J. /1978/: Regionális környezetvédelmi döntési problémák matematikai modelljei /Mathematical models of regional environmental decision-making problems/. - Computing Center of Eötvös Lóránd's University, Budapest, 55 p. /Manuscript./

PLÓSZ, S. /1979/: A Balaton ökológiai védelme. Magyar Hidroló-
     giai Társaság, Budapest /Ecological Protection of the Ba-
     laton/. - Hungarian Hydrological Society, Budapest, Meet-
     ing of Keszthely, 17-18 May 1979. III. A. 18, 9 p.

PRÉKOPA, A. /1973/: Stochastic programming models for inventory
     control and water storage models. - In: Prékopa A. /ed./:
     Inventory control and water storage. North Holland Pub-
     lishing Co., Amsterdam, 229-245.

RINALDI, S.--SONCINI-SESSA, R.--STEHFEST, H. /1975/: Optimal
     sequencing in installing wastewater treatment plans. -
     Laxenburg, IIASA, 35 p. /IIASA RM-75-77./

SOMLYODY, L. /1979/: Hydrodynamical aspects of the eutrophica-
     tion modelling in the case of Lake Balaton. - Laxenburg,
     IIASA, Collaborative Paper CP-79-1, 37 p.

TÓTH, L. /1972/: Reeds control eutrophication of Balaton Lake.
     - Water Research, 12, 1533-1539.

MANAGING THE PROBLEMS OF BROADLAND

T. O'RIORDAN

This is a brief synopsis of the history of administrative arrangements to manage the problems of the Broads.

In a nutshell the "problems" of the Broads stem from conflicting uses of a natural resource region. This is partly due to the fact that society collectively is usually unwilling to "pay" for all the demands it makes on its natural resources and partly because the governing institutions of the area have no clear and consistent policy toward conservation and landscape protection and cannot act as a single body capable of undertaken executive action without being forced into prolonged negotiation and compromise.

The nature of the environment problems facing Broadland are summarised in Figure 1. Basically demands on the productive use of the area's resources /more agricultural output, more use of the rivers for recreation /boating and fishing/, more use of water for domestic and industrial consumption/ creates two undesirable side effects a. eutrophication /the accelerated enrichment of the watercourses by nutrients which in turn leads to algal growth and decay and associated loss of interesting vegetation and organic decay/ and b. changes in the characteristic landscape of the region /in the form of loss of reedbank, quay-heading of river banks, changes in agricultural land, and loss of natural habitats for interesting insects and birds/. If we did not worry about landscape alteration and the destruction of wildlife, there would be no "problem" in Broadland. So we have first to ask ourselves why should these changes worry

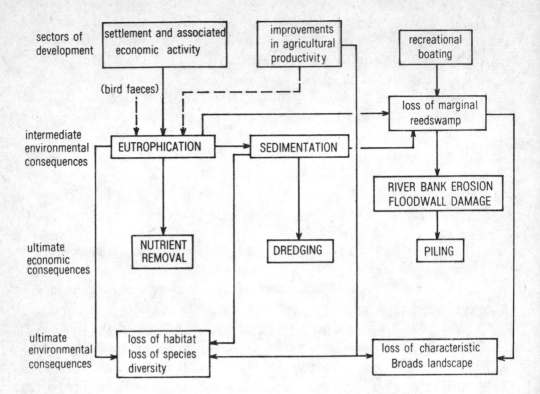

Fig. 1. The environmental problems facing Broadland

us? and to what extent is it worth controlling economic act.-
ivities such as agriculture and pleasure boating in order to
protect and improve nature conservation and landscape amenity?

Formation of the Broads Authority

This is an unique organisation established under sections
101 and 102 of the Local Government Act 1972 which is run primarily with local authority support, but backed financially by
the Countryside Commission. The Commission is a form of part-
ner, looking at the wider national significance of the Broads,
but is has a relatively minor say in the actual operations of
the Authority. The three major differences between this Authority and previous attempts to manage the Broads are

a. though membership of the Authority is voluntary, not statutory, a sense of collective responsibility should encourage its constituent bodies to work together and to coordinate their activities in a manner not yet achieved. Its membership is loaded towards the District Councils because of their special interests in planning and recreation matters which they have devolved to the Authority. Of the 26 members 12 are from the 6 district councils, 5 from Norfolk County Council, 2 from Suffolk County Council, 2 from the Anglian Water Authority[x], 2 from Great Yarmouth Part and Harbour Commissioners[xx] and 3 from the Countryside Commission. Its primary responsibilities are /i/ to prepare a management plan for the area /based on the old Broadland Study Plan/ /ii/ to deal with all planning matters /iii/ to deal with all recreation matters, and /iv/ to comment on, advise on and generally ensure that any proposals from other constitutent authorities /county councils, Anglian Water Authority, Great Yarmouth Port and Harbour Commissioners and Countryside Commission are in accord with its management plan.

b. It has powers to appoint a Broads officer and small staff. The costs of the salaries will be jointly shared by the Broads Authority and the Countryside Commission. The Broads officer will be the chief executive officer of the authority.

c. It has its own financing powers amounting to a levy of 30,000 per year per district council, and 70,000 for the Norfolk County Council and 30,000 for the Suffolk County Council. This money will help /i/ to pay for administration including the secondment of local authority officers and /ii/ to pay for works of improvement. These will generally be related to recreation but it is possible that some of this money will also be available for water management including navigation.

---

[x]The Anglian Water Authority is responsible for water supply, pollution control, recreation and fisheries, land drainage and flood protection

[xx]The Great Yarmouth Part and Harbour Commissioners are responsible for navigation, licensing of boats, dredging, provision of mooring facilities and speed limit bye-laws.

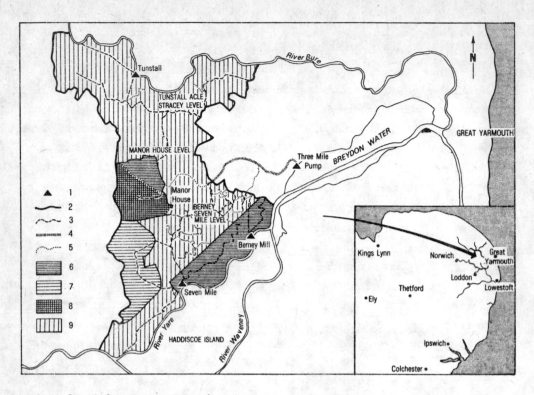

Fig. 2. Halvergate Marshes
         1 = site of pumping station; 2 = area boundary; 3 =
         new low level drain; 4 = existing high level drain;
         5 = existing dykes; 6 = safeguarded permanent pasture
         with award; 7 = permanent pasture /no award/; 8 =
         safeguarded sites of special scientific interest; 9 =
         voluntary contracts for compulsory notification

        Annual expenditure of the Authority in 1981/2 was 485,000
of which about 130,000 was spent on administration, 200,000
on projects including research and 110,000 was placed in reserve for future expenditures. It is estimatd that annual costs
to maintain the area in roughly its present state will not be
less than 500,000 annually and could be as much as 750,000.
This expenditure could be cost effective in the in the saving
of future costs on remedial work caused by inconsiderate use
of the area and should also indicate what British society is
willing to invest in conservation and amenity. The present
state of Halvergate Marshes is shown in Figure 2.

DRAINAGE BASIN PLANNING, WATER RESOURCES AND ENVIRONMENTAL MANAGEMENT IN GREAT BRITAIN

C. C. PARK

This paper has two broad aims: a. to examine the environmental impacts of existing and proposed water resource management policies and drainage basin changes in Great Britain, and b. to explore the implications and applications of these impacts on environmental management.

A. INTRODUCTION

Environmental management represents the interface between human use systems and natural environmental systems.[1] The environment offers both opportunities /resources/ and constraints /hazards and reduced environmental quality/; these influence population and society. Feedback occurs through resource use and man-made hazards and changes in environmental quality, so that the man-environment relationship in practice is a symbiosis /man affects environment and environment affects man/. This paper concentrates on water resources and drainage basin changes as an illustration of this symbiosis. It also forms a basis for exploring the environmental impacts of planned water resource management systems and of unplanned drainage basin changes in particular within the context of Great Britain.[2]

B. THE IMPORTANCE OF WATER

Water provides a useful example of an environmental resource which requires careful management because, while occur-

ring in limited quantities demand for water of specified qualities has been rising throughout the present century. Water-
created hazards, such as river flooding, pose additional problems for the resource manager.[3] In addition water is valued
in many ways. Water's ecological, economic and cultural values
include freshwater supply, maintenance of hydrological balance,
food production, visual and recreational amenity, high biological productivity of wetland habitats and the provision of gene
pools for freshwater aquatic species.[4] Water occurs in the environment in many habitats, and freshwater wetlands include
estuaries, rivers, streams, lakes, reservoirs, canals, flooded
gravel pits, ponds, bogs and other marshy areas. Pressures on
wetland resources in the United Kingdom comes from many sources
- such as freshwater pollution, urban and industrial development, agricultural improvement, flood protection schemes, water
supply and recreational use of wetland areas.

C. WATER AND ENVIRONMENTAL MANAGEMENT

Water and environmental management in Great Britain are
related in two broad ways. The first is purposeful management
of water resources,[5] and the second is the impacts on water and
wetlands of environmental management geared towards other objectives /such as agriculture and urban development/.[6] The differences between the two are important - resource management is
planned while indirect impacts are not; the former involves conscious decisions according to defined objectives whereas the
latter is incidental, and in reality is an environmental exter-
nality /in the sense used by economists/.

D. WATER MANAGEMENT

Water management is a major area of public responsibility
in resource management in the United Kingdom.[7] Water is only
available in limited quantities, but demand continues to rise;
it is often most readily available in locations distant from
the main centres of demand; it is also required for a variety
of purposes only some of which are compatible with one another.

114

i. The water resource system

Three characteristics of the water resource system are of particular importance:

a. opportunities exist for successive downstream use of the same water and resource managers need to adopt a "drainage basin" approach to management;

b. groundwater and river flows are intimately associated and groundwater and river systems must therefore be managed together;

c. water resources are unevenly distributed in the United Kingdom so that water storage and distribution are of central importance.

There are three broad functions for water management in the United Kingdom - development of new resources, allocation of available resources and recycling of water. The supply of water to agriculture, industry and domestic users is a central function of the water industry; the others are flood damage reduction, effluent disposal, navigation, Hydro-Electric Power, amenity and recreation. This multi-functional nature of water resources gives rise to special management problems, because the same water is often called upon to meet more than one function. Complementary uses of water create relatively few problems for water managers, whereas incompatible or conflicting uses need to be reconciled, zoned or otherwise managed.

ii. Geography of water resources

The geography of water resources in the United Kingdom reflects a spatial imbalance between areas of supply and areas of demand.[8] Sufficient water exists to cater for demand overall, but costly water redistribution schemes are required to match supply and demand. The principal surface water supply areas /with high precipitation, and impermeable rocks/ are in the north and west of mainland Britain, while groundwater storage in aquifers beneath much of eastern and southern England contributes to supplies. The major areas of demand are in central

England, East Anglia, southern England, the North West and extreme North East - largely reflecting the distribution of major centres of population and industrial activity, and the patterns of variations in agricultural practice.

iii. Levels of water use

Levels of water use in England and Wales have grown steadily since 1960[9] in response to growth in overall population, increasing per capita levels of consumption, increasing industrial activity and changing agricultural practices. Large industrial users of water are metered, whereas most households, small shops and businesses are not. There are 5 classes of water use:

    a. domestic use;

    b. industrial use;

    c. agricultural use;

    d. public use;

    e. losses.

iv. Administration and legislation

Water management systems have evolved differently in Scotland and in England and Wales.[10] In Scotland the water supply industry is dealt with by the Regional and Island Councils, while water pollution is the concern of the River Purification Boards.[11] A multi-functional and more co-ordinated management system exists in England and Wales, where the unit of management is the regional Water Authority /based largely on drainage basin units/. The system in England and Wales has evolved through four phases this century:[12]

a. Before 1945 the water industry was fragmented, diversified and unco-ordinated.

b. The 1945 Water Act brought about improvements which included the introduction of standardized codes of practice, and aggregation of small water supply units into larger and more efficient units /River Boards were set up under the 1948 River Boards Act/. A series of River /Prevention of

Pollution/ Acts were introduced between 1951 and 1961 to deal with problems of water quality. By the late 1950's the industry was still fragmented, largely unifunctional /water supply/ and lacking a long-term co-ordinated framework for planning future water resource developments.

c. The 1963 Water Resource Act replaced river boards by regional River Authorities and also created the Water Resources Board. River Authorities were designed to be much more multifunctional than the River Boards, while the Water Resources Board was created to co-ordinate the activities of the individual River Authorities, and to prepare a strategic plan for water developments in England and Wales up to the year 2000 A.D. /see section vi/.

d. The 1973 Water Act designated ten new Water Authorities, which are still in existence, to replace the existing River Authorities in order to maintain the hydrological continuity of the catchment systems, and to create largely autonomous authorities. Their responsibilities are much broader and include water quality management and amenity use of water, in addition to their water supply role. The multifunctional character of the Water Authorities includes responsibility to measure, licence abstractions and to augment water resources; to supply water; to provide sewers and sewage disposal works; to regulate discharges of effluent; to maintain and develop fisheries; to direct land drainage functions; to exercise these functions so as to allow recreational use of water; to have due regard to the desirability of preserving the amenities of, and public rights of access to areas of natural beauty, historical and other interest; and to survey water quality, use and estimated future demand and to make plans for new water resource developments.

v. Water quality

A series of surveys of water pollution in England and Wales were carried out by the Department of the Environment during the 1970s.[13] /Table 1/ Although over 70% of the total

Table I. Statistics for river pollution in the United Kingdom

Area	Year	Unpolluted per cent of total	doubtful polluted in per cent	poor	grossly	Total in km
		Unpol-luted per cent of total	doubt-ful	poor	gross-ly	in km
England and Wales /total/	1975	75.6	15.8	4.8	3.8	38,989
Non-tidal		77.6	15.1	4.0	3.3	36,123
Tidal		49.6	25.1	14.8	10.5	2,866
Scotland /total/	1974	95.1	3.6	0.9	0.4	47,772
Non-tidal		95.3	3.4	0.9	0.4	47,279
Tidal		65.5	20.5	6.3	7.7	493
Northern-Ireland /non-tidal/	1978	95.9	3.1	1.0	0.0	994

Source: Based on surveys by the Department of Environment /England and Wales/, Scottish Development Department, and Department of the Environment for Northern Ireland. Summarised in: D.E. Walling and B.W. Webb /1981/: Water Quality, pp. 126-172. In: J. Lewin /ed./: British Rivers /George Allen and Unwin, London/.

length of non-tidal rivers were classed as "free from serious water pollution", the "poor" and "grossly polluted" rivers provide numerous problems for downstream water use, landscape and amenity planning, and biological conservation. Most of the polluted stretches are located in the more traditionally industrial parts of Britain - these include rivers such as the Clyde in Scotland; the Tyne in north east England; the Douglas and the Mersey in the north west; the Humber and Don in Humberside; parts of the Trent and Severn in the Midlands; and numerous streams in South Wales. Success stories in cleaning up previously polluted rivers in sections of the River Severn and the Warwickshire Avon and much of the tidal River Thames.[14]

6. National Water Plan

Long-term forward planning has become an integral component of water resource management in Great Britain. In the early 1970s the Water Resources Board published a national strategic plan for water resources which sought to ensure reliable supplies up to year 2000 A.D.[15] The Water Plan assumed that most of the predicted increase in industrial demand for water could be met from private sources /through improved recycling by industrycoupled with repurification of water carrying effluents/. Expected increases in domestic demand were to be met by a combination of additional surface storage, improved uses of exsisting storage capacity, and a more co-ordinate use of underground storage. The Plan aimed to inter-link major river systems in England and Wales /by aqueduct where necessary/ to form a water grid, and to generate an optimal pattern of water storage.[16] The plan involved four types of improvement:

    a. river regulation and inland reservoir storage;

    b. groundwater developments;

    c. inter-basin transfers;

    d. estuary storage and desalination.

E. DRAINAGE BASIN CHANGES

The drainage basin provides a convenient basin on which to evaluate man-induced environmental changes. The water cycle serves to link to other major environmental systems /the energy system, nutrient cycles, and sediment system/, and all parts of the land surface in temperate areas belong to one drainage basin or another. The drainage basin is a process-response system[17] so that the effects of a man-induced change at some point in the system can be transmitted over a wide area /in particular downstream/, via impacts on the movement of water and sediment through the system.

From the point of view of environmental management, two broad types of drainage basin change can be recognised - direct modifications, and indirect changes.[18]

i. Direct drainage basin change

Direct modifications relate to purposeful action on the stream channel or drainage basin. These are often engineering schemes designed to alleviate existing or impending threats of flooding, erosion or deposition; examples include canalization, channel stabilization and channel straightening.[19] Direct channel changes involve both realignment and stabilization. Realignment /or channelization/ is designed to improve channel efficiency and so assist in flood protection, and might involve either the dredging of a new channel to replace an existing inefficient one, or the straightening of an existing stream.[20] Environmental impacts include increased stream gradient, increased velocity and channel erosion, which in turn threaten structures downstream, lead to loss of valuable floodplain land, and promote deposition and increased flooding downstream. Direct channel controls are often required in flood-prone areas, in reaches subject to excessive bed and bank erosion, in land drainage schemes, and in areas undergoing urban and suburban development.

ii. Indirect drainage basin change

Indirect changes generally arise as a side effect of other resource-using schemes or resource management systems which occur within the drainage basin and pose special problems for environmental management. The indirect impacts are not planned, and often the environmental manager is not aware of the impact until it reaches a critical dimension, or until costly remedial measures are required. Indirect changes are generally pervasive and cumulative, and the impacts are often experienced either upstream or downstream from the initial change. It is perhaps convenient to consider three broad categories of indirect drainage basin change:

a/ Land management

Vegetational removal

Vegetation removal often induces accelerated erosion. Impacts in the sediment source areas produce problems for soil management and conservation, so that land treatment practices and structural controls are often required.[21] Downstream impacts stemming from increased sediment load and changes in streamflow include induced channel changes and instability, and accelerated deposition /which in turn might promote increased overbank flooding/.[22] One common feature of sediment removal is gully development, and there are many areas in Great Britain where this has been induced in historical times through partial or complete destruction of former heathland vegetation.[23]

Land use and river systems

The association between land management practices and land use regimes, and river systems has attracted much attention. In Great Britain information has been derived from small experimental catchments, where measurements of contemporary processes /water and sediment transport/ under various land uses and management regimes can be used to detect changes induced by land management. The best documented example is the Plynlimon experimental catchment operated in Mid-Wales by the Institute of Hydrology since the early 1970s.[24] The experiment is designed to evaluate the hydrological differences between a wooded catchment /the upper River Severn/ and an adjacent grassland catchment /the upper River Wye/. Early results suggest that annual evapotranspiration loss from the forested Severn in about 280 mm /10% of net precipitation input/ greater than from the grassland Wye. Forest reduces water yields because of reduced albedo, increased air turbulence under the canopy, interception of precipitation by leaves and branches, and drainage of soil moisture via deep tree roots.[25] Results from sediment measurements suggest that a forested sub-catchment of the Severn produces up to four times the amount of bedload produced by a pastureland sub-catchment /probably because of forest drainage ditching/.[26] Observations from Coal Burn experimental catchment in Northumberland show that the process of ditching and planting a former moorland catchment with coniferous forest has increased sediment concentrations in rivers by two orders of magnitude.

Forestry

Most large forests are in upland Britain, and most areas favoured for new planting are in upland moorland, where there are few competitors for economic and extensive land use. Thus the paradox arises that the most important source of water supplies in Britain is the uplands, yet these are also the areas favoured for increased forestry operations /which might reduce water yields by up to 20%/.

Studies of the environmental impacts of forestry /particularly Sitka Spruce and other coniferous species/ on upland Britain[27] show that the early phases of the forest life-cycle increase water yields in streams /through ditching and drainage/; increase nutrient concentrations in drainage waters /derived from fertilizer applications on the young tree crop/; and lead to temporary increases in erosion and suspended sediment yield /through road construction/. When the tree crop starts to grow, water yield falls. Studies of forest felling highlight the impacts of logging and clearcutting. These include increased peak flows in river systems; increased streambed deposition from the use of bulldozers for road building, and forest traffic during operations on site; and increased incidence of hillslope erosion and landslide on unstable sites.[28]

Land drainage

Land drainage has affected extensive areas in Great Britain since 1945. Recent years have seen extensive installation of field drains to improve drainage in existing fields, and to reclaim large tracts of agriculturally marginal land subject to water logging.[29] Two types of land drainage are employed most widely in Great Britain - improvement of water courses /surface drainage/ and field drainage /under-drainage/.[30] Arterial drainage involves the regulation of major watercourses by straightening, deepening, embanking, and sometimes by wholesale pumping of water from wetlands /such as the Fenlands of East Anglia/.[31] The primary impact of surface drainage is to increase the drainage density of land tributary to river systems and this serves to speed runoff from the drained area. Streamflow is thus increased. Recent increases in the frequency of flooding along the upper River Severn in Wales have been related in part to the combined effects of land drainage, peat drainage and forestry practices /which include drainage/ in the tributary catchment.[32] Underdrainage has different environmental impacts - it reduces the frequency and amount of surface runoff, increases runoff volumes but reduces "flashiness" in stream response. Some parts of Britain have witnessed heated debate over wetland drainage, particularly when agriculture and nature conservation interests are in direct conflict.[33] One such case concerns the Somerset Levels, an extensive area of low-lying peat and wetland near the Bristol Channel, threatened during the 1970s, with increased rates of commercial peat extraction and increasing use of drainage to reclaim land for agriculture.[34]

b/ Water resource management

Reservoir developments

A large number of reservoirs have been built in Great Britain since the late nineteenth century; most were built by public or private water authorities, and most are located in upland areas. A reservoir can induce a series of interrelated environmental impacts in the drainage basin.[35] First order impacts relate to process alterations; second order impacts relate to changes in channel size and form, and changes in stream invertebrate populations; while third order impacts relate to longer term adjustements in channel morphology and stream ecosystem populations. Observations from a series of British reservoirs exhibit reduced annual runoff and reduced magnitude and frequency of peak flow events downstream, promoted by absorption of flood discharges by reservoir storage. The evidence suggests reductions of between 9 and 70% in predicted pre-dam flows.[36] Reservoirs also effectively trap sediment which would otherwise be carried downstream, and this has two main consequences - the likelihood of scouring of the channel bed down-stream /because of the release of sediment-free water/, and the isolation of upstream sediment sources.[37] Second order changes include those related to channel adjustment to reduced water and sediment discharges. Evidence is available from a wide range of upland reservoirs in Britain to show how alluvial channels reduce their cross-sectional size as a response to reduced magnitudes of bankfull discharge.[38] Most of the channel adjustment tends to be via reduced channel widths.

Inter-basin transfers

The direct transfer of water between two drainage basins is a basic element of many water resource management schemes. This might include enclosed pipelines, or artificial feeder channels. The net effect is a reduction in flow in the donor stream down-stream from the point of abstraction, and a corresponding increase in flow in the receiver stream downstream from the point of input. A small field study in Devon identified a marked increase in channel size triggered off by the import of water into the drainage system from an adjacent catchment /in the form of road drainage/.[39] The possibility of large scale inter-basin transfers for water supply purposes raises the possibility of widespread and perhaps irreversible impacts through increased flooding, increased erosion, and perhaps even inadvertent modification of local or regional climates.[40] The 1974 Water Plan envisaged the construction of a series of new upland reservoirs, the enlargement of some existing ones, and the transfer of water between catchment areas for supply purposes.

c/ Urban development

Perhaps the most important form of drainage basin change is that related to building activity and urban development, because this is a final and generally irreversible change in land use.[41] It is estimated that by 2000 A.D., urban land will occupy 14% of the land surface of Great Britain.[42] Urban development can induce water-related environmental impacts in two basic ways - through creating a demand for water supplies /thus the impacts arise through water resource management schemes/, and through the effects of building activity and urbanization on water and sediment movement in host drainage basins. There are four main areas of urban environmental impact.[43] Modified runoff patterns are brought about by increases in the impervious cover of the drainage basin and increased speed of water movement into channels. The general effect is an increase in the volume of streamflow, with decreased base flows but marked increases in peak flows. The second group of impacts arise via increases in sediment yields during construction, caused by the exposure of soil on construction sites to storm runoff. Further impacts relate to the introduction of effluent from sewage disposal plants, which affect water quality, trigger off changes in stream flora and fauna, and reduce the recreational value of the river systems. The fourth area of environmental impact is amenity, because urban streams often suffer from channel instability, the accumulation of human artefacts and the disruption of stream ecosystems. Each can reduce the scenic attractiveness and utility of riverscapes.

Process measurements of water and sediment changes have been collected from a number of "urban" or "urbanizing" experimental catchments[44] of which the best known is the Rosebarn catchment on the margins of Exeter in Devon.[45] Early results /with 25% of the catchment influenced by building activities/ show increases of between 2 and 4 fold in strom runoff volumes and peak flows; increases of about 5 fold in suspended sediment concentrations; increases of between 5 and 10 fold in sediment loads overall; and increases of the order of 30% in specific conductance levels.

Urban development generally follows a two-phase cycle, made up of the initial phase of constructional activity, followed by the longer period when the entire catchment, or a portion of it, is urbanized and building activity has ceased. Phase one often produces massive increases in stream sediment loads, valley floor deposition, reduced channel size and stream infilling. Phase two often sees a marked decrease in sediment yields, increases in impervious areas in the catchment, and increased streamflow related to operation of storm drains /and

the impervious surface cover /.[47] Channel enlargement associated with urban development has been detected and quantified downstream from a number of urban areas in Great Britain.[48] The implications for environmental management of these induced channel changes include channel instability downstream from the urban areas; loss of visual quality and amen   value of the altered channel systems; threat of collapse to downstream structures such as bridges, embankments and floodplain buildings
close to the enlarging channel.

F. CONCLUSIONS AND IMPLICATIONS

The paper has illustrated how man uses environmental resources, and how environmental impacts arise as side-effects
of other resource using activities within the context of water
in Great Britain. Clearly the environmental management implications of water resource use need to be evaluated with care, and
the evidence from Great Britain suggests that the multi-functional basis of water management does at least go some way towards including environmental consideration when resource-bas-
ed decisions are being made. The environmental impacts of indirect drainage basin changes, however, are somewhat more difficult to detect and isolate and are rarely recognised let alone
catered for in environmental management and planning. Whilst
environmental resource-using activities such as agriculture and
forestry have significant effect on both water and sediment
yields from catchments, both national and local policies ignore
the wider environmental impacts of large scale drainage, planting and land management schemes. Environmental management must
recognise the significance and widespread nature of these forms
of indirect impacts on river systems, along with the side-effects of water resource management policies /such as reservoir
development and inter-basin water transfers/ and urban and suburban development.

NOTES AND REFERENCES

1. Environmental management is difficult to define unambiguously - see R. Lorrain-Smith /1982/: The nature of environmental management. Journal of Environmental Management, 14,
   229-236; and C.C. Park /1981/: Ecology and Environmental
   Management, Butterworth, London, 272 p.

2. A general review is offered in C.C. Park /1981/: Man, river
   systems and environmental impacts. Progress in Physical Geography, , 1-31. Recent books include G.E. Hollis /ed./ /1979/:
   Man's Impact on the Hydrological Cycle in the United Kingdom /Geo-Books, Norwich/ and J. Lewin /ed./ /1981/: British
   Rivers /George Allen and Unwin, London/.

3. See, for example, R.C. Ward /1978/: Floods - a geographical
   perspective - /Macmillan, London/; and K. Smith and G.A.
   Tobin /1979/: Human adjustment to the flood hazard /Longman,
   London/.

4. Recent books which concentrate on rive ecology include H.B.
   N. Hynes /1970/: The Ecology of Running Waters /Liverpool
   University Press, Liverpool/; and R.T. Oglesby, C.A. Carlson
   and J.A. McCann /eds./ /1972/: River Ecology and Man /Aca-
   demic Press, New York/.

5. Water resource management in the United Kingdom is described
   by C. Kirby and J.C. Rodda /1974/: Managing in the hydrological cycle, 73-84 in A. Warren and F.B. Goldsmith /eds./:
   Conservation in Practice /Wiley, London/, and by T.R. Wood
   /1981/: River Management, 173-194 in J. Lewin /ed./: British
   Rivers /George Allen and Unwin, London/.

6. See, for example, C.C. Park /1981/, note 2

7. Useful reviews are given by K. Smith /1972/: Water in Britain /Macmillan, London/; E. Porter /1978/: Water Management
   in England and Wales /Cambridge University Press, London/;
   C. Kirby /1979/: Water in Great Britain /Penguin, Harmonds-
   worth/; and D.J. Parker and E.C. Penning-Rowsell /1980/:
   Water Planning in Britain /George Allen and Unwin, London/.

The wider setting of water management within resource management is detailed by C.C. Park and P.J. Cloke /forthcoming/: Resource Management in the Countryside /Croom Helm, London/.

8. Water resource in Great Britain are described by K. Smith /1972/, Note 7, and C. Kirby /1979/, Note 7. Geographical patterns of water resources are illustrated in R.C. Ward /1975/: Principles of Hydrology /McGraw Hill, London/. Implications of the spatial imbalance between water demand and supply are explored by J.A. Rees /1976/: Rethinking our approach to water supply provision. Geography, 61, 232-245.

9. Data are available from several sources, including Central Water Planning Unit /1976/: Analysis of Trends in Public Water Supply /CWPU, Reading/; Central Water Planning Unit /1977/: Public Water Supply in 1975, and Trends in Consumption /CQPU, Reading/; Water Data Unit /1978/; Water Data 1976 /Water Data Unit, Reading/. Analysis are given in C.C. Park /1980/: Water Demand, in J.C. Doornkamp, K.J. Gregory and A.S. Burn /eds./: Atlas of Drought in Britain 1975-76 /Institute of British Geographers, London/, and in C.C. Park /1983/: The supply of and demand for water, in R.J. Johnston and J.C. Doornkamp /eds./: The Changing Geography of the United Kingdom /Methuen, London/.

10. The evolution of water management systems in the United Kingdom is outlined by D.J. Parker and E.C. Penning-Rowsell /1980/, Note 7 and E. Porter /1978/, Note 7. Detailed reviews are offered in Her Majesty's Stationery Office /1973/: A Background to Water Re-organisation in England and Wales /HMSO, London/; B.M. Funnell and R.D. Hey /eds./ /1974/: The Management of Water.

11. The system in Scotland is described by K. Smith /1977/: Water Resource Management in Scotland. Scottish Geographical Magazine, 93, 66-79.

12. These phases are described in detail by C.C. Park /1983/, Note 9.

13. The surveys are described in Department and Environment
    /1971/: Report of a River Pollution Survey of England and
    Wales, 1970 /HMSO, London/; Department of Environment /1972/:
    River Pollution Survey of England and Wales, updated 1972
    /HMSO, London/; and Department of Environment /1978/: River
    Pollution Survey of England and Wales, updated 1975 /HMSO,
    London/.

14. The recovery of the River Thames is described by J. Har-
    rison and P. Grant /1976/: The Thames transformed: London's
    river and its waterfowl. /Deutsch, London/.

15. The Plan is described in Water Resources Board /1973/: Water
    Resources in England and Wales /HMSO, London/; implications
    of the Plan are explored by J.A. Rees /1976/, Note 8.

16. One of the initial components of the national water grid is
    the Yorkshire grid described by V. Gardiner /1980/: The
    Yorkshire Water Gird. Geography, 65, 134-136; and by R.
    Dobson /1980/: The River Ouse Water Supply Scheme. Journal
    of the Institute of Water Engineers and Scientists, 34,
    265-290; C.C. Park /1983/: Note 9 describes a recently com-
    pleted water gird system in Lancashire /The Lancashire Con-
    junctive Water Use Scheme/.

17. Reviews of drainage basin systems are offered by R.J.
    Chorley /1962/: Geomorphology and General Systems Theory.
    United States Geological Survey Professional Paper, 500B,
    10 p.; A.D. Howard /1965/: Geomorphological Systems - equi-
    librium and dynamics. American Journal of Science, 263,
    303-312; J.R.L. Allen /1975/: Reaction, relaxation and lag
    in natural sedimentary systems - general principles, ex-
    amples and lessons. Earth Science Reviews, 10, 263-342;
    K.J. Gregory and D.E. Walling /1973/: Drainage basin form
    and process /Arnold, London/; and S.A. Schumm /1977/: The
    Fluvial System /Wiley, New York/.

18. A general review of man-induced changes is offered by C.C.
    Park /1981/, Note 2.

19. Early British studies include those by G.W. Lamplugh /1914/: On the taming of streams. Geographical Journal, 43, 651-656; and B. Smith /1910/: Some recent changes in the course of the Trent. Geographical Journal, 35, 568-579. A recent study is that of G.D. Gaunt /1975/: The artificial nature of the River Don north of Thorne, Yorkshire. Yorkshire Archaeological Journal, 47, 15-21.

20. For details of the various approaches adopted, see Task Committee on Channel Stabilization Works /1965/: Channel stabilization of alluvial rivers. American Society of Civil Engineers, Journal of Waterways, Harbours and Coastal Engineering Division, WW1, 91, 7-37.

21. See, for example, M.A. Stocking /1978/: A dilemma for soil conservation. Area, 10, 306-308, and D.A. Davidson /1980/: Soils and Land Use Planning /Longman, London/.

22. See, for example, C.B. Crampton /1969/: The chronology of certain terraced river deposits in the south east Wales area. Zeitschrift für Geomorphologie, 13, 245-259.

23. See, for example, studies by J. Radley /1962/: Peat erosion on the high moor of Derbyshire and West Yorkshire. The East Midland Geographer, 3, 40-44; and J.H. Tallis /1965/: Studies on southern Pennine peats IV. Evidence of recent erosion. Journal of Ecology, 53, 509-520.

24. Results are summarised by R.T. Clarke and J.S.G. McCulloch /1970/: The effects of land use on the hydrology of small upland catchments, 71-80 in G.E. Hollis /ed./: Man's Impact on the Hydrological Cycle in the United Kingdom /GeoBooks, Norwich/. More detailed results are available in R.T. Clarke and M.D. Newson /1978/: Some detailed water balance studies of research catchments. Proceedings and Transactions of the Royal Society of London Series A 363, 21-42; and M.D. Newson /1979/: The results of ten years' experimental study of Plynlimon, mid Wales, and their implications for the water industry. Journal of the Institute of Water Engineers and Scientists, 33, 321-333.

25. These changes are suggested by W.D. Binns /1979/: The hydrological impact of afforestation in Great Britain, 55-70
in G.E. Hollis /ed./: Man's impact on the Hydrological Cycle
in the United Kingdom /GeoBooks/, Norwich/.

26. R.B. Painter, J. Blyth, J.C. Mosedale and M. Kelly /1973/:
The effect of afforestation on erosion processes and sediment yields. International Association of Scientific Hydrology, Publication 113, 62-67.

27. See, for example, W.D. Binns /1979/, Note 25; and M.D. Newson /1979/, Note 24.

28. See, for example, American Studies by J.W. Burns /1972/:
Some effects of logging and associated road construction on
northern California streams. Transactions of the American
Fisheries Society 101, 1-17; and F.J. Swanson and C.T.
Dyrness /1975/: Impact of clear-cutting and road construc-
tion on soil erosion by landslides in the western Cascade
Range, Oregon. Geology, 3, 393-396.

29. F.H.W. Green /1979/: Field drainage in Europe - a quantitative survey. Institute of Hydrology Report, 57, 79 p. Environmental impacts are summarised by A.R. Hill /1976/: The
environmental impacts of agricultural land drainage. Journal of Environmental Management, 4, 251-274; and S. Swales
/1982/: Environmental effects of river channel works used
in land drainage improvement. Journal of Environmental Management, 14, 103-126.

30. See, for example, F.H.W. Green /1973/: Aspects of the
changing environment - some factors affecting the aquatic
environment in recent years. Journal of Environmental Management, 1, 377-391; and F.H.W. Green /1979/: Field underdrainage and the hydrological cycle, 9-17 in G.E. Hollis
/ed./: Man's Impact on the Hydrological Cycle in the
United Kingdom /GeoBooks, Norwich/.

31. Fenland is described by H.C. Darby /1956/: The Drainage of
the Fens. /Cambridge University Press, London/. Wider impacts of pumping and arterial drainage are described by

G.J. Thomas, D.A. Allen and M.P.B. Grose /1981/: The demography and flora of the Ouse Washes, England. Biological Conservation, 21, 197-229.

32. These changes are described by G.M. Howe and H.D. Slaymaker and D.M. Harding /1966/: Flood hazard in mid Wales. Nature, 212, 584-585; and by the same authors in /1967/: Some aspects of the flood hydrology of the upper catchments of the Severn and Wye. Transactions of the Institute of British Geographers, 41, 33-58.

33. See, for example, E.C. Penning-Rowsell /1980/: Land drainage policy and practice - who speaks for the environment? Ecos - A Review of Conservation, 1, 16-21.

34. The Somerset wetlands controversy is described by M. Shoard /1980/: The Theft of the Countryside /Temple Smith, London/. See also reports by the Nature Conservancy Council /1977/: The Somerset Wetlands Project; a consultative paper /NCC, Taunton/; and /1978/: The Somerset Wetlands Project; Summary of responses to the consultative paper /NCC, Taunton/.

35. This scheme is proposed by G.E. Petts /1980/: Long-term consequences of upstream impoundment. Environmental Conservation , 7, 325-332.

36. These changes are summarised in G.E. Petts and J. Lewin /1979/: Physical effects of reservoirs on river systems, 79-92 in G.E. Hollis /ed./: Man's Impact on the Hydrological Cycle in the United Kingdom /GeoBooks, Norwich/.

37. See, for example, D.L. Grimshaw and J. Lewin /1980/: Reservoir effects on sediment yield. Journal of Hydrology, 47, 163-71.

38. Studies include those by K.J. Gregory and C.C. Park /1974/: Adjustment of river channel capacity downstream from a reservoir. Water Resources Research, 10, 870-873; K.J. Gregory and C.C. Park /1976/: Stream channel morphology in north west Yorkshire. Revue de Geomorphologie Dynamiquw, 25, 63-72; C.C. Park /1977/: Man-induced changes in stream channel capacity, 121-144 in K.J. Gregory /ed./: River Channel

Changes /Wiley, London/; G.E. Petts /1979/: Complex response of river channel morphology subsequent to reservoir
construction. Progress in Physical Geography, 3, 329-362.

39. K.J. Gregory and C.C. Park /1976/: The development of a
Devon gully and man. Geography, 61, 77-82.

40. Such environmental impacts are summarised by H.H. Lamb
/1971/: Climate-engineering schemes to meet a climatic emer-
gency. Earth Science Reviews, 7, 87-95.

41. Reviews of the environmental impact of urbanization include
those by R.U. Cooke /1976/: Urban geomorphology. Geographical Journal, 142, 59-65; I. Douglas /1976/: Urban hydrology. Geographical Journal, 142, 65-72; and I. Douglas
/1981/: The city as an ecosystem. Progress in Physical Geography, 5, 315-367.

42. Data are derived from R.H. Best /1976/: The extent and
growth of urban land. The Planner, 62, 8-11.

43. These changes are summarised by L.B. Leopold /1972/: Hydrology for urban land planning - a guidebook on the hydrolog-
ic effects of urban land use. United States Geological Survey Circular, 554, 1-18.

44. Studies include those by G.E. Hollis /1974/: The effects of
urbanization on floods in the Canons Brook, Harlow, Essex.
Institute of British Geographers Special Publication, 6,
123-140; K.J. Gregory /1974/: Streamflow and building activity. Institute of British Geographers Special Publication, 6, 107-122; D.E. Walling and K.J. Gregory /1970/: The
measurement of the effects of building construction on
drainage basin dynamics. Journal of Hydrology, 11, 129-144.

45. The Rosebarn experimental catchment is described in papers
by K.J. Gregory /1974/, Note 44, and D.E. Walling /1979/:
The hydrological impact of building activity - a study near
Exeter, 135-152 in G.E. Hollis /ed./: Man's Impact on the
Hydrological Cycle in the United Kingdom /GeoBooks, Nor-
wich/.

46. These data are summarised in D.E. Walling /1979/, Note 45. More details are given by D.E. Walling /1974/: Suspended sediment and solute yields from a small catchment area prior to urbanization. Institute of British Geographers Special Publication, 6, 169-192; and D.E. Walling /1974/: Suspended sediment production and building activity in a small British basin. International Association of Scientific Hydrology Publication, 113, 137-144.

47. See, for example, G.E. Hollis /1974/, Note 44 and K.J. Gregory /1974/, Note 44. This theme is also covered by J. C. Packman /1979/: The effect of urbanization on flood magnitude and frequency, 153-172 in G.E. Hollis /ed./: Man's Impact on the Hydrological Cycle in the United Kingdom /GeoBooks, Norwich/.

48. Studies include those by C.C. Park /1977/, Note 38; K. J. Gregory and C.C. Park /1976/, Note 38; and C. Knight /1979/: Urbanization and natural stream channel morphology - the case of two English New Towns, 181-198 in G.E. Hollis /ed./: Man's Impact on the Hydrological Cycle in the United Kingdom /GeoBooks, Norwich/.

LAND EVALUATION AS A PRECONDITION FOR ENVIRONMENTAL MANAGEMENT

L. GÓCZÁN

The organization of collective farms in Hungary was followed by decades of wasteful land management because land was considered a free gift of nature. Moreover, since the Second World
War the agricultural area of the country has decreased by more
than 10 per cent through dereliction. This has meant the loss of
about 650,000 ha of cultivated land, more than half of it irre-
vocably lost to food production. If a realistic land evaluation
system had been in operation in Hungary at that time, it is likely that poorer quality land of low rentability would have been
subsituted instead. In other words, the lack of a suitable system of land evaluation resulted in wasteful land management that
caused thousands of millions of forints of damage to the country's economy.

Rocketing oil prices have made intensive industrialized agricultural production systems extremely expensive to maintain,
while at the same time Hungary, with its open economy, is compelled to sustain or even raise the quality of agricultural exports in spite of rising costs of production. Such an economic
path can be followed only if our natural resources, particularly
those relating to agriculture, are rationally managed.

The government has acknowledged the problem and, as a first
step, commissioned experts to devise a new, scientifically based
method of land evaluation. Although the method was not fully a-
vailable when the government passed legislation to enforce the
introduction of a new national land evaluation system, the Land
Evaluation Decree of April 2nd 1981 has created a new climate
for purposeful environmental management.

The new system of land evaluation will impinge upon environmental management in a number of ways. Firstly, it will be possible to employ real land values when assessing the cost-benefit analysis of investment. Secondly, it will be possible to relate the cultivation of crops to agro-ecological endowments at both national and farm level, resulting in the optimum pattern of cultivation and of costs. Thirdly, a reliable appraisal of land values will aid the realistic assessment of national wealth. Fourthly, when prepared, the new cadastre of land quality will enable the identification of areas requiring soil conservation and chemical and physical soil amelioration as well as portraying the regional pattern of land use. Fifthly, dereliction will be regulated through minimising land loss and preventing the alienation of land of good quality. Lastly, the new system of land evaluation may stimulate the exchange of land between collective farms, and thereby create a regulated land market within the socialist sector of the economy.

Until recently the land evaluation system introduced last century at the time of the Austro-Hungarian Monarchy was still universally applied in Hungary. This system was based on cadastral net income expressed in terms of gold korona /crowns in the currency of the time/, but is now gradually being superceded by the first phase of the new complex land evaluation. This latter comprises the rating of agricultural production sites on a scale ranging from 100 to 1. An economic evaluation of land will be derived from this and the two together will be used to establish real land value in the form of a new land price. The Geographical Research Institute of the Hungarian Academy of Sciences is actively participating in the elaboration of the new land evaluation system and in the drafting of the legislation on land evaluation. In the following the method devised by the Institute which, as yet, is the only complex proposal for a land evaluation procedure in Hungary, will be outlined. The method involves the identification of three indices:

1. the numerical value of the production site;
2. the elasticity coefficient of the production site;
3. the value per unit area of land in forints.

1. DETERMINATION OF THE NUMERICAL VALUE OF PRODUCTION SITES

An agricultural production site is a relatively homogeneous area as regards agro-ecological endowments, and such factors as soil-forming material, the soil itself, topography, ag-
ro-climate and water availability are generally different from
neighbouring areas. In the case of natural grassland, the particular association of grass species is also counted as one of
the ecological factors determining the value of the site for
agricultural production. The basic areal unit for agricultural
production is the elementary agricultural production site which
is homogeneous as far as soil fertility is concerned. Within
the Hungarian system of genetic soil classification 17 properties are considered altogether when assessing soil value.

The evaluation of production site is carried out on maps
at a scale of 1 to 10,000 and is based on elementary agricultural production sites of a quarter of a hectare, i.e. 2,500 m^2.
The scoring is relative. The most fertile soil subtype occurring in Hungary is assigned the score of 100 provided its quality is unimpaired by any property it may possess or by any other
agro-ecological factor. If any negative soil property or other
restrictive factor occurs at a site being evaluated, the score
is reduced in proportion to the extent of the restriction.
Based on this principle, a range of score is assigned to each
subtype, the upper limit of which serves as a marker for the
assessment of negative soil properties.

In the second phase of the evaluation, the numerical value
assigned to a particular soil type is assessed against the effect topography might have on fertility. If topography is considered to restrict fertility, a topographic correction value
is applied which reduces further the numerical value of the
soil. The impairment of soil fertility by topography is measured by the amount of surface runoff from a bare cultivated soil

given rainfall ranging from 1 to 40 mm per hour on slopes of 0 to 5, 5 to 12, 12 to 17, 17 to 25, and 25 per cent and over. Topographic correction values are derived from the computer processing of the results of artificial rain experiments, which are then applied to the slope categories mapped at a scale of 1 to 10,000 for the area concerned.

The third step of the evaluation involves a similar correction for water capacity, calculated as the reciprocal of useful water capacity for a soil block 1 m thick given a rate of infiltration appropriate for the various slope categories. Similarly, the fourth step is a climatic correction taking into account the parameters for climatic regions and the negative effect of exposure.

The fifth and final phase of the evaluation is the summation of the correction values for topography, water capacity and climate which are then subtracted from the numerical value of the soil. In this way an ecological numerical value is obtained for each production site which falls within a range between 100 and 1.

2. CALCULATION OF THE ELASTICITY COEFFICIENT OF A PRODUCTION SITE

The numerical value of a production site by itself does not represent the real value of land since land value has economic as well as fertility /ecological/ components. But whereas the ecological components are enduring, the economic components are liable to relatively rapid change. It is for this reason that the elaboration of a complex land evaluation method, capable of identifying both components, is necessary.

Such a complex index of land value has been constructed by the Geographical Research Institute of the Hungarian Academy of Sciences based on the land and capital components per unit area of collective farm incomes from crops. It is this capitalized gross crop production value per unit area that represents the real price of land.

The procedure is realized through cost-benefit analyses for the individual areal units making up a collective farm, the

is an index of the coefficient of elasticity of the production site,

K is the rate of interest for long-term deposits.

During our investigations, the data base for the establishment of the numerical value of a given production site was produced by ourselves through a detailed soil and production site
survey, while the quantification of the data through the cost-
benefit analysis of production per unit area was realized in
collaboration with the chief accountants of the farms concerned.

The results of the land evaluation experiment have been demonstrated in map form for two farms. On the one the average
price of land with high-quality chernozem soils of medium humus
content was 65,000 forints per hectare at 1972 prices, while on
the other, which has an eroded chernozem soil, the value was
33,000 forints per hectare.

Planned environmental management can only be pursued if
the beneficial and adverse natures of resources and potentials
are appreciated by the various branches of the economy. In Hungary the most important natural resource is fertile land and
its evaluation is an indispensable task of environmental management.

3. THE APPLICATION OF AUTOMATED DECODING OF SPACE IMAGES IN AGRO-ECOLOGICAL MICROREGIONALIZATION

In resolution No. 2012/1981/May 16th, the Hungarian Government commissioned the Hungarian Academy of Sciences to establish a production-ecological regionalization of the country,
in which the Geographical Research Institute is participating.

As industrial-like systems are widespread in Hungarian agriculture, the assumption that the regional pattern of cultivation adjusts to the available ecological endowments and also
reflects their profitable use seems to be well founded.

The regional pattern of agricultural land use is recorded
on tape, which can then be decoded automatically and represented on maps. The production-ecological regionalization of agricultural land can be realized through mapping the ecological

outcome being a data matrix comprised of area units in the rows
and the following production data weighted by the areal units
in the columns:

Column 1 : gross crop production value in forints
Column 2 : the numerical value of a production site
Column 3 : labour input in forints
Column 4 : inputs of fixed assets in forints
Column 5 : inputs of working capital in forints

Of the various relationships experimented with, a modified
variety of the Cobb--Douglas production function provided the
most successful fit viz.:

$$Y = a \cdot S^{\alpha} L^{\beta} C^{\gamma}$$

where

Y is column 1 of the matrix,
a is a coefficient,
S is column 2 of the matrix,
L is column 3 of the matrix,
C is columns 4 and 5 of the matrix,
α, β, γ are coefficients of elasticity showing the percentage change in the dependent variable required
to produce a 1 per cent increase in the corresponding independent variables,
$\alpha + \beta + \gamma = 1$ are coefficients of production volume elasticity.

Through the computer solution of the function, the coefficient of elasticity of a production site can be obtained from
which land value per unit area in money terms can be calculated
according to the formula:

$$\text{basic price of land} = \frac{Y}{T} \cdot \alpha \frac{1}{K}$$

where

Y is the gross crop production value,
T is the area in hectares,

suitability of areas of varying agro-ecological endowments and then comparing this with the regional distribution of the most profitable crops averaged over a number of years. However, this method necessitates such time-consuming and expensive work that it is virtually impossible to carry it out in practice.

As an alternative the procedure will be applied to certain agricultural test areas only, and crop patterns reproduced from Landsat images through digital interpretation using a colour plotter. A probability relationship may then be established between the regional pattern of land capability for crop cultivation and the average annual crop pattern shown by the Landsat image.

Hungary is covered by eight separate Landsat scenes, and the representation of crop patterns on maps would therefore substantially reduce the costs and time needed to produce a regionalization of agricultural land. The plotter image presented here shows one of the test areas. For decoding an improved version of Bayes' digital recognition method was applied.

THE ROLE OF ASSESSMENT IN ENVIRONMENTAL MANAGEMENT: AN EVALUATION OF THE PHYSICAL ENVIRONMENT FROM AN AGRICULTURAL VIEWPOINT

D. LÓCZY

It is quite common for regional planners to be faced with the dilemma of adjudicating between various conflicting uses for a given area of land. Given this situation decision making should be preceded by a determination of the relative value of land for several competetive uses. Land is suitable for a particular use if production is enhanced or if little damage is caused by that use /Howell 1981/. Ideally, both conditions should be fulfilled.

Although it is eventually social demand which settles the debate, applied physical geography has a valuable contribution to make in reaching rational land use decisions. The trend in our discipline towards the establishemnt of exact parameters to describe environmental phenomena and processes enables researchers to set up an inventory of the state and dynamics of the major physical factors of the environment and to evaluate their inherent potential for various activities.

The purely financial cost-benefit analysis of investment cannot alone detect all the indirect man-induced impacts on the physical environment and which also bear on future exploitation. The physical environment has been transformed to such a degree /Pécsi 1979/ that exploitation and protection can no longer be separated, and an approach should be made towards creating a uniform framework of environmental management. A comprehensive assessment of human intervention should be part of this process as well as acquiring an all-round knowledge of the components and processes of the environmental system. An assessment of environmental quality at any date and through time is therefore an important preparatory task for any system of environmental management.

TOWARDS THE PLANNING OF OPTIMUM LAND USE

Availability highly influences the value of land as of all other commodities. Densely populated countries cannot reach self-sufficiency in food expect by massively increasing per unit output in agriculture through more and more intensive land management. As a consequence, the environment becomes particularly precious.

Apart from ensuring indigenous food supply, Hungary, as a country favourably endowed from the point of view of agriculture, is also interested in the quantitative and qualitative development of agriculture for balance of payments reasons. The products of agriculture and of the food processing industry comprise about 20 per cent of exports.

The appreciation of natural resources is reflected in the Environmental Protection Act of 1976 and in the Land Evaluation Decree of 1981, while a survey assessing the agricultural potential of Hungary in the year 2000 is also indicative of the growing concern about the food economy and its environmental background.

Agricultural land made up 70.4 per cent of the area of Hungary in 1980, and although this value is decreasing by some 0.3 to 0.5 per cent per year, the importance of evaluating the environment is not diminishing. On the contrary, for when any proposal is made to transfer a particular cultivated area to non-agricultural use it is essential to know the relative environmental value of that land when making the decision /Pécsi 1980/. Relative evaluation helps prevent the expropriation of precious land for new roads, for new industrial plants, for open cast mines and even for recreational use.

PRINCIPLES OF AGRO-ECOLOGICAL EVALUATION

In developing our technique for evaluation the aim was not to accomplish as comprehensive a synthesis as that attempted at the Institute of Experimental Biology and Ecology in Bratislava, Czechoslovakia /Ruzicka and Miklós 1981/. Our investigation was restricted to an assessment of the agro-ecological potential of the landscape and of land capability for the cultivation of major field crops.

It was based on the following assumptions:

1. Although the ecological requirements of field crops are broadly similar and are related to relief, availability of water, climate and soils, differences exist in two respects. There are those crops that are especially sensitive to water supply while others are sensitive to temperature or soils. Moreover, within each category there are variations in the preference for humid or arid conditions during certain phenological phases or for calcareous as opposed to acid soils and so forth.

2. Information concerning ecological requirements is assumed to be available in proper detail from the agronomic literature or through consultation with experts and from the field data of ecology-oriented soil surveys and meteorological observation series etc.

3. It has been assumed that areas of average fertility by Hungarian standards exist for almost all environmental factors to which the suitability of land under investigation can be related.

4. Environmental data are so abundant that any method of storage and processing other than by computer is not feasible. As a result the evaluation itself should also be automated.

It is hoped rather than presumed that agriculture will make use of our research.

METHOD

The steps in the procedure /Lóczy 1982/ for the assessment of land capability for crop cultivation are set out below.

1. Specification of an evaluation goal

Although the method can be applied to almost any type of land use, we decided to restrict it to the cultivation of the five major crops in Hungary, excluding grassland.

Table I. Distribution of major field crops by harvested area
/1980/

Winter wheat	26.8%
Maize	26.4%
Lucerne	8.1%
Sunflowers	5.8%
Sugar-beet	2.2%

The crops in Table I represent three main types of field crops - grain, fodder and row crops. An alternative would be to investigate other forage or row crops and propose which of those that are ecologically most suitable should be included in the rotation.

2. Compilation of the field data base for computer storage

The information essential for an assessment of agricultural potential was collected from maps depicting the principal physical factors. Ideally the parameters should be independent of one another but, as a matter of course, almost all factors are interrelated.

The relief parameter selected was the angle and exposure of slope while climate was measured as the character of the mesoclimatic region, comprising mean monthly temperature values and an indicator of water availability during the growing season /Petrasovits 1981/. Soils were represented by general genetic types taking note of parent material, and soil properties like humus condition, texture and pH value. Most of these parameters characterize the state of the environment at a given time and need periodic revision to take account of dynamic changes.

Cartographic data were digitized by grid square and thereby converted into data matrices of coded parameter values which preserved the uniformity of the data /Table II/. The value falling into the fifth category of the sixth environmental factor is identified at 6/5, regardless of whether it was mean temperature or quantitative description of soil texture. Factors which are in close mutual interaction are coded together. The computerized storage and retrieval system can be visualized as a series of data matrices of environmental factors superimposed upon one another. Further parameters may be added later and information regarding partial environmental quality printed out for regionalization purposes.

3. The establishment of "suitability indicators"

As is clear from the above, the stored information by itself does not involve any kind of preliminary evaluation, and represents the "supply" side of the utilization of the environment. Is is only at a later and separate stage of the procedure that the ecological demands of cultivated crops are introduced. The "suitability indicators" are environmental statements, categorizing environmental conditions into the quality grades excellent, favourable, neutral, restrictive, highly restrictive and unsuitable. Each parameter occurring in Hungary is treated in this way. These partial suitability scores are eventually combined to determine the overall suitability of an areal unit for a given land use. As measurement data are available only in limited amounts, the use of a more refined system of "suitability indicators" does not seem well founded as yet.

Table II

Coding of genetic soil types

Genetic type and depth of humus layer /cm/	Humus content of topsoil /%/		
Brown forest soil with residual carbonate	<1.5	1.6--3.0	3.1<
0--30	96.	97.	98.
30--60	99.	100.	101.
60 <	102.	103.	104.
Chernozem brown forest soil			
0--30	105.	106.	107.
30--60	108.	109.	110.
60 <	111.	112.	113.
Chernozem soils with forest	<2.0	2.1--3.5	3.6<
0--40	114,	115.	116.
40--80	117.	118.	119.
80 <	120.	121.	122.
Leached chernozem soils			
0--40	123.	124.	125.
40--80	126.	127.	128.
80<	129.	130.	131.
Calcareous chernozem soil			
0--40	132.	133.	134.
40--80	135.	136.	137.
80 <	138.	139.	140.
Meadow chernozem soil			
0--40	141.	142.	143.
40--80	144.	145.	146.
80 <	147.	148.	149.

4. Evaluation programming

Still outstanding is the translation of the indicators into computer language, the weighting of the factors and the in-
structions as to how the partial scores are to be summarized.
The subsequent stages of evaluation are fully automated. The
program ranks the areal units on a scale of O-9, O denoting the
least suitable areas and 9 the most suitable areas. This device
yields comparable scores for the various crops.

5. Automated drawing of the "map" of suitability

The end product of the evaluation is a matrix of rank
scores for each crop /Fig. 1/. In order to facilitate visual interpretation, the matrix of numerical figures can be transformed into a colour mosaic.

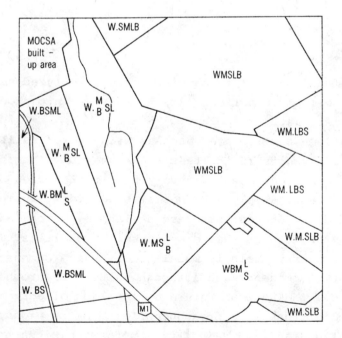

Fig. 1. Land capability map for the five major field crops
/by fields/
W = winter wheat; M = maize; L = lucerne; S = sun-
flower; B = sugar-beat

TEST AREAS

Two areas in County Komárom were selected to test the method, the one being within the administrative limits of the historical town of Tata, and the other in the vicinity of the village of Mocsa. Both are rolling lowland areas on the terrace plain of the Danube with a warm, moderately dry, continental climate, and chernozem soils derived from a sandy parent material. Since detailed environmental data were available based on the results of a earlier large-scale soil survey /Góczán, Marosi, Szücs and Szilárd 1969/, the evaluation was performed on the basis of areal units of one hectare in size.

These areas are also of interest since they are traversed by sections of the new M1 Motorway which has taken up much valuable agricultural land. The results of our investigation should therefore provide arguments for or against such road construction.

RESULTS

Ecological suitability maps are either analyzed separately or, for purpose of comparison, are integrated into a combined land capability map.

Apart from some isolated patches with poorer soils, the ecological endowments in the test areas are above the national average. Winter wheat displayed very high rank scores due to an advantageous water supply and thermal conditions, whereas sugarbeet recorded the highest standard deviation, which reflects the high sensitivity of this crop to soil properties. The pattern of low quality areas is mosaic-like. Maize demonstrated the greatest homogeneity and although values are around or only slightly above the national average, the lack of extreme environmental conditions is a great benefit to maize producers.

The integrated land capability map for the Mocsa agricultural produce co-operative /Fig. 2/ places the major crops in preferential order by agricultural fields, the various tints showing crops for which suitability is much higher or lower

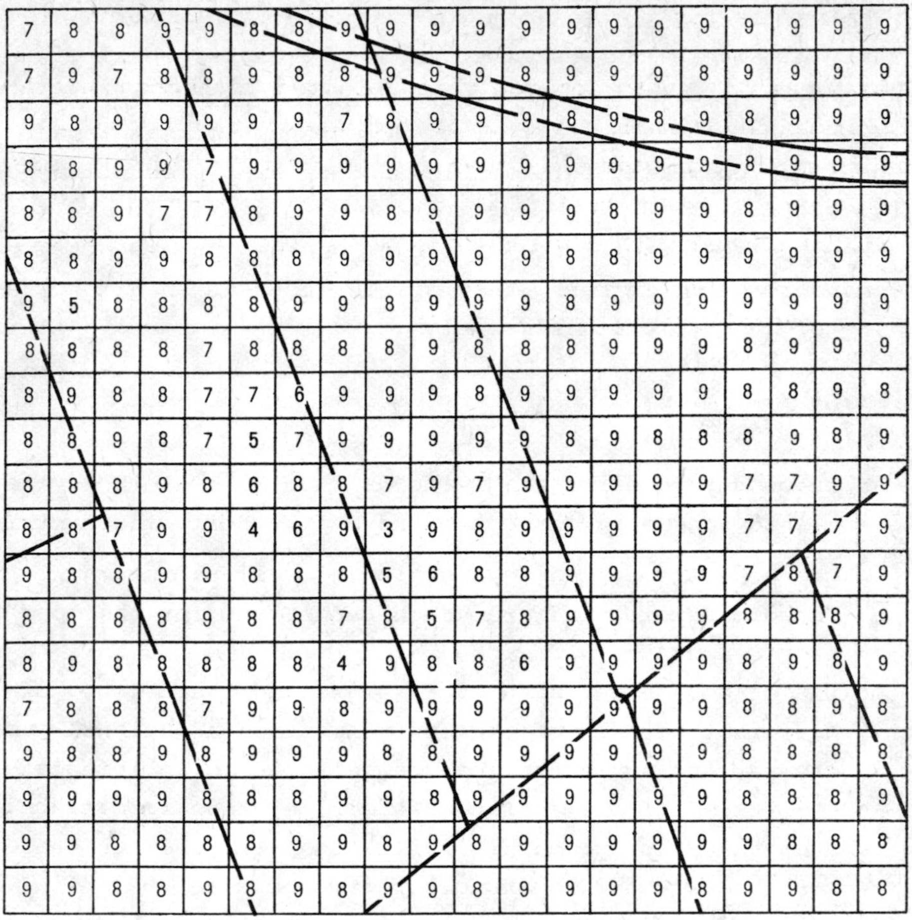

7	8	8	9	9	8	8	9	9	9	9	9	9	9	9	9	9	9	9	9
7	9	7	8	8	9	8	8	9	9	9	8	9	9	9	8	9	9	9	9
9	8	9	9	9	9	9	7	8	9	9	9	8	9	8	9	8	9	9	9
8	8	9	9	7	9	9	9	9	9	9	9	9	9	9	9	8	9	9	9
8	8	9	7	7	8	9	9	8	9	9	9	9	8	9	9	8	9	9	9
8	8	9	9	8	8	8	9	9	9	9	9	8	8	9	9	9	9	9	9
9	5	8	8	8	8	9	9	8	9	9	9	8	9	9	9	9	9	9	9
8	8	8	8	7	8	8	8	8	9	8	8	8	9	9	9	8	9	9	9
8	9	8	8	7	7	6	9	9	9	8	9	9	9	9	9	8	8	9	8
8	8	9	8	7	5	7	9	9	9	9	9	8	9	8	8	8	9	8	9
8	8	8	9	8	6	8	8	7	9	7	9	9	9	9	9	7	7	9	9
8	8	7	9	9	4	6	9	3	9	8	9	9	9	9	9	7	7	7	9
9	8	8	9	9	8	8	8	5	6	8	8	9	9	9	9	7	8	7	9
8	8	8	8	9	8	8	7	8	5	7	8	9	9	9	9	8	8	8	9
8	9	8	8	8	8	8	4	9	8	8	6	9	9	9	9	8	9	8	9
7	8	8	8	7	9	9	8	9	9	9	9	9	9	9	9	8	8	9	8
9	8	8	9	8	9	9	9	8	8	9	9	9	9	9	9	8	8	8	8
9	9	9	9	8	8	8	9	9	8	9	9	9	9	9	9	8	8	8	9
9	9	8	8	8	8	9	9	8	9	8	9	9	9	9	9	9	8	8	8
9	9	8	8	9	8	9	8	9	9	8	9	9	9	9	8	9	9	8	8

Fig. 2. Computer map of relative environmental quality /ecological suitability of the Tata test area for winter wheat growing, by one hectare units/
Grades: 0 = unsuitable; 1--8 = values indicating increasing suitability; 9 = excellent /most valuable under the conditions in Hungary/

than average. Capital letters indicate the order of suitability and points separate ranks of suitability. W.SLM.B. on a red colour background means that the field is excellent for winter wheat, good for sunflowers, lucerne and maize, but is only of intermediate quality as far as the cultivation of sugar-beet is concerned.

The map serves to pick out the fact that rank scores are generally higher in the western than in the eastern half of the Mocsa test area. Even the pasture along the Kocs-Mocsa stream is shown to be of ecological value and with appropriate treatment could be converted into arable land of high productive potential.

The orders of preference displayed on the map are not meant to be mandatory for farmers; they are intended as an aid to the planning of crop rotation systems.

CONCLUSION

As opposed to other rating methods /Góczán et al. 1979/ the above outlined scheme is characterized by the following features:

a. the objective of the evaluation is well-defined;
b. the parameters used are unambiguous, and for the most part measured;
c. the data base can be used for repeated evaluations of different aspects of the environment on a national basis;
d. the particular factors can be weighted in an integrated evaluation in proportion to their relative importance;
e. the evaluation proper is fully automated and can therefore be executed in a short period of time.

Although the results achieved so far are promising, further experimentation is required to improve and test the usefulness of the method.

REFERENCES

Agricultural Land Classification Map of England and Wales /1 inch to 1 mile/ with Explanatory Note. - Ministry of Agriculture, Fisheries and Food, 1977.

GÓCZÁN, L. et al. /1979/: A természeti környezet ökológiai tényezőinek értékrend szerinti minősitése /Rating of the ecological factors of the physical environment/. MTA FKI, Budapest, 195 p. + suppl.

GÓCZÁN, L.--MAROSI, S.--SZÜCS, L.--SZILÁRD, J. /1969/: A mocsai
"Buzakalász Mgtsz" területéről készitett genetikai talaj-
térképet és kartogramsorozatot magyarázó és a laborató-
riumi vizsgálati eredményeket ismertető szakvélemény /Re-
port explaining the genetic soil map and thematic map
series of the "Ear of Wheat" Agricultural Producer Cooperative of Mocsa and containing results of laboratory
investigations/. MTA FKI, Budapest, 63 p. + suppl.

HOWELL, E.A. /1981/: Landscape design, planning and management:
an approach to the analysis of vegetation. - Environmental Management, 5, 3, 6 p.

LÓCZY, D. /1982/: A természeti környezet integrált, számitógé-
pes minősitése egy kisalföldi mintaterületen /An integrated, computerized evaluation of the physical environment
in a Little Hungarian Plain test area/. MTA FKI, Budapest,
69 p. + suppl.

PÉCSI, M. /1979/: A földrajzi környezet uj szemléletü regionális vizsgálata /summary in English: A new regional approach to the geographical environment/. - Geonómia és
Bányászat, 12, 1-3, 163-176.

PÉCSI, M. /1980/: Value oriented quantitative mapping of the
ecological factors of the physical environment. - Symposium de l'Union Géographique Internationale de la Carto-
graphie de l'Environnement et de sa Dynamique. Caen 18-
23 June 1979, Univ. de Caen, 55-63.

PETRASOVITS, I. /ed./ /1981/: Magyarország mezőgazdasági viz-
használati adattára. I. Szántóföldi növénytermesztés
/Data of agricultural uses of water in Hungary. I. Field
crop cultivation/. Agrártudományi Egyetem, Mezőgazdaság-
tudományi Kar, Gödöllő, 107 p.

RUZICKA, M.--MIKLÓS, L. /1981/: Methodology of ecological landscape evaluation for optimal development of territory. -
Proc. Int. Congress Neth. Soc. Landscape Ecology, Veldho-
ven, 1981. Pudoc, Wageningen, 99-107.

ENVIRONMENTAL QUALITY CONTROL POLICY IN AN ECONOMIC AND REGIONAL CONTEXT

D. KULCSÁR

This paper provides a general evaluation of Hungarian environmental quality control policy. It analyses the socio-economic conditions of the evolution, the aims and the results of
environmental policy and touches briefly on its future tasks
and problems. From among various protective activities, it emphasises water and air quality control. Finally, it overviews
the relationship between regional economic development and environmental quality control.

A. THE EVOLUTION OF ENVIRONMENTAL QUALITY CONTROL POLICY IN HUNGARY

The development of productive forces, urbanization, the
scientific and technological revolution have also damaged the
natural environment in Hungary. It follows from the economic-
historical characteristics of this country that urbanization developed within relatively short period of time. /One can mention as an example that industrial output has increased eight
times during the past thirty years. The relative weight of the
engineering and chemical industries and power generation have
increased considerably within total industries output./ Similar
to general international experience, the extensive use of chemicals in agriculture has also added to the tasks of environmental protection. It is a historical fact that accelerated economic development, forced industrialization and rapid urbanization have tended to force environmental issues into the back-

11*

ground as have economic difficulties and the lack of careful perspective planning.

The beginning of the formulation of a comprehensive environmental quality control policy in Hungary can be placed in the mid-1970s. There was earlier legislation concerning the protection of water, productive land and the atmosphere, but one can only speak of a comprehensive policy since 1976 when the Environmental Quality Control Act was passed. It is only since 1976 that environmental protection has figured as a major task in national plans.

The background to the formulation of a comprehensive environmental policy in Hungary can be summarized as follows:

1. By the beginning of the 1970s, socio-economic development had reached that stage at which environmental damage was beginning to hamper further economic development. /For instance, in certain regions the lack of clean water presented itself as an obstacle to industrial development./ The need to stress the importance of environmental quality control was also forced on the country by future economic development requirements.

2. The early 1970s were characterized by economic prosperity in Hungary. Measures in great number were taken to improve the quality of life, and environmental protection has also become a social need at that time. It was also a time when the Hungarian Government planned a stable and constantly high pace of economic growth. It was only later that an unfavourable world economic situation affected the national economy and the realization of the tasks related to environmental protection.

3. The formulation of an environmental quality control policy in Hungary was also facilitated by the fact that environmental protection was becoming a major concern all over the world. Lessons drawn from international experience made the need for comprehensive environmental management obvious.

156

When establishing the objectives of environmental policy, the aim was to achieve considerable progress in the field of environmental quality control within the limits made possible by the economy. Given the difficulties faced by the Hungarian economy during the second half of the 1970s, environmental policy could only set a minimal target. The plan for the year 1976 as well as the present plan have been concerned with environmental quality preservation. Besides this general target, considerable progress has of course been made in some regions and towns in improving water and air quality standards, in refuse disposal and reuse, but all in all, environmental quality conservation remains the realistic objective of the overall plan.

In setting this not too ambitious target as the objective for environmental quality control policy and practical environmental management, the responsible governmental agencies had to take account of the following circumstances:

a/ Advanced processes are not widely used in Hungarian industry and most of the existing technologies are pollutive. Although environmental protection technologies are being developed a fall in the general level of investment has also slowed down activities in this field.

b/ The system of environmental management so far has relied on penalties as the major regulator. Due to the increasing demands based on the state budget, the state can only offer limited support to enterprises and cooperatives in solving the tasks relating to environmental protection. Since state subsidies are not expected to increase significantly in the future only a halt to further aggravation can be planned. A rapid solution to environmental problems would require more state subsidies but this course is subject to economic constraints.

c/ When defining the objectives of environmental policy, government bodies also considered the fact that the economic situation of neighbouring countries does not allow a substantially reduction in imported pollution, and Hungary therefore stresses the urgency of international cooperation.

B. ENVIRONMENTAL PROTECTION FROM A REGIONAL PERSPECTIVE

1. The present situation

    In spite of the fact that environmental quality preserva-
tion was formulated as the major objective of Hungarian environmental policy, one can also observe improvements, particularly in the field of investment serving environmental protection purposes. /This paper limits itself to a discussion of the
questions relating to water and air quality./

    The quality of the environment is fundamentally affected
by the characteristics of regional development. In Hungary, the
most polluting industries have come to be concentrated in the
Budapest agglomeration and in the Hungarian Central Chain of
Mountains. Although there have been important changes in the
spatial structure of industry during the past thirty years, it
is in these traditional industrial areas that pollution still
cause most trouble. Present environmental quality standards
were established during earlier stages of industrialization,
the period before 1970 was therefore decisive.

    The relationship between the location of industry and the
distribution of air pollution is shown in Figure 1. Contiguous
zones of polluted air are associated with the totality of the
metal, engineering and chemical industries and with power generation, the major source of air pollution being coal-based
energy production. Most settlements suffering from air pollution are characterized by the prevalence of various pollutants,
typically of suspended particulates and sulphur dioxide. It is
very regrettable that air quality control has not yet been rig-
orously applied in the new towns which rapidly developed during
the period of forced industrialization, i.e. Tatabánya, Komló,
Oroszlány, Dunaujváros, Kazincbarcika and Várpalota.

    Contiguous zones of polluted air cover 8 per cent of the
national territory, but this understates the extent of the problem because 40 per cent of the total population live in these
areas.

    Surface water quality in Hungary is not only effected by
the location of industry and population but also by imported

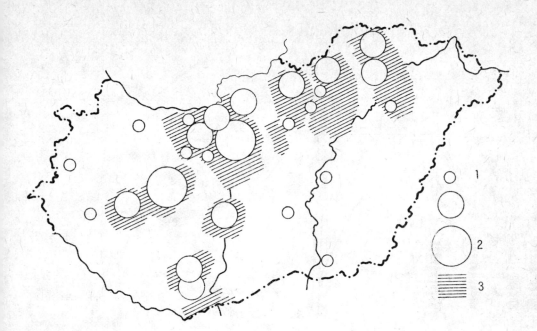

Fig. 1. Air pollution /1981/
   1 = areas of lesser pollution; 2 = areas of considerable pollution with a variety of material; 3 = areas
   of contiguous pollution

pollution from abroad. 95 per cent of all surface waters orig-
inate outside the national borders and rivers are already polluted when they enter the country. Organic river pollution is
shown in Figure 2 according to CMEA/Comecon/ water quality
standards. Physical pollution and non-organic pollution would
show a similar picture.

   Water pollution can be briefly characterized by two statements. Firstly, of the major rivers, the Danube, Raab and Dra-
va are extremely polluted. They are already polluted when they
enter Hungary and receive heavy extra loading as they flow
through the country. Secondly, most of the smaller rivers which
have their sources inside Hungary are also strongly polluted,
due to their small discharge.

   It should be noted that the Sajó is by far the most polluted Hungarian river, and in reality is little more than a

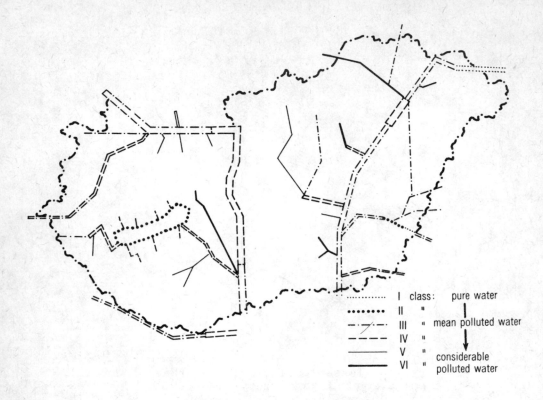

....	I	class:	pure water
••••••••	II	"	
–·–/·–·–	III	"	mean polluted water
– – – –	IV	"	
—————	V	"	considerable
▬▬▬▬	VI	"	polluted water

Fig. 2. The quality of surface water /1980/. Water quality
based on organic chemical indices /CMEA's water quality classification of 1978/

sewer. She arrives at the Hungarian border over-polluted and
further discharge from riverside industry adds to her pollution. The Sajó adversely effects the water quality of the moderately polluted Tisza which has a much larger discharge.

2. The results of environmental quality control

In spite of the ground that environmental protection has
gained, the state of affairs has not essentially changed since
1975. The results of environmental protection are expressed in
the fact that - in conformity with the objective - quality
standards overall have not deteriorated, although this covers
both positive and negative changes, as shown by air and water
quality data. Changes in air quality in Budapest and in other
five large cities may be taken as examples /Fig. 3/. Suspended

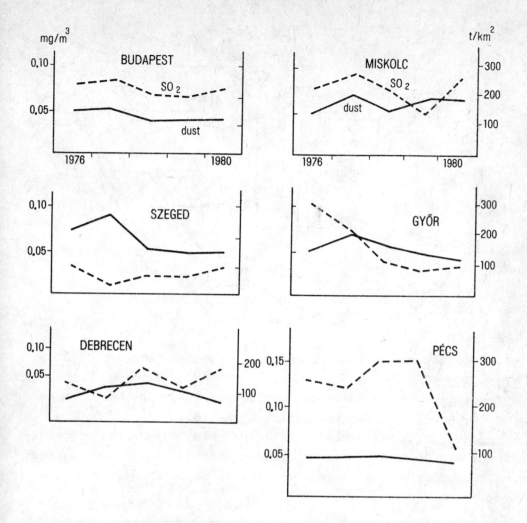

Fig. 3. Changes in air pollution in the major cities between 1976 and 1980

solid particulates and sulphur dioxide concentration decreased in a number of cities but nowhere radically. Changes in regional air pollution show a similar picture. Moreover, it follows from the spatial location of productive forces that the differences in air quality among the economic planning regions have not been reduced during the past decade either and the industrial zones of the northern part of the country are still the most polluted areas. Figure 4 presents the regional breakdown

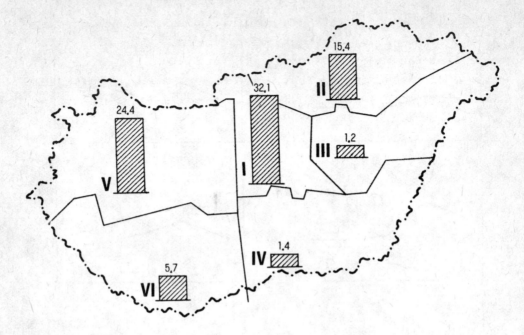

Fig. 4. Quantity of deposited SO_2 by economic regions /1980/

of sulphur dioxide emissions per square kilometre based on average annual data for the period 1976-1980.

As far as water quality is concerned, only slight improvements can be observed as is demonstrated in the following table which summarizes the amount of certain pollutants in Hungarian waters.

Indicator	Chemical oxygen requirement		Total amount of dissolved solids		Oil	
			/thousand tons/day/			
	1975	1980	1975	1980	1975	1980
Pollution from abroad	7.4	7.4	76.6	84.3	0.8	0.8
Inland discharge	1.1	1.1	2.4	2.7	0.09	0.06
Assimilation /+, - /	+0.5	+0.5	-12.0	-13.2	+0.14	+0.11

The amount of pollutants remain practically unchanged between 1975 and 1980. Although the proportion of treated waste water from the major industrial emitters rose, the amount of sewage increased considerably, and the loading in absolute terms has not esentially changed. Figure 5 shoes how the proportion of treated industrial waste water changed over time. The proportion of fully or partially treated water within the total amount of industrial sewage increased considerably but the proportion of untreated waste water at 26.6 per cent is still large.

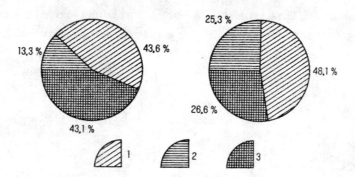

Fig. 5. Structure of industrial effluent by degree of treatment in 1975 and 1980
    1 = fully treated sewage; 2 = partially treated sewage;
    3 = untreated sewage

3. Investment in environmental quality control

Environmental investment has gradually increased since 1976 as a result of Hungarian environmental quality control policy, but their effect will be only felt in the longer term. Present investment serves mainly to counterbalance the increasing amount of pollutants and only if the present level of environmental investment can be maintained or eventually raised, will notable improvements eventually be forthcoming in environmental quality, since one cannot, even with increasing investment, rapidly offset earlier neglected.

In term of the level of investment in environmental quality control, given the country's level of economic development, Hungary stands, at present, about the mid-way in the interna-

tional league table. Future result in environmental protection
depends firstly on the present level of investment in the field
and this doubted between 1976 and 1980, when 0.3 per cent of
total Gross National Product was spent on environmental investment. It should be noted that this is rather low by international standards but the increase is very significant when we
take account of the fact that in 1976 only 0.16 per cent of GNP
was set aside for this purpose. It is an encouraging sign that
investment in environmental quality control grew much more rapidly between 1976 and 1980 than investment in other sectors:
the average annual increase in total national investment amounted to 5.7 per cent while that in environmental investments was
25 per cent /Fig. 6/.

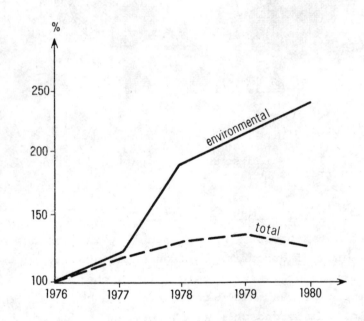

Fig. 6. Change in total and environmental investments between
1976 and 1980 /1976 = 100%/

Of the investment of environmental purposes, that serving
water quality control takes up the largest proportion and dis-
plays, at the same time, the most dynamic increase /Fig. 7/.
The primacy of water quality control is closely related to the
fact that a lack of pure water directly jeopardizes industrial

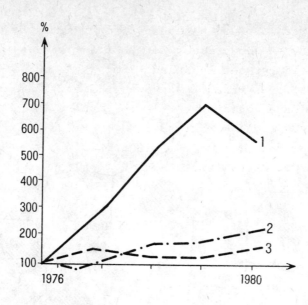

Fig. 7. Change in environmental investment by purposes between
1976 and 1980 /1976 = 100%/
1 = investment in water quality protection; 2 = investment in air quality protection; 3 = investment in disposal of refuse

development and the supply of water to the population. An increase in the investment devoted to in air quality control is
an objective of future investment policy.

A regional breakdown of environmental quality data has
been recorded since 1978. In general it can be stated that the
proportion of environmental investment is higher in those regions where pollution is concentrated than elsewhere, the
largest in Budapest and Northern Hungary /Fig. 8/. Nevertheless
the share of environmental investments is smaller than is required in the counties of Komárom and Veszprém where a high
level of water and air pollution calls for more attention. Between 1976 and 1980 almost half of all environmental investments - in monetary terms - was spent in Budapest, while from
among 19 counties, Borsod-Abauj-Zemplén ranks in first place.
Both are two of the most polluted regions where the safeguard-

ing of public health also requires redoubled efforts in environmental protection.

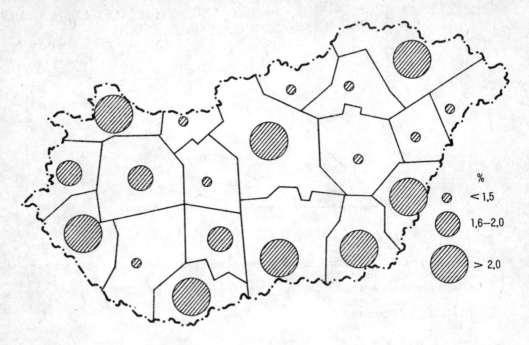

Fig. 8. Geographical distribution of investment in environmental protection as a proportion of total investment by counties /%/, 1980

CONCLUSION

Hungarian environmental policy has a short history, but it is an important advance that environmental quality control is now a major concern of economic planning and state economic management. A practical result is that actual environmental quality standards are being maintained while in the most polluted regions enterprises are compelled to increase their activities in the field of environmental protection. If economic conditions allow the maintenance of the present level of investment in environmental quality control, it is reasonably certain that the natural environment will be able to withstand economic development in the future, while harmful environmental effects on the quality of life should decrease.

ENVIRONMENTAL PROBLEMS OF THE OLD AND NEW COALFIELDS IN THE UNITED KINGDOM: MANAGING THE COAL REVIVAL

D. J. SPOONER

I. RETROSPECTIVE: THE COALHOUSE DOOR

> Close the coalhouse door, lad
> And stay outside
> Geordie's standing at the dole
> and Mrs. Jackson like a fool
> complains about the price of coal
> Close the coalhouse door, lad
> There's blood inside
> There's bones inside
> There's bairns inside
> So stay outside.
>
> Alex Glasgow, 1968

The play, Close the Coalhouse Door /Plater 1969/, was first performed in Newcastle-upon-Tyne in 1968. Its theme song captures the bitter but ambivalent attitudes towards the demise of coal in a mining region like North East England in the 1960s - a decade when the rapid contraction of the industry was closing the coalhouse door in many communities. 1968 was a particular bitter year for the miners of Nort East England. The government announced its decision to build a nuclear power station at Hartlepool on the ege of the Durham coalfield. The grip of coal on the power station market was being loosened even close to its own heartland. It was ironic that the announcement fell to a Labour Minister of Power, Mr. Roy Mason, himself an ex-miner, a Member of Parliament sponsored by the National Union of Mineworkers.

That period represents the trough of the coal industry's fortunes. It reflects the impact of ruling ideas about energy futures which were characterised by a belief that cheap abundant imported oil would continue to be available; a view shared by government and by many academic commentators. As late as 1971 the geographer Manners /later a fierce critic of plans to mine the Vale of Belvoir/ concluded that there would be "a continuing downward drift in the real price of oil f.o.b." and "no grounds" for believing that the expansion of the oil industry's markets will not continue.

Mitchell /1979/ suggested that "unified field theory" /Jones 1954/ is an appropriate conceptual tool or structure for analysing the evolution of an idea and associated events in the field of resource analysis. Stated briefly the unified field theory suggests the chain of linkages from an initial "idea", through a "decision" to "movement" and "circulation fields" and finally to an "area". This idea-area chain can be loosely adapted in the context of coalfield "development" and "de-development". Acceptance of the conventional wisdom or idea of "Energy Abundance" in the 1960s led to a series of decisions to disinvest in coalmining. Because of the characteristics and history of working of individual coalfields these decisions were associated with the movement of capital and labour away from particular locations. The differential impact on the various coalfield areas was marked at both the inter- and intra-regional scales. While all coalfields shared to some extent in the decline, the colliery closure programme was heavily concentrated in the peripheral coalfields of Scotland, the North East, Lancashire and South Wales. In the central coalfields of Yorkshire and the East Midlands, with shorter working histories, better production conditions and more assured regional power station markets, decline was concentrated in the shallower exposed sections of the field, and some new investment continued to occur in new deep mines like Kellingley /Yorkshire/, Cotgrave and Bevercotes /Nottinghamshire/ /Spooner 1981a/.

In the 1960s witnessed the rapid "closing of the coalhouse door" in many areas, the 1970s were characterised by an abrupt turnaround in policy: the coalhouse door was swung wide open. The trigger was the 1973-74 oil crisis. Rapid acceptance of new

ruling ideas - oil shortage, energy crisis - led to a swift
government decision to support a new Plan for Coal. This was
translated into mining exploration movements and the circulation of capital and manpower resources to develop new projects
in both old and new coalfield areas. The speed of development
of this idea - area chain was remarkable. By 1980, just seven
years after the first major oil price hikes by O.P.E.C. upset
the conventional wisdom about energy futures, the National Coal
Board had completed over 50 investment projects at existing
collieries, embarked upon more than 100 others, opened 3 small
new mines, and started the massive project for the 10 million
tonnes per annum complex at Selby, North Yorkshire. However,
the preciseness of the sequence of development from ide to areal impact should not be exaggerated. The Plan for Coal was
being prepared before the 1973-74 oil price hikes and a pre-
scient National Coal Board had already embarked upon its major
exploration drive by that date. The onset of a crisis was perceived at different times by industry, government and the wider
public. The 1974 Plan for Coal set out a strategy for the coal
industry which involved essentially a stabilisation of production levels, with a target of 135 million tonnes set for 1985
/including 15 millions open-cast/ /National Coal Board, 1974/.
Because of exhaustion at old collieries this was seen as requiring the creation of 42 million tonnes of annual productive
capacity, of which 20 million tonnes was to come from new mines,
primarily at greenfield sites, with the balance coming from reconstruction projects and life extension schemes at existing
collieries, or blackfield sites. This strategy still holds,
though it was soon recognised that by 1985 only 10 million tonnes per annum would come from new mines, because of the length
of lead times in both gaining planning approval and constructing new capacity at greenfield sites /Spooner 1981a/. A more
ambitious Plan to 2000 was put forward in 1977 embodying much
higher targets for the end of the century - involving a major
expansion at numerous greenfield sites /Department of Energy
1977/. This Plan was apparently endorsed by the Government in
1978, though there have been protracted arguments about the

realistic size of the industry given the wide range of demand forecasts. It is now expected that the original Plan for Coal objectives will not be achieved before the late 1980s. In 1981 the National Coal Board produced 125 million tonnes of coal.

Decisions to "open the coalhouse door" in the 1970s have had precise locational results in investment projects, although on an areal basis these have done little to alter the trends established in the earlier phase when the coalhouse door was being shut. New greenfield sites are being developed or planned primarily in the Yorkshire, East and South Midland regions on the frontier of existing coalfield development /e.g. Selby, Belvoir, South Warwickshire/; blackfield site investment is occurring in all regions, but most heavily in Yorkshire, /where the "new Barnsley" field is being created out of the old/, and the Midlands /North and Spooner 1982a/. The divergence in the fortunes of the central and peripheral fields continues /Spooner 1981a/ /Fig. 1/.

However, while the 1960s and mid-1970s were periods when the ruling ideas were well defined /though dissenting voices could be heard in each case e.g. Schumacher 1961; Manners 1976, 1978/, these have been succeeded by a period when conflicting ideas have been forcibly expressed and fresh uncertainties have hampered the coal industry's progress to a more settled future. The problems faced by the National Coal Board in gaining planning permission for mines in North East Leicestershire /Vale of Belvoir/, the problems of marketing coal in a climate of recession /with big customers like the British Steel Corporation rapidly disinvesting/, the issue of competition from low-cost overseas suppliers and from nuclear power, and the problems of shedding high-cost marginal capacity, all suggest that in the 1980s the coalhouse door is swinging nervously on its hinges.

II. THE FRAMEWORK FOR RESOURCE/ENVIRONMENTAL MANAGEMENT

The 1974 Plan for Coal is essentially a programme for the /re-/ development of the coal industry. Taken in isolation it is not a programme of resource management.

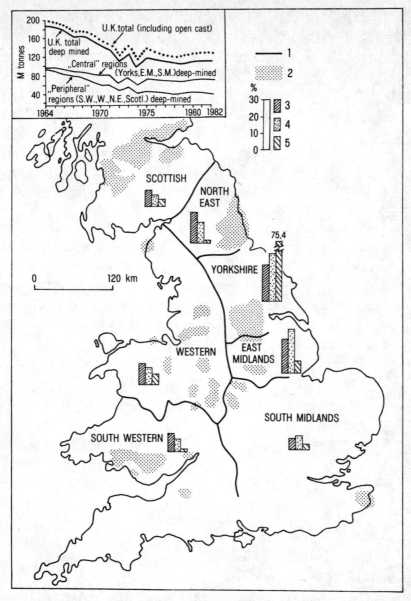

Fig. 1. The "ladder" of coal prospects in 1982.
1 = NCB administrative regional boundary; 2 = coalfields
in production: 1960; 3 = deep-mined output: 1960 /total:
186,7 m tonnes/; 4 = deep-mined output: 1981-82 /total:
108,9 m tonnes/; 5 = capital investment in progress: 1982
/total: £1981,6 m/
Source: Commission on Energy and the Environment /1981/
        /adapted/.

According to O'Riordan /1971/, resource management comprises "a process whereby resources are allocated over space and time according to the needs, aspirations and desires of man within the framework of his technological inventiveness, his political and social institutions, and his legal and administrative arrangements." It must be stressed that this process is as much political as it is economic; it has to resolve conflicts between rival interest groups. It is particularly concerned with balancing the benefits of resource use against the costs of environmental disruption. The process of coal resource management will involve not only the National Coal Board, the developer, but also those governmental bodies who make decisions to allocate resources, to permit, modify or prevent development. These decisions will also be influenced by a series of interest groups operating at both national and local levels. Environmental management or planning can be interpreted as the process relating to the areas in which coalmining is located, and will again involve interaction between the developer and public authorities with statutory responsibilities for land-use planning and environmental protection. Within the coalfield areas a variety of activities and interests may exist with which "accommodation" must be reached.

Thus the processes of coal resource development and management take place in a context of administrative and institutional complexity. There are large number of actors. National government is strongly involved, primarily through the Department of Energy /since 1974/, which has the responsibility for policies towards the individual energy sectors /coal, oil, gas etc./ and for an overall strategy towards the national energy mix. This department also authorises directly the working of coal on open-cast sites, though this may change if the government accepts the recent recommendation of the Flowers Commission that applications for open-cast working be dealt with under the normal minerals planning machinery /Commission on Energy and the Environment 1981/. A second department frequently involved with coal problems is the Department of the Environment with its responsibilities in the field of physical planning and environmental protection. The Department of the Environment will normally be called upon to adjudicate on planning applications for new underground mines through the public inquiry procedure. Conflicts of interest between Energy and Environment Departments can occur, which may have to be resolved in the forum of the Cabinet. This was rumoured to be the case with the application to mine the Vale of Belvoir /North East Leicestershire/ - supported by Energy, opposed by Environment - with the inevitable result a compromise, deferred decision /Arnold and Cole 1982/.

It is interesting that the aforementioned Flowers Commission on Energy and the Environment was established jointly in 1978 by the Secretaries of State for Energy, Environment, Scotland and Wales, with a remit that included examination of the interface between energy policies and land-use planning - critical to the resource management problem. The first task tackled by this "quango" was an examination of the environmental implications of coal production and use; this may also prove to be its last as the Government has let the Commission "fall into abeyance."

If Energy and Environment are the two major departments involved in the process of decision making in the coal context, others may play an important role. The financing of the National Coal Board is of vital concern to the Treasury, in its attempt to allocate scarce resources and control public expenditure. The present government's commitment to a reduction of public spending has crucial implications for the coal industry's investment plans. Under the 1980 Coal Industry Act the coal industry faced a withdrawal of subsides by 1983-84. The Treasury sets limits on the external borrowing of the nationalised industries. Thus the pace at which the investment programme can proceed will be critically determined by Treasury decisions - which are based on political priorities as much as the particular needs of the coal industry itself. Several other government departments also have interests in decisions concerning coal, including for example Employment, Transport and Agriculture. For example, the last's determination to preserve good quality farmland may bring it into conflict with Energy. To these national government influences must now be added those of E.E.C. Institutions, including the European Coal and Steel Community.

The prime actor in the coal management process, the National Coal Board, assumed responsibility for coal production in 1947, and suffers from the persistently ambivalent stance towards nationalised industries in the United Kingdom. As a nationalised industry it is expected to pay its way taking one year with another but at the same time has not been given a free hand on pricing policies /Buxton 1978/ and the cheap fuel policies adopted by governments in the past have forced the industry into indebtedness. According to one interpretation, this is because nationalised industries are meant to facilitate capital accumulation by capitalists by providing cheap fuels, but not be capitalist in themselves /Krieger 1979/. Nor have nationalised industries been able to resolve the dilemma between the needs of efficiency and the issue of social costs and responsibilities. Other state industries play a crucial role in the process of energy resource management. The National Coal Board's largest customers are the Central Electricity Generating Board /and the South of Scotland Electricity Board/ and the British Steel Corporation. /Between them these consumed 78 per cent of coal in the United Kingdom in 1980-81/. However, because of the /financial/ pressures exerted upon these industries too, conflicts with the interests of the National Coal Board can, and frequently do, occur. At the present time the disinvestment plans of the ailing British Steel Corporation are fast reducing the markets for coking coal /and adding to pressures to buy cheaper foreign supplies/. In the case of the Central Electricity Generating Board, an emphasis upon investment in nuclear power stations is threatening to limit coal markets in the longer term /Manners 1981/. Co-ordination between the plans of these state industries is surprisingly limited.

While the prime actors in coal development and management are the nationalised industries and central government, an im-

portant role at the local and regional level is played by local
planning authorities, at both county and district level. Here
too the process remains essentially political /Blowers 1980/.
The attitude of local authorities towards coal development is
conditioned by their political make-up, by the financial problems arising from relationship with national government, as
well as by the environmental planning context in which proposals
are set. Attitudes can change with the shift in the balance of
political power in local government; for example Leicestershire
County Council has shifted from a stance of opposition to the
Vale of Belvoir development at the time of the public inquiry
to one of support for mining - reflecting a loss of control by
the Conservative party. At this level demployment opportunities
and local economic impact become significant factors which have
to be weighed against negative environmental effects.

Finally one must recognise the role of interest groups in
the process of decision-making. This occurs most obviously in
the public representations made by such groups in the forum of
planning inquires, but this is only one aspect. Particularly
powerful nationally - organised interest groups operate in this
field. The National Union of Mineworkers has been rejuvenated
as a political force since the 1972 and 1974 strikes revealed
its power to halt economic life and change the course of political history. It is particularly effective in slowing the process of disinvestment in the older coalfields, but is also vocal
in supporting investment schemes at greenfield sites which offer replacement jobs for those being lost elsewhere. However,
the militancy of the National Union of Miners may be ultimately
counter-productive to its own interests; leaked Cabinet minutes
indicate that current government preference for nuclear power
may reflect in part "the advantage of removing a substantial
proportion of electricity production from the dangers of disruption by industrial action by coalminers or transport workers" /Raphael 1979/.

Arrayed against the coal industry in debates over new
greenfield sites may be the powerful National Farmers' Union,
undoubtedly one of the most successful pressure groups in Brit-

ain /Newby 1979/. This has strong links with the Department of
Agriculture and with local government. According to Shoard
/1980/ farmers constitute 35 per cent of all rural district
councillors in England and Wales.

Although there is no strongly anti-coal national environ-
mentalist lobby, individual coal proposals are frequently opposed by environmental groups, and more particularly by local
community groups with vested interest in property values and
maintenance of the status quo. Interest groups operating in the
environmental field are classified by Muir and Paddison /1981/
into two categories - sectional groups /out to promote private-
oriented wants/, and principle groups /interested in public-
oriented wants and a more ideological form of conservation/.
Those fighting coal development tend to fall into the first category with fairly selfish interests /"don't dig it here, dig it
elsewhere"/, but it is not always clear-cut. The "Alliance"
which fought mining proposals in the Vale of Belvoir was primarily attempting to protect local and sectional community interests, being formed by the Vale Parish Councils Committee,
the Vale Protection Group, and the National Farmers Union /North
and Spooner 1982b/.

This bewildering array of actors and influences provides
the cast for the process of decison-making and resource management in the coal industry /Table I/. Within this context the
British "style" of policy-making tends to lead to compromise,
though the strength of the pro-coal influences in the 1970s at
least meant that the process took on some of the characteristics of an "accommodation" exercise to serve the interests of
the state in maintaining secure energy supplies.

The central management problem arises from the difficulty
of reconciling policies emanating from a perception of national
need with the problems of mitigating and controlling environmental impact - largely at the local or sub-regional level.
/There are also national and international environmental problems associated with coal use - for example air pollution or
acid rain - but these have not yet forced their way into a high
position on the political agenda in the United Kingdom.

Table I.

ATTITUDES TO GREENFIELD PROJECTS	PRO	NEUTRAL	ANTI
NATIONAL GOVERNMENT		◄———— THE CABINET ————►	
		TREASURY ————►	
	DEPARTMENT OF ENERGY ◄————	DEPARTMENT OF THE ENVIRONMENT ————►	
	◄————	Department of Employment	
		Department of Transport	
		Department of Agriculture ————►	
NATIONALISED STATE INDUSTRY	NATIONAL COAL BOARD ◄—	ELECTRICITY BOARDS	
		British Steel Corporation	
LOCAL GOVERNMENT PLANNING AUTHORITIES		◄———— COUNTIES ————►	
		◄———— DISTRICTS ————►	
		Parishes ————►	
INTEREST GROUPS /examples/		ENVIRONMENTAL GROUPS SECTIONAL	
	◄————	PRINCIPLE	
		NATIONAL FARMERS UNION	
	NATIONAL UNION MINEWORKERS		
	Local Labour Parties		
		Local Conservative Parties	
	◄———— Local Liberal Parties		

177

Resource management and the coal industry: attitudes to Greenfield Projects

The chart suggests the probable stance of different "actors" - "pro", "neutral" or "anti" towards proposals for major greenfield underground coalmines. It draws upon recent experience in the United Kingdom but remains hypothetical.

The arrows indicate that the position of particular actors may change through time - with respect to different projects or even the same project.

We now consider briefly the two interacting elements of national energy policy and the local planning system.

a/ National energy policy/strategy

In the United Kingdom, energy policy has evolved piecemeal. Given the range of external influences it is necessarily formulated in flexible terms rather than as a rigid blueprint. Its primary objective remains the provision of adequate and secure energy supplies at the lowest practicable cost to the nation, but in fact any energy policy decision is likely to involve a wide range of considerations - industrial, political, social, environmental, macro-economic. The last major government document on energy policy in the United Kingdom emanated from the Department of Energy in 1978 /Secretary of State for Energy, 1978/; the present government has not yet published an equally full statement. It has, however, publicly endorsed the determination of western governments to support investment plans for their coal industries, declared at successive 7-nation summits in Tokyo and Venice. Ostensibly Britain is committed to the Co-Co-Nuke /coal, conservation and nuclear power/ policy recommended by the International Energy Agency as the best route to freedom from oil dependence /International Energy Agency 1979/, though this acronym tends to overlook the considerable role of gas.

Whatever the grand words about overall strategy, these have to be translated into a series of policies for the individual energy sectors. Here it becomes clear that in practice

the strategy is rather NUKE-CO /in that order/, with the second
CO, conservation, left well behind in commitment of government
resources. The recent report of the House of Commons Select
Committee on Energy /1982/ pointed out that only 7 million
out of 667.5 million in the Department of Energy's estimates
for 1981-82 was allocated to support research into reducing demand. The strategy in practice is heavily supply-oriented; it
is also "technocentric" /O'Riordan 1976/, favouring large-scale
high-technology centralised energy production, and this techno-
centrism /large is beautiful/ is carried forward into the policies of individual sectors, especially electricity and coal
production.

Government policy ostensibly supports the Plan for Coal
and modernisation and expansion of coal production. However,
policies in the electricity industry, also supported by government - "most of us agree we will not have enough fuel unless we
go nuclear on a larger scale than we are now" /Thatcher 1979/ -
do not appear compatible with the long-term plans of the coal
industry. The reluctance of the electricity boards to invest in
further coal-fired capacity /well illustrated by their attitude
towards the ordering of Drax "B", the only coal-fired station
currently being built/ suggest long-term difficulties for the
coal industry in retaining its present scale of sales to power
stations /Manners 1981/.

b/ The local planning system

A perceived national need for coal production has to be
reconciled at local level with other diverse interests through
the normal operations of the town and country planning system,
and its development control procedures. The Flowers Commission
recently concluded that this system did not require radical
change, despite the problems that arise at public inquiries
from the interweaving of local and national issues /Commission
on Energy and the Environment 1981/. This overall complacency
is perhaps unnecessarily generous to the interests of the coal
industry /North and Spooner 1982b/.

A notable feature of the present system /and one to which
Flowers did recommend amendment/ is the discrepancy between
procedures at greenfield and blackfield sites. Under the General Development Order system, the National Coal Board has comparative freedom of operation at sites which were being worked
before 1948 /the vast majority of blackfield sites fall into
this category/, and is deemed to have been granted planning
permission for both underground and ancillary pithead development. The Board has been able to exploit this softness in the
planning system to proceed very rapidly with development at existing sites. A spectacular example is Thorne /Yorkshire/, where
£211 million is being spent on a virtually new mine and associated preparation plant at the site of a previous mine closed
in 1956. Its ability to proceed rapidly at such sites without
the delay of a public planning inquiry has been some compensation for the problems of time lost in the planning process when
major new greenfield sites are contemplated. At greenfield
sites the Board must seek planning permission from the local
planning authority, and this authority is likely in most cases
to refer the application to the Department of the Environment.

A public inquiry will normally be called. The Vale of Belvoir case /North East Leicestershire/ is an excellent example
of the potential delays at greenfield sites; the National Coal
Board's intentions to apply for mines in that area were first
declared in 1976; the planning inquiry was held in 1979-80 and
the decision /negative/ not announced until 1982 /revised in
early 1983 and one mine is now to go ahead/. Even if a revised
application is successful the length of construction time makes
it unlikely that any mine could now be in production before
the early 1990s.

At existing sites the Board has considerable freedom of
operation; this, together with the exemption of open cast mining from the normal system, makes it difficult for planning
authorities fully to control the industry's operations in the
older mining districts, and the effect on the landscape can be
little short of devastating.

III. OLD FIELDS, NEW FIELDS: THE LADDER, THE LIST AND THE
     LEGACY

The operation of the system of resource management outlined above, and the interaction between national energy policy
requirements and local environmental planning considerations,
is resulting in a modern pattern of development in the coal industry which exhibits a distinctive spatial arrangement, and is
associated with problems of a different nature and intensity in
the old and new coalfield areas. These can be summarised briefly:

1. Greenfield sites

The exploration programme of the National Coal Board has
identified plentiful supplies of coal, often at considerable
depth, in a wide range of locations. However, the majority of
the biggest and best finds lie in "frontier" locations at the
margin of areas already worked. This is particularly evident a-
long the eastern edge of the Yorkshire-Nottinghamshire-Derbyshire field where a whole series of new "blocks" of deep coal
have been found from north of York down through Selby, Thorne
etc., to North East Leicestershire. The Board have developed
the concept of the "Ladder of Exploration" - a sequence of
stages through which any prospect must pass before mining can
begin /including exploration, feasibility study, planning and
development, Fig. 2/. The only greenfield site to have reached
the development stage is Selby. Individual prospects may move
up or down the ladder as their appraisal is progressively refined.

The Flowers report /Commission on Energy and the Environment 1981/ clearly favoured a steady build-up of new capacity
at greenfield sites as part of the modernisation strategy; it
supported the development of large new mines of the Selby/Bel-
voir type. Lord Flowers, speaking in a debate on his own report
in the House of Lords, declared himself surprised by the Secretary of State for the Environment's decision in 1982 to reject
the National Coal Board's application for 3 mines in North East

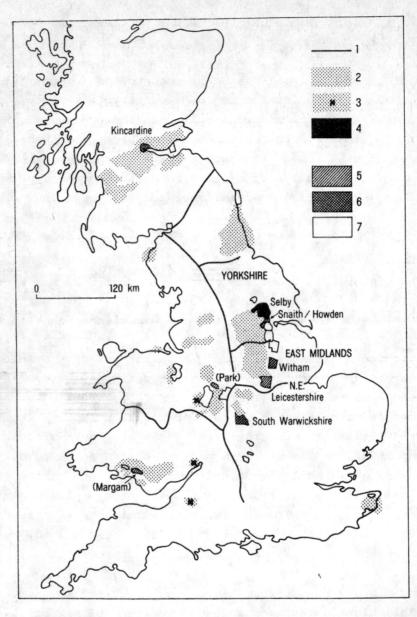

Fig. 2. United Kingdom coal production by major region 1960–82
1 = NCB administrative regional boundary; 2 = coalfields;
3 = coalfields ceased NCB operations since 1960; 4 =
new coalfield under development; 5 = planning stage –
/Park/ denotes application withdrawn,/Margam/ in abeyance; 6 = feasibility study stage; 7 = exploration
stage

Source: National Coal Board /NCB/ Reports and Accounts.

Leicestershire at Hose, Asfordby and Saltby: "I find it hard to believe that the Secretary of State could have discovered in our report any substantial grounds for rejecting the Board's submission" /Parliamentary debates 1982/. This decision, taken contrary to the recommendation of the Inspector at the public inquiry, was explained by the Secretary of State as due to his lack of conviction that the degree of need outweighed the adverse environmental effects. Disposal of waste spoil was cited as a crucial problem. This, however, was not a final refusal; the Board were encouraged to submit revised applications and indeed have already done so for Asfordby. This "half-way house" solution suggests that the decision was really shaped primarily by national and international factors, including the effects of the recession and a perception of the political power of the miners /Arnold and Cole 1982/.

Thus Selby remains unique - the only greenfield site to gain approval for development in the 1970s. At this, and other potential lowland sites coalmining is entering a zone of large-scale modern capitalistic farming, and accommodation between energy and agricultural interests is a critical problem. Subsidence of high quality farmland was a major issue at Selby, where the National Caol Board were, however, fortunate in being able to avoid the use of spoil tips or a coal preparation plant - it was able to project the image of "an environmental mine".

Notes: /Fig. 2/.

i/ The map relates only to deep-mined output; figures for open-cast output are not available on a regional basis.

ii/ Note the regional figures refer to share of national output and not to absolute quantities. Absolute measures are used in the inset graph.

iii/ Figures for capital investment in progress give only an approximate indication of the regional distribution of investment under the 1974 Plan for Coal, as many schemes have already been completed. Nevertheless the dominance of Yorkshire is striking

In the greenfield areas, village and small town communities are disturbed by the prospect of social and environmental change consequent upon introduction of coalmining and miners, and are fearful of an erosion of property values. These interest groups therefore attempt to promote an image of their areas which distances them from the coal culture. It is interesting for example that the South Warwickshire prospect, high on the "ladder", is already being referred to as "Shakespeare country". Images projected of the Vale of Belvoir are loosely based on reality /North and Spooner 1978/. Despite much rhetoric about the environment, the chief protesting groups in the Vale of Belvoir were privately oriented sectional groups rather than ideological conservationists.

Although there is much scope for improvement in the procedures for assessing environmental impact at greenfield sites, and the question of public inquiry procedure still raises important issues, the major environmental management problems associated with the coal revival occur not at greenfield sites but rather in the old coalfields.

2. Blackfield sites

The old coalfield areas present major challenges in both the regional development and environmental fields; they have long dominated the map of regional policy's assisted areas and have a disastrous legacy of environmental dereliction. At present two aspects of the modernisation programme embodied in the Plan for Coal are of particular significance - firstly the continuing problem of colliery closures, secondly the environmental impact of new investment projects.

a/ Colliery closure

While communities sited in potential greenfield areas frequently oppose the opening of new mines, those sited in existing blackfield areas oppose the reverse process of colliery closure. This process occurred on a massive scale in the 1960s bringing despair to many communities in the peripheral coalfields especially; it destroyed both their highly simplified economic base

and their social cohesion. Paynter /1972/ described it graphi-
cally and emotionally - "the death of a creation that gave the
community life and sustained that life no matter how deprived
and anguished it might sometimes have been".

While colliery closure no longer occurs at the rate and
scale of the 1960s, the phasing out of spent and obsolescent
capacity remains the most politically charged element in the
process of change.

The explanation why closures occur in an extractive industry is superficially a simple one; the coal has run out. Reality is rarely so simple. Decisions about closure are made on
economic grounds; it is rarely the case that there is literal-
ly no coal left to work, but rather that the marginal cost of
each additional ton produced will increase /Town 1978/. The market situation at a particular time may be the factor that pre-
cipitates a decision to close the least economic collieries -
or perhaps those producing a particular type of coal. A point
may be reached in the operation of the mine whereby future production can only be sought by substantial further investment and
with no guarantee of adequate returns. Contention between the
Coal Board and the miners' union often revolves around the com-
mital of expenditure by the Board to open up new underground
areas; future production prospects being dependent upon further
investments.

In the 1970s, with the prospects for coal production apparently improved most closures that did take place /there were
40 between 1975 and 1980/ attracted comparatively little controversy, though ritual resistance was undertaken by miners.
Normally a regular set of procedures would be followed to review
the position of threatened collieries, over a period sometimes
of several years. In the 1980s the problem re-emerged with the
recession. The build-up of coal stocks, and new financial stric-
tures imposed by the 1980 Coal Industry Act, forced the National Coal Board to attempt to speedup the closure of the most
marginal set of collieries. A list of 23 doomed collieries was
dramatically announced. This short-circuiting of the normal procedures brought a stormy reaction from the coalfields and with

a national coal strike threatened the Government made additional finance available and the "list" was withdrawn. /In the 1960s
the Board had published a list of all collieries categorised as
A Continuing, B Doubtful, and C Imminently Closing Pits, but had
shifted away from this to a generally more discreet approach./

The 23 collieries had an average age of 93 years, a total
production of only 4.27 million tons in 1980-81 and were expected to lose 74 million in 1980-81. 14 out of the 23 lay in the
peripheral fields of Scotland, South Wales and North East England with South Wales especially hard hit. A National Coal Board
spokesman for South Wales succinctly summarised the situation in
his area - "all the best coal has gone from these pits and what's
left is difficult to mine" /The Guardian, 17-2-81/. Closure of
3 of the 23 pits had in fact already been agreed with the National Union of Mineworkers through the normal negotiating machinery; in fact by March 1982 9 of the 23 pits on the list had
closed or been agreed for closure. The Government decision to
back down on the closure programme and provide extra funds was
heavily criticised by a House of Common's Select Committee /1982/;
there had been no proper calculation of the trade-off between
the extra cost of keeping open uneconomic pits and the resultant
savings on social payments. The Flowers report is also clearly
in favour of phasing out heavily loss-making capacity - "failure to face this challenge would be to tether the United Kingdom to the industry's past" /Commission on Energy and the Environment, 1981/.

With the National Union of Miners and its new leader Arthur
Scargill committed to an increasingly militant posture on closures, the reality of this challenge cannot be in doubt. Back in
1967 Cabinet Minister Richard Crossman wrote in his diary of an
earlier pit closure crisis that "after 3 years the Labour Government had evolved neither an instrument for assessing the social impacts of its actions nor an instrument for ameliorating
that impact upon the community" /Crossman 1976/. Fifteen years
later governments are little further forward.

b/ Impact of new investment projects

While the spectre of the closure list haunts some blackfield areas, especially South Wales, it is the scale of new investment in others that poses serious environmental problems.
This is especially true of parts of the Yorkshire coalfield
where the programme for re-structuring the industry is creating vast quantities of spoil in areas with a huge legacy of dereliction from past mining. Here the environment is already
overstressed. The Yorkshire-Nottinghamshire-Derbyshire field
contains 69 per cent of the total area of England affected by
active spoil tips, lagoons and plant buildings, 28 per cent of
the area of derelict spoil tips and accounted for 62 per cent
of national colliery waste in 1978-79 /Commission on Energy and
the Environment 1981/. The county planning authorities fear that
"the communities in the Yorkshire coalfield face having as much
waste dropped on their doorsteps in the next two decades as has
been tipped there over the last 200 years' /Strategic Conference of County Councils in Yorkshire and Humberside 1979/; they
calculate that a minimum of 500 million tonnes of colliery
waste will be created in Yorkshire by the year 2000 - plus substantial quantities of power station ash. Spoil tips are only
the most visible aspects of the environmental impact in these
areas - lagoons, noise, air and water pollution and subsidence
damage all also have to be contained.

It is scarcely surprising that the local authorities in
such areas have been disappointed by the mildness of the Flowers' proposals for reforming planning procedures and imposing
better standards: "the Commission does not go far enough in re-
cognising the effects of mine subsidence in terms of economic
and environmental loss"... "have not appreciated the full extent of the problems" /West Yorkshire Metropolitan County Council 1981/.

Moreover the strength of opposing interest groups in the
greenfield areas and their success in delaying or preventing
new mine development may increase the pressures on the blackfield areas. Interest groups opposed to mining /particularly to
open cast mining and to spoil tipping/ do occur in these areas

too, but their strength is limited by the crucial role played by coalmining in the local economy.

In summary, the problems of the greenfield sites like Selby or Belvoir, appear almost insignificant comparad with those that exist in areas like South Wales or the Barnsley district of Yorkshire. The real challenges of environmental management in relation to coalmining occur in the old coalfields which have to face the problems of closures and the large scale impact of re-structuring on top of a legacy of environmental misuse stretching back over many decades. A regional development dimension is added by the poor image these areas present to the outside investor /Spooner 1981b/. New initiatives may be needed to cope with the problems of such areas. One such initiative proposed by the Flowers Commission is the creation of a regional development agency for Yorkshire. This proposal may threaten to create another layer of bureaucracy and has been emphatically rejected by the local authorities in the region, but certainly merits closer scrutiny.

Baroness White, speaking for South Wales interests in the House of Lords, neatly summarised the fears of the older districts: "we are concerned that we shall not be left behind while attention is focussed on how best to handle the developing areas in the Midlands, Oxfordshire and parts of Yorkshire." /Parliament Debates 1982./

REFERENCES

ARNOLD, P.--COLE, I. /1982/: The political motives of the Belvoir Truce. - Town and Country Planning, 51, 8, 207-208.
BLOWERS, A. /1980/: The Limits of Power. - Pergamon, Oxford.
BUXTON, N. /1978/: The Economic Development of the Coal Industry. - Batsford, London.
Commission on Energy and the Environment /1981/: Coal and the Environment. - H.M.S.O., London.
CROSSMAN, R.H.S. /1976/: Diaries of a Cabinet Minister. - Hamish Hamilton and Jonathan Cape, London.

Department of Energy /1977/: Coal for the Future, Progress with
the Plan for Coal and Prospects to the Year 2000. - H.M.
S.O., London.

GUARDIAN /1981/: Five doomed Welsh pits "little more to offer".
17th February.

House of Commons Select Committee on Energy /1982/: The Department of Energy's Estimates for 1981-82. - H.M.S.O.,
London.

International Energy Agency /1979/: Principles for I.E.A. Action on Coal. - O.E.C.D., Paris.

JONES, S.B. /1954/: A unified field theory of political geography. - Annals of the Association of American Geographers, 44, 111-123.

KRIEGER, J. /1979/: British colliery closure programmes in the
North East: from paradox to contradiction. - In CULLEN, I.
G. /ed./: London Papers in Regional Science, 9, Pion,
London, 219-232.

MANNERS, G. /1971/: Some economic and spatial characteristics
of the British energy market. - In CHISHOLM, M. and MAN-
NERS, G.: Spatial policy problems of the British economy.
C.U.P., Cambridge, 146-179.

MANNERS, G. /1976/: The changing energy situation in Britain.
- Geography, 61, 4, 221-231.

MANNERS, G. /1978/: Alternative strategies for the British coal
industry. - Geographical Journal, 144, 2, 224-234.

MANNERS, G. /1981/: Coal in Britain: an uncertain future. -
George Allen and Unwin, London.

MITCHELL, B. /1979/: Geography and Resource Analysis. - Long-
mans, London.

MUIR, R.--PADDISON, R. /1981/: Politics, Geography and Behaviour. - Methuen, London.

National Coal Board /1974/: Plan for Coal. - London.

NEWBY, H. /1979/: Green and pleasant land: social change in
Rural England. - Hutchinson, London.

NORTH, J.--SPOONER, D.J. /1978/: On the coalmining frontier. -
Town and Country Planning, 36, 3, 155-163.

NORTH, J.--SPOONER, D.J. /1982a/: The Yorkshire, Nottingham-
    shire and Derbyshire coalfield: the focus of the Coal
    Board's investment strategy. - Geographical Journal, 148,
    1, 22-37.

NORTH, J.--SPOONER, D.J. /1982b/: A future for coal. - Town and
    Country Planning, 51, 4, 93-97.

O'RIORDAN, T. /1971/: Perspectives on Resource Management. -
    Pion, London.

O'RIORDAN, T. /1976/: Environmentalism. - Pion, London.

Parliamentary Debates /Hansard/ /1982/: House of Lords Official
    Report, 18th May. - H.M.S.O., London.

PAYNTER, W. /1972/: My Generation. - George Allen and Unwin,
    London.

PLATER, A. /1969/: Close the Coalhouse Door. /Song by Alex
    Glasgow./

RAPHAEL, A. /1979/: Go-ahead for 15 nuclear reactors. - The Ob-
    server, 9th December.

SCHUMACHER, E.F. /1961/: Prospect for coal. - National Coal
    Board, London.

Secretary of State for Energy /1978/: Energy policy: a consul-
    tative document. - H.M.S.O., London.

SHOARD, M. /1980/: The Theft of the Countryside. - Temple
    Smith, London.

SPOONER, D.J. /1981a/: The Geography of Coal's Second Coming.
    - Geography, 66, 1, 29-41.

SPOONER, D.J. /1981b/: Mining and Regional Development. - O.U.
    P., Oxford.

Strategic Conference of County Councils in Yorkshire and
    Humberside /1979/: Proof of Evidence for the Coal Study
    by the Flowers Commission on Energy and the Environmnet.

THATCHER, M. /1979/: speaking in House of Commons, 26th June.

TOWN, S.W. /1978/: After the Mines: changing employment op-
    portunities in a South Wales valley. - University of
    Wales Social Science Monograph 4, Cardiff.

West Yorkshire Metropolitan County Council /1981/: Report on
    Coal and the Environment: views of the West Yorkshire M.
    C.C.

URBAN CLIMATE AND URBAN PLANNING IN BUDAPEST

F. PROBÁLD

1. URBAN STRUCTURE AND ENVIRONMENTAL PLANNING: PROGRESS REPORT

Budapest occupies a prominent place in the settlement network of Hungary. 19.2 per cent /2,060,000 people/ of the country's population live there and in spite of major efforts in
recent years to realize a more proportionate regional economic
structure, a quarter of all industrial workers are still engaged in the factories of the capital. The environmental problems of Budapest are rooted in the large-scale concentration
of both population and industrial activities there.

Budapest evolved rapidly during the second half of the
19th century when much of the present urban structure took
shape. The development of the various urban zones and neighbourhoods was influenced by the capital's position at the boundary between two different landscape types - the Great Hungarian Plain and the Transdanubian Mountains. Pest, to the east of
the Danube, has been built on an almost featureless surface
of gently sloping Quaternary fluvial terraces and its structure can be described by Burgess' model of concentric zones.
West of the Danube, in the Buda Hills, the urban pattern is
less regular and more closely approximates Hoyt's sector model.
As a consequence environmental problems as well as the value
and character of residential areas differ strongly according
to whether one is on the Buda or Pest side of the city.

Environmental protection is hindered by the intermingling
of various urban functions and related land use belts. The

fifth district of the city is roughly coincidental with the central business district but, although dominated by administrative, commercial and cultural functions, still houses 50,000 people. 186,000 people or 11.3 per cent of the capital's population reside in industrial belts or in mixed residential belts, i.e. in areas directly exposed to the environmental hazards caused by industry. The distribution of the city's population is also highly varied. 25 per cent of the inhabitants are concentrated in closely built-up areas at population densities of more than 550 people per hectare. By contrast, 63 per cent of residential areas are composed of family homes with an average population density of only 45 people per hectare. Such areas house a mere 27 per cent of the total population. Large-scale housing projects are relatively new components of the urban structure. These are characterized by system-built housing in which 10-storey blocks dominate and are provoking an increasing amount of public criticism. 30 per cent of the capital's population live on these new estates. The first steps in regulating the development of Budapest were taken as early as the 19th century but large-scale comprehensive plans were not perfected and projects in preparation were not realized because of the Second World War. The first master plan for Budapest and its environs that was approved by the Council of Ministers was elaborated as late as 1960 by the Budapest Planning Enterprise for Urban Construction appointed by the Metropolitan Council. The same enterprise may supervise and update the master plan every ten years. Related to the master plan is the Code for Urban Construction in Budapest, first issued in 1959 and amended in 1981, which among other things establishes building regulations for the various zones.

Reflecting a predominantly technical attitude, the first master plan for Budapest hardly touched upon the problems of environmental protection. Sites for huge housing projects were selected on the basis of technical and economic considerations and their possible impact on the environment was neglected. Moreover, in practice exemptions from the building regulations were often granted and the observance of the prescribed pro-

tection belts around industrial plants that could prove harmful
to the environment was sometimes relaxed. Thus, new housing estates and district centres have been constructed in areas exposed to serious environmental damage.

An approach requiring the conscious and organized protection and development of the environment spread widely in Hungary during the 1970s. A comprehensive Environmental Act was passed by Parliament in 1976 and the National Environment Protection Concept, setting out the direction and long-term purpose
of particular measures, was submitted to the Council of Ministers in 1980. As part of the 1980 revision of the structure
plan for Budapest, a long-term environmental protection concept
for the period up to the year 2000 was prepared in 1981. Measures for its implementation, which will be re-examined every
five years, are now being worked out.

In 1960, when the structure plan was elaborated, scientific research regarding the state of the urban environment was in
its initial stages. The first network of air pollution gauging
stations, for instance, was established by the National Institute for Public Health as late as 1958. Moreover, data from only one station of the National Meteorological Survey were available for the description of the climate of Budapest and it is
only since the 1960s that a programme aimed at revealing local
climatic differences has been realized.

The new environmental protection concept for Budapest is
founded on scientific research carried out by numerous institutions including geographers, and in the following some examples of the author's own investigations into the atmospheric
environment of the city are outlined. These investigations are
connected with the problems of urban planning and their results
have been incorporated into the environmental protection concept for the capital.

2. URBAN CLIMATOLOGY IN THE SERVICE OF TOWN PLANNING

2.1. An assessment of urban climate from a human bioclimatological viewpoint

In cities, the built environment, polluted atmosphere and anthropogenic thermal emissions generate a local climate substantially different from the macroclimate of the natural environment. The extent to which individual climatic elements are modified in the city is well documented in the international literature /for instance, Chandler 1965, 1970 and 1976/ and from related studies in Budapest /Probáld 1974/. There is general agreement that the typical urban climate forms an unfavourable environment for man. However, the impact on man of the modification of the various meteorological elements in the city varies according to the background climate and even the season in one and the same place. Consequently, an assessment of urban effects needs a more differentiated approach, based on a knowledge of the particular background climate, exactly which climatic factors can be regarded as adverse and the means whereby urban planning can reduce unfavourable impacts. With this purpose in mind the characteristics of the urban climate of Budapest were assessed from the human bioclimatological viewpoint. The appraisal covered the major climatic elements of temperature, humidity, wind, rainfall and radiation as reflected in three to five indicators that were as far as possible independent of each other. Local variations during the winter and summer halves of the year were evaluated separately and assigned a score ranging from -3 to +3 depending upon their bioclimatological significance /Table I/. The main findings of the study /Probáld 1976/ can be summarized as follows:

a. the city has a beneficial effect on certain climatic elements, and an adverse impact on others, although the nature of the deviations may differ with the seasons;

b. features that are unfavourable from the human bioclimatological aspect dominate throughout the year. It is primarily radiation change that is disadvantageous in winter, and temperature variation during summer. A change in wind is also unfavourable at any time of the year, but the effects of

Table I. The appraisal of urban climate from the viewpoint of
human bioclimatology

Elements of climate	Appraisal of the urban deviation		
	summer	winter	total
I. Radiation			
sunshine duration	∅	---	-3
global radiation	+	--	-1
light	+	--	-1
UV-radiation	∅	---	-3
	+2	-10	-8
II. Temperature			
surface temperature	---	+	-2
mean annual temperature	--	+	-1
mean minimum "	--	+	-1
mean maximum "	--	+	-1
diurnal temperature range	+ -	+	+1
	-9	+5	-4
III. Humidity, pre-cipitation			
relative humidity	+	+	+2
vapour pressure	+	∅	+1
frequency of fog	∅	---	-3
amount of precipitation	∅	∅	∅
	+2	-2	O
IV. Wind			
mean annual wind speed	--	+ -	-2
frequency of strong gusts	+	+	+2
frequency of calms	---	---	-6
	-9	-9	-18

Legend:
      - = slightly unfavourable,
    -- = unfavourable,
  --- = strongly unfavourable,
   + = slightly favourable,
 + - = ambivalent effect,
   ∅ = indifferent

local deviations in rainfall and humidity are negligible;

c. although urban climate is less advantageous for human comfort than the natural background climate, it cannot be considered harmful to health in itself, with the exception of pollution;

d. the negative features of urban climate can be reduced or eliminated by adequate urban planning, although this would necessitate the weighing up of construction alternatives with the likely climatic impacts in mind when planning decisions are being made.

Although the consideration of climatic factors is not a guaranteed part of the environmental protection concept for Budapest, further microclimatic investigations are being urged in order to reveal causal relationships. Even with the present level of knowledge, a number of the basic principles necessary to improve climate conditions in open urban areas are already appreciated. In this respect the proportion and distribution of green areas have an important role to play.

2.2. Green areas - tools for the improvement of urban climates

High temperature is the most uncomfortable characteristic of an urban climate in summer; along with the radiation from heated surfaces and reduced air motion it produces thermal discomfort. The origin of the urban heat island is related to the lack of biologically active evaporating surfaces. As far as the beneficial effects of green areas are concerned, the following facts deserve notice in the course of planning:

a. the intensity of the urban heat island, which varies from place to place, depends on building density in an area of 500 m radius from the point of observation;

b. the expansion of continuous green zones up to 100 hectares in area has a very favourable climatic effect but beyond that areas of larger size have hardly any further influence;

c. there is a close correlation between the proportion and temperature reducing effect of uniformly distributed biologically active surfaces. Some investigations show that where up to 20-30 per cent of the total area is covered by biologically active surfaces the temperature is rapidly affected but over that limit the effect is greatly moderated;

d. in well-forested green areas the reduction of temperature is greatest during those very hours of the day and exactly in those weather situations when it is most desirable for thermal comfort.

Although biologically active surfaces make up about 50 per cent of the total area of Budapest the distribution is very uneven. In the densely built-up city core green areas comprise only 1 per cent of the total area, while 20 to 25 per cent of the area of the many small parks is covered with gravel or asphalt-paved walks and playgrounds. Moreover road-side trees are in a poor state due to the spreading of salt against ice in winter and because of air pollution and repeated road construction works. The situation on new housing estates is more favourable but still far from being satisfactory, and although green areas make up 30 to 35 per cent there, it means only 6 to 10 m^2 per capita owing to the high density of population.

The first step with new construction is always the complete destruction of vegetation, while subsequent replanting is invariably less than necessary. Moreover, it takes 15 to 20 years for new trees to grow to a size where there is a perceptible microclimatic influence. A considerable part of green areas originally planned for housing projects are later released for other purposes, for instance, car parks, shops and stores, while in the Buda Hills the planting of trees around new buildings makes little progress.

The long-term environmental protection concept for Budapest lays particular stress upon the climatic effect of green areas. The desirable proportion of biologically active surfaces is specified as 60 per cent. The amount of green area per person should reach a value of 50 m^2, with the target that 28 per cent of it should be proportional to population density, i.e. in the residential areas. During the redevelopment of residential neighbourhoods parks must now be planned, while the importance of woodland screens especially around industrial plants, where hardly any trees were planted before, is underlined. If the guidelines laid down in the environmental protection concept are realized, the negative features of the urban climate of the city will be largely ameliorated.

2.3. Protection and use of natural climatic features

In cities with diverse relief and building density numerous mesoclimatic regions can be delineated. In the early 1970s the atmospheric environmental regions of Budapest were mapped by the author from two quantitative parameters - heat island intensity and sulphur-dioxide concentrations as a reflection of air quality /Fig. 1/. In a somewhat expanded form this map was used in determining the location of sites most suitable for concentrated housing development as part of the general planning programme of the Budapest agglomeration prepared in 1975. There are two types of mesoclimatic region in Budapest which, due to their natural endowments, mitigate the effects of the urban climate and are therefore especially valuable for the inhabitants of the city.

The first of these comprises the banks and islands of the Danube, where average summer temperatures are 1.5 to 2 °C, and on cloudless days 3 to 4 °C, cooler than the inner city, thus providing favourable possibilities for recreation. Unfortunately, the banks of the Danube are densely built-up; the establishment of public green areas is hindered by industrial plants, shops and busy roads. The existing riverside recreational areas are neglected and their value is also reduced by the increasing pollution of the river. An achievement of the last decade is the conversion of a good part of the Óbuda Island into a park serving the capital's population.

The Buda Hills, particularly those areas above 400 m above sea level, are of exceptional climatic value for the capital with their coolness in summer, long hours of sunshine in winter

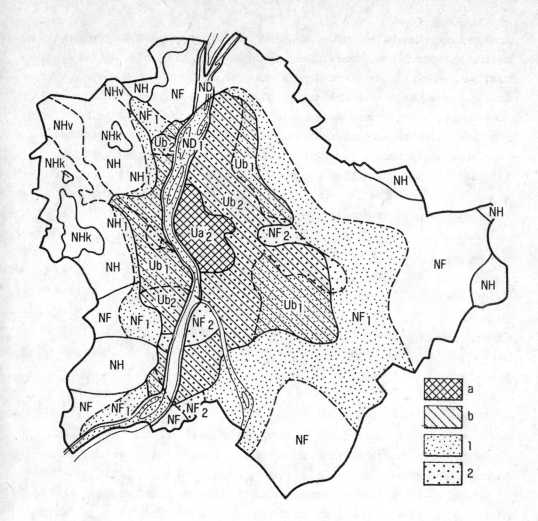

Fig. 1. The mesoclimatic regions of Budapest
NF = natural climates of flat areas; NH = natural climates of hilly areas; NHk = natural climate of the highest part of the Buda Hills; NHv = natural climate of the valleys; ND = natural climate of the Danube River; U = urban climates; a = densely built-up area; b = less densely built-up area; 1 = heavily polluted area; 2 = less heavily polluted area of the city

and clean air throughout the year. The dominant north-westerly
winds and the breeze at night produced by the circulation of
air in the hills and valleys mean the Buda Hills also influence
the climate of the inner city. Unfortunately, during the last
two decades large-scale housing development that have impeded
air motion have taken place in the hills. Hillslope vegetation
has been removed as part of the construction process and has
frequently exceeded the limits permitted by the construction
code, while public forest has also receded. During the last decade two positive developments have occurred that are worth
mentioning. Firstly, in 1974 the residential areas of the Buda
Hills were designated with fuel containing more than 1 per cent
sulphur has to cease by 1985. Secondly, the new urban construction code introduced in 1981 reduced the area of any hillside
plot that can be built on from 20 to 15 per cent. Although this
measure is quite belated, a new effort to preserve the climatic
character of the Buda Hills in the public interest is therefore
now discernible.

2.4. Typology of surface wind fields

According to the long-term environmental protection concept for Budapest, wind channel modelling should be applied
more frequently than before when planning large scale residential units in order to achieve the optimum location of buildings and green areas from the climatic point of view. Such modelling, however, is only meaningful when the natural frequency
of various wind directions in the area to be built-up is known.
Moreover, the application of transmission models to describe the
spread of air pollution also requires information on the frequency of wind direction. In areas of complex physiography such
as Budapest, wind shows great variability from place to place
and extrapolation of data from one or two stations may consequently lead to major blunders. Regarding the above, a new method has been worked out by the author which enables the determination of wind direction frequencies for any parţicular place
in the city. The procedure is based on the typology of surface
wind fields /Probáld 1979/.

During the investigation the surface wind field was mapped for each hour during the year. In order to establish trajectories, data from the 9 anemographs and 2 climatic observation stations operating in the municipal area of Budapest were used in conjunction with a consideration of the influence of relief. An analysis of the map sheets, about 8,7000 in all, enabled the definition of 26 types of wind field. Knowing the frequency of occurrence of each type and associated wind directions, the distribution of wind direction frequencies can be determined for any point in the city. Should it prove possible to include a station with a longer series of measurements in the investigation, the climatological reliability of the method would be increased. Although further processing of data is under way to establish the level of accuracy, it is already certain that the method yields more useful results than those obtained from regional extrapolation. Investigations have also established which wind fields have the highest frequency of occurrence and how frequently mountain and valley breezes and local circulation induced by the urban heat island occur /Figs 2-4/.

Notwithstanding the fact that the major part of urban climatological research is basically theoretical in approach and is aimed at a better understanding of climatic process, we hope that the examples chosen on this occasion have demonstrated the applicability of climatic research to urban planning. It is undoubtedly the case that during recent decades the efforts made to satisfy the demands for housing have generally ignored environmental considerations. With the gradual elimination of the housing shortage, however, the demand for a healthy and pleasant environment will certainly grow. Changes in attitude are already apparent and this means a further challenge to geographical research to serve the interests of urban planning.

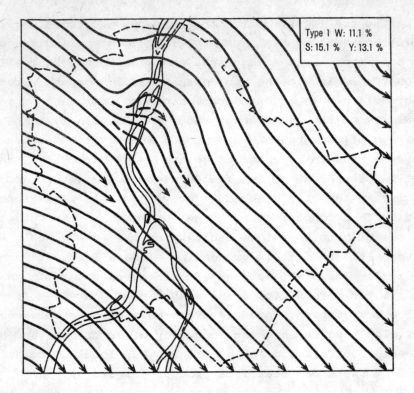

Fig. 2. The most frequently occurring type of wind field in
Budapest /type 1/
W = frequency of given type during the winter half-
year; S = frequency of given type during the summer
half-year; Y = annual frequency of given type as a
percentage of total number of hours

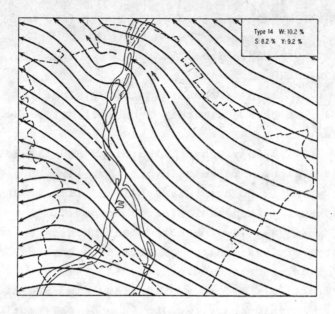

Fig. 3. The second most frequently occurring type of wind field
in Budapest /type 14/. Legend: see Fig. 2

Fig. 4. Wind field type 13 reflecting convergence above the
downtown area due to the combined effect of the urban
circulation system and the mountain breeze. Legend:
see Fig. 2

REFERENCES

CHANDLER, T.J. /1965/: The Climate of London. - Hutchinson,
    London.

CHANDLER, T.J. /1970/: Urban Climatology: Inventory and Pros-
    pect. - In Urban Climates, Technical Note, No. 100. WMO,
    Geneva.

CHANDLER, T.J. /1976/: Urban Climatology and its Relevance to
    Urban Design. - Technical Note, No. 149. WMO, Geneva.

PROBÁLD F. /1974/: Budapest városklimája /The Urban Climate of
    Budapest/. - Akadémiai Kiadó, Budapest.

PROBÁLD, F. /1976/: The Role of Green Areas in Planning the
    Atmospheric Environment of Cities. - Annales Univ. Sc. Bp.
    R. Eötvös, Sectio Geographica, XI. 141-159.

PROBÁLD, F. /1979/: Typology of Surface Wind Fields in Buda-
    pest. - Annales Univ. Sc. Bp. R. Eötvös, Sectio Geographi-
    ca, XIII-XIV. 84-105.

THE DEVELOPMENT OF THE COUNTRY PARK CONCEPT WITH SPECIAL REFERENCE TO NOTTINGHAMSHIRE

P.T.WHEELER

THE DEVELOPMENT OF NATIONAL POLICIES

Since the Industrial Revolution, Britain has become one of the most densely populated and most heavily urbanised countries in the world; at least 80 per cent of the population must be counted as urban by any standards, and yet about 80 per cent of the surface of the land is in some kind of agricultural use. Furthermore, one effect of this strict planning legislation required to deal with shortage of space has been to restrain the spread of settlement and to emphasise the contrast between the built-up and the rural areas. The result is a relatively wealthy, relatively mobile, highly urbanised population, anxious to spend significant parts of its growing leisure time beyond the urban fringe. Because of the uneven distribution of that population, the pressures thus produced upon the countryside tend to be strongly concentrated, especially mear large towns, in areas accessible to improved road transport, or around the coasts. However, mass ownership of the private car[1] has diffused pressure more widely, and a large proportion of all recreational visits to the countryside consist of leisure motoring.[2] Nonetheless, more active pursuits, especially walking, continue extremely popular. Thus, amenity pressures[3] have become a significant factor /some would say an unjustifiable intrusion/ in agricultural and silvicultural development.

Formal attempts have been made to increase legal freedom of access to the countryside since at least 1882, but the two most important measures were the "Town and Country Planning

Act" of 1947, which established planning control over all land uses even in rural areas, and the "National Parks and Access to the Countryside Act" of 1949, which established the "National Parks Commission" for England and Wales.[4] By 1957 all ten National Parks had been established. These are extensively rural areas of attractive natural and cultural landscape, largely formed by agricultural and silvicultural uses, and mainly in private ownership, where all forms of landscape change are strongly controlled, and where public access and recreation is encouraged. The National Parks cover nine per cent of England and Wales and are situated chiefly in the upland areas of the north and west /Fig. 1/. Subsequent declaration of the "Areas of Outstanding Natural Beauty", where planning controls are less emphasis is placed on public access, has done something to redress this regional imbalance. The "Countryside Act" of 1968 transformed the National Parks Commission into the "Countryside Commission", with concern for all rural areas and not just the National Parks, and with much increased funding. In addition, the Act embodied the new idea of the Country Park, which was intended to make it easier for those seeking recreation to enjoy their leisure in the open without travelling too far and without adding to congestion on the roads; to ease the pressure of the more remote and solitary places; and to reduce the risk of damage to the countryside, aesthetic as well as physical, resulting from recreational pressures.[5] Given these requirements, it was clear that Country Parks would have to be sited more with regard to the major centres of population than with regard to the distribution of attractive landscapes.

What, then, is a Country Park? It is "an area of land, or land and water, normally not less than 25 acres /10 ha/ in extent, designed to offer to the public, with or without charge, opportunity for recreation pursuits in the countryside". Only a small part of the area may be covered with buildings; the area may be a coastal site; and there may be facilities for a variety of recreational pursuits, for specialised interests or for quiet enjoyment of the country. Such Parks may be owned and managed by statutory bodies or private agencies or a combina-

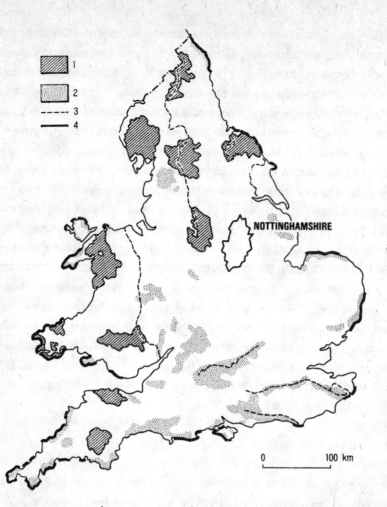

Fig. 1. National Parks, Areas of Outstanding Natural Beauty,
Long-distance Paths and Heritage Coasts in England and
Wales, 1981 /N.B. Coastal Long-distance Paths omitted
for clarity./
1 = National Parks; 2 = Areas of Outstanding Natural
Beauty; 3 = Long-distance Paths; 4 = Heritage Coasts

tion of both, but to qualify for grants administered through
the Countryside Commission /and therefore for the status of
Country Park/ they must be readily accessible for motor vehicles and pedestrians, and be provided with an adequate range
of facilities, including as a minimum parking facilities, lavatories, either within or adjacent to the Park, and a super-
visory service.[6] As a further condition of grant is that a Country Park must be "freely available" to the public, it has also

come to be accepted that entrance must be free, although charges may be made for individual facilities such as parking, and for special services.[7] The early emphasis was upon the provision of quiet, rural surroundings with the minimum facilities, but from 1974, with more stringent financial conditions and perhaps a more sensitive response to the actual desires of the public, a greater emphasis has been placed upon the provision of specialised facilities and a promotional strategy. At the same time, locational emphasis has changed from rural areas,of the accessible only by car, to urban fringe areas, closer to deprived city populations and often accessible by public transport.[8] By 1981 the Countryside Commission had recognised 166 Country Parks in England and Wales, 27 of which were run by non-public bodies /Fig. 2/.[9] However, it must be realised that these form only part of a spectrum of public amenity provision in rural areas, ranging from National Parks to recognised Picnic Sites /212 in 1981/, quite apart from provision by such bodies as the National Trust and many private organisations.[10] Indeed, the total provision of amenity-cum-conservation sites is almost impossible to plot on one map.

NOTTINGHAMSHIRE

Nottingham and Nottinghamshire have a long and honourable history in the provision of facilities for recreation. The very first municipal park was established in Derby in 1840, and Nottingham followed suit in 1852.[11] In 1924 Nottingham City Council bought the outstanding Elizabethan mansion of Wollaton Hall and its park, just west of the then City boundary, which now provides museums in the Hall, and facilities ranging from formal gardens to open parkland on 200 ha of land. Shortly after, the City was given Newstead Priory, the poet Byron's home, together with 132 ha of land, including woods, parkland and important formal and water gardens. Gedling Borough Council more recently /1979/ acquired Bestwood Lodge Park on the northern fringe of the City. It has 30.3 ha of ornamental gardens, formal recreation areas and parkland, with a large Victorian man-

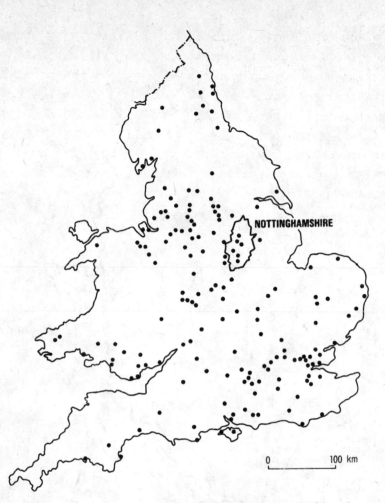

Fig. 2. Country Parks in England and Wales, 1981. Source:
Countryside Commission Annual Report 1980-1981

sion /now a hotel/. Although Wollaton now lies within the urban area, Bestwood is just on its edge, and even Newstead, 19
km north of the City, is not without some suburban development,
all three properties effectively function as Country Parks, although they lack the formal status. This is largely because ne-
gotiations with the Countryside Commission after 1968 were more
concerned with the creation of new development than with improvements to existing facilities; it is possible, however,
that Wollaton in particular may qualify for a grant in the future.

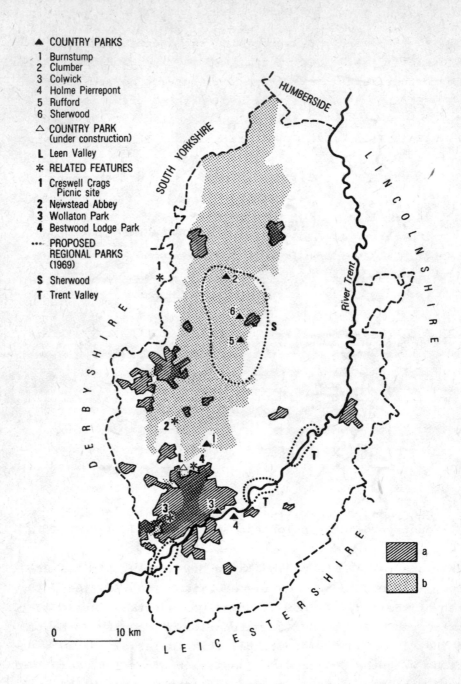

▲ COUNTRY PARKS
1 Burnstump
2 Clumber
3 Colwick
4 Holme Pierrepont
5 Rufford
6 Sherwood
△ COUNTRY PARK
(under construction)
L Leen Valley
✳ RELATED FEATURES
1 Creswell Crags
Picnic site
2 Newstead Abbey
3 Wollaton Park
4 Bestwood Lodge Park
⋯ PROPOSED
REGIONAL PARKS
(1969)
S Sherwood
T Trent Valley

a
b

Fig. 3. Country Parks and related features in Nottinghamshire, 1982. Source: see text.
a = urban areas; b = Bunter sandstone

210

It is, therefore, not surprising that Nottinghamshire
County Council should have inherited this tradition and developed it further, and in 1969 the "Nottinghamshire and Derbyshire Sub-regional Study" distinguished three areas suitable
for "Regional Parks" - in Derbyshire the Matlock Hills area,
and in Nottinghamshire /Fig. 3/ the Sherwood Forest and Trent
valley areas.[12] Regional Parks were intended to be rather like
National Parks, but whereas the latter always contained a significant area of wild land, and the preservation of landscape
and of the interests of the local inhabitants were to be paramount in case of planning conflict, Regional Parks were to be
located primarily with regard to the urban demand for recreational facilities rather than with regard to the presence of
beautiful landscape, and in the case of planning conflicts recreation was to be paramount. As with National Parks, public
access would not be universal, but there would be concentration on selected sites where specifically recreational provision could be made. This was known as the "honey pot" approach, and it was hoped that it would not only satisfy the
rising demands for facilities, but would also draw off some
people who would otherwise visit the National Parks, where visitor pressure was in places and at times becoming a serious
problem. In fact, in the end only two Regional Parks were created, the Lea Valley /London/ and the Colne Valley /Essex/
Parks, both by special Act of Parliament, but the so-called
"honey pots" emerged as Country Parks, both nationaly and specifically in Nottinghamshire.

Geographically, the six existing and one proposed Country
Parks in Nottinghamshire fall into two groups /Table I/. In
the south, Colwick, Holme Pierrepont and Leen Valley Country
Parks lie in the urban fringe /as do Wollaton and Bestwood/,
and the first two are also located in the suggested Trent Valley Regional Park area. In the north, Clumber, Sherwood Forest
and Rufford Country Parks lie within the proposed Sherwood Forest Regional Park area /and the popular Cresswell Crags Picnic
Site in Derbyshire is nearby/. Burntstump Country Park is almost on the Nottingham fringe, but by geology and general characteristics is best grouped with the northern Country Parks

Table I. Country Parks and analagous parks in Nottinghamshire in 1982

Country Park	Date	Area ha	Type of location	Main geology	Former use	Main features
1. Burntstump	1974	24	Rural	Bunter Sandstone	Parkland	Rolling parkland, woodland; cricket ground
2. Clumber	1972	1,544	Rural[x]	Bunter Sandstone	Former mansion, gardens, home farm, park	Chapel, refreshments, shop; gardens, lake, woodland, parkland, farmland; bicycle hire
3. Colwick	1978	1o5	Urban[o] fringe	River terraces	House, woods and lakes; sand and gravel working	Refreshments; woods, parkland, lakes; playgrounds, swimming, boating, fishing, riding; water events
4. Holme Pierre-pont	1971	16,2	Urban[o] fringe	River terraces	Sand and gravel workings	Refreshments; parkland, lake, fishing, nature reserve
5. Leen Valley /in preparation/	1984/5	170	Urban fringe	Bunter Sandstone	Neglected farm and woodland; old industry	Woodland and parkland; interpretation industrial archaeology and agriculture
6. Rufford	1969	61	Rural[x]	Bunter Sandstone	Mansion, gardens and park	Mansion /in preparation/, refreshments, shop; craft centre, interpretation /in preparation/; gardens, lake, woods
7. Sherwood Forest	1969	143	Rural[x]	Bunter Sandstone	Ancient woodland and scrub	Visitor centre /interpretation, shop; refreshments/; woodland, Major Oak, waymarked paths with interpretation; cricket ground and fair
Analagous parks						
a. Newstead	1931	132	Rural	Bunter Sandstone	Priory, mansion, gardens and parks	Priory ruins, mansion /Byron relics/, refreshments; gardens, with lakes etc., parkland and woods
b. Wollaton	1924	200	Urban	Bunter Sandstone	Mansion and park	House and museums; refreshments; gardens, parkland and woodland with deer, lake and fishing; golf course /club/

Sources: see text.   x = within area of proposed "Sherwood Forest Regional Park"
o = within area of proposed "Trent Valley Regional Park"

Neighbouring attractions	Access	Users /generalised/	Administration
Public house	Car	Number uncertain; local inhabitants	Gedling Borough Council
	Car, coach	1.2 m.; mainly S. Yorks. and Notts.	National Trust
Race course; greyhound stadium; River Trent	Foot, bus, car	Number uncertain; inhabitants central and SE Nottingham	Nottingham City for City and Severn-Trent Water Authority
National Water Sport Centre; River Trent	Car	0.25 m.; inhabitants West Bridgford plus spectators NWSC	National Sports Council for NSC and Nottingham County Council
	Foot, car	Number uncertain; inhabitants N.Nottingham, schools	Nottingham City
	Car, coach	0.35 m.; mainly S. Yorks. and Notts.	Nottinghamshire County Council
	Car, bus	0.42 m.; mainly S. Yorks. and Notts.	Nottinghamshire County Council /on lease from private estate/
	Car, bus	House 19,540 visitors 1981; mainly Nottingham and Notts.	Nottingham City
	Foot,	Museums 666,800 visitors 1981; mainly western parts Nottingham conurbation, schools	Nottingham City

/as is Newstead/. However, examination shews that historical accident has been influential as planning strategy in location, although it is true that the hinterlands of the two main groups show distinct southern and northern biases.

THE SOUTHERN COUNTRY PARKS

1. Holme Pierrepont

The earliest Country Park to be established in the south was at Holme Pierrepont in 1971, and this was really as an adjunct to the new National Water Sports Centre /NWSC/.[13] Figure 4 shows this clearly, with the Country Park as an elongated feature of 16.2 ha between the main rowing course and the Trent, as does the managerial organisation, by which the NWSC is largely run by the /national/ Sports Council /under the direction of a joint committee with the County Council/, with the Country Parks as, in effect, a sub-department.

The decision to build the NWSC at Holme Pierrepont was taken in 1969 because:

a. There was no alternative existing national centre;

b. The low-lying gravel workings by the Trent offered a cheap site for development, while requirements for preliminary restoration and landscaping could be written into the grant of planning premission for the remaining commercial extraction of gravel from the site;

c. Nottinghamshire County Council and the Sports Council were prepared to share the building and running costs, while the inclusion of the Country Park ensured a contribution from the Countryside Commission;

d. Heavy demand for water sports facilities was predicted at local, regional and national level.

This complex of considerations enabled Holme Pierrepont to beat a rival proposal for the Lea Valley, and work was sufficiently advanced for use to be made of some facilities in 1972, although official opening took place the following year. By 1978

the NWSC had approximately 78,850 visitors, exclusive of spectators, visitors to the Country Park proper, anglers etc., who
were estimated at 262,419.

It is clear, therefore, that the Holme Pierrepont complex
has to be managed in a rather special way. When there are no
water sports events, the Country Park functions conventionally,
with a normal range of facilities, somewhat strengthened by the
possibilities of private use of the water sports facilities and
angling along the Trent, in the lake, and even in the main 2,000
metre course, whereas, when there are events, the presence of
the Country Park enables the Water Sports Centre proper "to cater
for the total family".[14] A bank beside the rowing course provides a stand for spectators, but also shelters the quieter,
more informal Park. The main car park for the latter lies near
the western entrance, with the adventure play area, pets' corner,
shop, ranger post, toilets and picnic area close by. This was a
specific element of design to concentrate family pressures where
they could be most easily served; the contrast is with the nature reserve at the opposite end of the Park where fewest family
users penetrate. An interesting point is that the fishing lagoon
in between was subsidised and is supported by a private firm.

2. Colwick

Colwick Country Park, like Holme Pierrepont, lies along-
side the Trent within the south-eastern sector of the Nottingham fringe, although its position north rather than south of
the river does much to explain differences in local user patterns.[15] Like Holme Pierrepont, too, it is under joint management, in this case Nottingham City Council and the Severn-Trent
Water Authority /STWA/. The present Country Park covers 105 ha,
and consists of land owned by the two controlling bodies. The
City bought the Colwick estate in 1965, including:

a. The race course /one of the major national courses/, now let.
  /Land inside the course is available for football and other
  activities when there is no meeting./;

b. The greyhound stadium, also let;

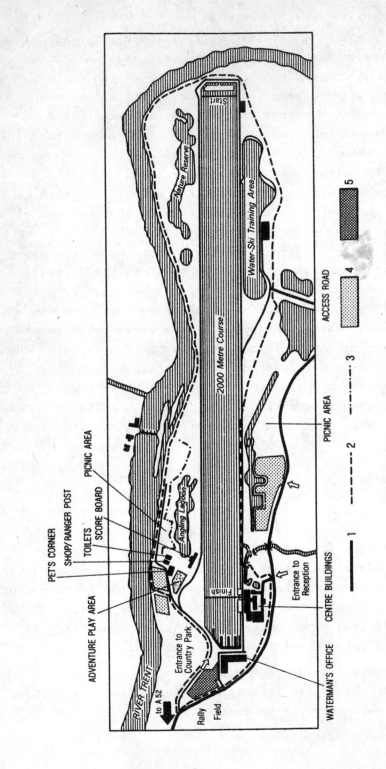

Fig. 4. Holme Pierrepont National Sports Centre and Country Park
1 = roadways; 2 = boundary walk; 3 = adventure play trail; 4 = car parks;
5 = trailer park

c. An area of 13 ha between the present Park and Mile End Road
   subsequently developed by a housing association;

d. Land within the Country Park:
   /i/ Colwick Hall, Colwick Hall Pool, and woodland, covering
       5.5 ha. The Hall is a "listed" building /1776/,[16] and
       has been restored by a local brewery as a hotel and res-
       taurant. The neighbouring ruins of a former parish
       church have been repaired and gardens laid out;
   /ii/ Washlands, covering 60.7 ha, bounded by an old course of
        the Trent which ran roughly through the Marina, round
        the western edge of Colwick Lake, and then through The
        Loop and along the Line of Colwick stream to the present
        river.

The Country Park was brought up to its present area by an additional purchase of about 8 ha next to Colwick Road, and by
about 30.7 ha of STWA washlands lying between the City property and the river.

     The original proposals were that the two authorities should
develop the Park jointly from 1977 to 1978. Gravel working was
not completed when improvements began in 1977, and /as with
Holme Pierrepont/ advantage was taken of the granting of planning consents to insist on partial restoration and landscaping
by the gravel company. The major development programme has been
completed /1982/, although minor works are likely to continue
for sometime. The lake and woodlands east of the Hall form a
quit area and nature reserve, with a picnic area and children's
playground close to the Hall car park. The 10.1 ha West Lake is
for casual sailing, wind surfing, model boat sailing and angling, and also has a swimming area. Colwick lake /26.3 ha/ is
also designed for sailing and angling, and has a shallow area
with paddle boats for children, but the Lake is also available
for special events /19 in 1981/, especially at week-ends.
Colwick Marina consists of a mooring basin of 2.4 ha with
berths for 200 cruisers. There are associated picnic areas,
car parks, play areas, perimeter paths and a horse trial.
     There are interesting points of comparison with Holme
Pierrepont. There is a major specialist attraction immediately

adjacent to the Park /the race course/, and events in the Park
are arranged to fit in with race meetings, as congestion would
otherwise be severe on approach roads. There is a great emphasis on the provision of specialised facilities, notably with
the Marina. One interesting pecularity of Colwick, however, is
that, apart from the people attendig special events, a very
substantial proportion of its users are of local origin, one-
third being from the adjacent parts of Nottingham, and a quarter from the deprived areas of the City centre.[17] Similar data
are not available for Holme Pierrepont, but it would seem that
Colwick in some ways functions more like an urban park /and
specifically, it might be guessed, like Wollaton Park, its municipal counterpart in the west of the City/ than a Country
Park, a feature emphasised by the provision of facilities. Perhaps the outstanding feature to an outsider, however, is the
lack of coordination between these two important amenity areas,
both of which have very strong /and potentially complementary/
water elements.

3. Leen Valley

The Leen Valley Country Park, due to be opened in 1984/5,
should be mentioned here, as it will occupy a position on the
northern edge of the built-up area of Nottingham, helping to
produce a ring of such features, if Wollaton and Bestwood be included.[18] The Leen is a small river flowing from Newstead to
the Trent and lying immediately west of nineteenth-century Nottingham. Its valley was intensively developed for textile working and processing in the eighteenth and nineteenth centuries,
and now presents considerable problems of industrial dereliction. Adjacent to its central stretch lay Bestwood Colliery,
with extensive tips. It was originally proposed in 1975 that
the tips and valley should be reclaimed to provide a strip of
open land which could be made to stretch to Newstead. Work began in 1981, with 500,000 raised by the City and Countryside
Commission. Figure   5 shows the present plans. Big Wood is a
historic remnant of a deer park formerly belonging to the Dukes
of St. Albans, and will need considerable management and resto-

ration. Bestwood Colliery tip has been landscaped and planted, and forms a pleasant hill. The Mill Lakes area, formerly occupied by textile industries, is being reclaimed and landscaped. These properties cover 170 ha, and further acquisitions are in negotiation, particularly of the lands of Forge Farm, which will form a connecting fulcrum. Specific features will be the use of the old Bestwood Colliery Winding Engine as an interpretive element[19] on coal mining, the development of Forge Farm with some sort of farming-related educational activity, and /in the more distant future/ the acquisition of Forge Mill as a comparable feature on the textile industry. The Park, therefore, not yet officially in existence, will be a new creation, but will incorporate various historic features. It will have the additional advantage of effective contiguity with Bestwood Lodge Park. Although this belongs to Gedling Borough Council and is not officially a Country Park, there will in practice a continuous zone of parkland of at least 198 ha.

THE NORTHERN COUNTRY PARKS

The northern group of Country Parks in Nottinghamshire lie mainly on the rolling lands of the Bunter Sandstone, with poor, dry, sandy soils which naturally would be under scattered oak-birch wood and scrub. This is the ancient area of Sherwood. In the Middle Ages there were some important religious houses here, which were succeeded by a series of great mansions and their associated estates. These estates have been broken up in the twentieth century, making it possible to acquire parts for recreational purposes. They lie beyond the urban fringe, and in many ways conform to the pre-1974 Country Park concept much better than the southern group.

1. Clumber Park

Much the largest of the northern group is Clumber Park, covering 1,544 ha, including 245 ha farmland not open to the public, and approximately 882 ha of woodland, almost half of which is leased by the Forestry Commission.[20] The rest of the area is made up by formal gardens associated with the former mansion, open parkland and the 34.4 ha lake. This property was bought by the National Trust from the Duke of Newcastle in 1946, with grants from nine Local Authorities who formed a management committee with the Trust. Since 1980 the Trust has been solely responsible for management, though grants are still received from Mansfield District and the County of South Yorkshire, who retain an interest. Hence, it has become imperative to promote the Park in order to generate income, and support from the Countryside Commission has been welcomed /mainly in the form of a grant to dredge the lake, 1978/79/.

Very large numbers visit Clumber - 1.2 million day visits in 1979 and in 1982. Over a third of visitors come from South Yorkshire and the same proportion from Nottinghamshire /of which Nottingham contributes only 6 per cent/. A tenth come from Derbyshire. All except some coach parties travel by car. The attractions of Clumber are above all quiet farm landscape, parkland and the lake and woodlands. On permanent "feature" is a cycle hire scheme, supposedly the largest in Britain; eighty bicycles are available for hire in two-hourly periods between 11.00 and 16.00,and this is an extremely popular facility. There is also a long-established cricket pitch, and the Lake is a premier coarse fishing water. An experiment is being carried out in the provision of a specially designed, self-propelled invalid chair capable of traversing relatively rough terrain, which will be extended if successful. There is a shop, a cafe and a restaurant, and the Chapel of the former great house is an attraction. Some open-air theatre performances have taken place this year and a widely-publicised "water spectacular" is to be held for three days in July /1982/.

There are considerable problems of management. One is that of subsidence. Coal seams are worked by both the South Yorkshire and the Nottinghamshire Areas of the National Coal Board, and fears are entertained for both the lake and the Chapel, although eventual repair would follow damage.
The presence of a public highway /Limetree Avenue/ means that the Park can never be wholly closed, and there is risk of van-

dalism. The woodland areas leased to the Forestry Commission are managed commercially, but those run by the Trust are maintained for scenic purposes. Considerable planting takes place /2,000 trees in 1981/, but much care is required, although natural regeneration of birch and even of oak will take place freely if access is restricted by reduction of grass cutting or by leaving brushwood in situ. Management is potentially complicated by the proposed designation of about 400 ha including the lake and grasslands to the south as a Site of Special Scientific Interest.[21]

2. Rufford Park

Rufford Park, although at 61 ha much smaller than Clumber, is somewhat similar in origin, in that it contains the remains of a great house, with its gardens, park and lake, but the balance of features is very different.[22] Rufford began as a Cistercian house founded in 1148 and suppressed in 1536. It passed through various hands, coming to form the core of an estate of about 7,3000ha in Nottinghamshire. This was finally sold in 1938, and the property was broken up until the County Council bought the residual area in 1951, containing the mansion and associated buildings, the 8 ha lake, and the related grounds. Little active management took place and a large part of the mansion, neglected since 1938 and weakened by mining subsidence, was demolished in 1958. In 1969 Country Park status was approved, and the Department of the Environment[23] became responsible for the partial restoration of the remainder of the mansion, while the County Council, with Countryside Commission support, was responsible for the other buildings and the lake. Active development began in 1970, the immediate task being to restore the lake and buildings affected by subsidence /at one point the lake was emptied overnight by subsidence fractures in the clay lining/. Also included were supplementary landscaping, car parks, toilets, footpaths, improvement of the mill at the north end of the lake, and the reinforcing of the dam and sluices. A second phase of development, preceded by careful commercial analysis,[24] followed, including exhibition and auditorium space,

shops and refreshment facilities, new accommodation for the
park ranges, and four craft workshops. It is hoped that the mansion house may eventually form and interpretive centre for the
Park when restoration is complete. The mill is being renovated
and will serve as a museum and as a County centre for interpretive material. At the same time, work continues on the grounds.

That this programme was well conceived is proved by the
fact that visitors increased from an estimated 80,000 in 1978
to about 350,000 in 1981. Indeed, on the afternoon of 31st May
/Spring Bank Holiday/, 1982, access to the Park had to be closed as all car parks were full to capacity. This also brings out
the point that virtually all visitors to Rufford arrive by car,
except for a small number of coach parties, although a rather
higher proportion comes from within a radius of 60 km than is
the case with Clumber.[25] To some extent, the attractions of Rufford are the same as those of Clumber, with parkland, lake and
gardens, but the site is smaller, the facilities more concentrated, and much greater emphasis is laid not only upon related
features such as wardening services, waymarked trails, and interpretation of the Park, but also upon elements far removed
from the original concept of the Country Park, especially the
craft centre and catering facilities. Even so, a considerable
element of "tamed wilderness" remains, and the lake is a major
attraction.

3. Sherwood Forest

The Sherwood Forest Country Park attracts even more visitors than Rufford, about 425,000 a year. It was established in
1969 on land leased from a private estate by Nottinghamshire
County Council.[26] It is located in an area of ancient semi-nat-
ural oak and birch woodland and heathland known as the Birk-
lands, which is one of the last remnants of the former Royal
Hunting Forest of Sherwood, and is now a Site of Special Interest. The woodland includes the famous Major Oak, which is said
to be 600 years old, and which, because of its legendary associations with Robin Hood,[27] has for long been a focus of visitor interest. Indeed, it was partly pressure from indiscrimi-

nate car parking and the soil compaction and erosion on the network of tracks leading to the Major Oak, which led to County action. The "Sherwood Forest Study" of 1971 recommended the construction of proper landscaped carparks and picnic areas, the
provision aof adequate new footpaths and restoration of old e-
roding tracks, as well as the provision of a substantial Visitor Centre. The last was opened in 1976 and extended in 1978,
and includes a permanent exhibition, a sixty-seat auditorium, a
bookshop, cafeteria, toilets and the rangers' offices and accommodation. In addition, the southern extremity of the Park includes a cricket ground and pavillion, leased to Edwinstowe
Cricket Club, and a seasonal fair /the proprietors of which
claim rights dating from a mediaeval charter/. This area is due
for some improvement, but presents something of the appearance
of a "village green".

Sherwood Forest Country Park differs in significant ways
from Clumber and Rufford. It lacks associations of historic
buildings and it has no lake. The Visitor Centre with its car
parks and the Major Oak form the two main foci of interest. The
terrain is under such pressure that most paths are surfaced with
gravel and firmly enclosed by fencing or at least clearly de-
marcated. There is access to open land but even there waymark-
ing encourages estriction to selected routes. That this policy
is successful is shewn by the remarkable degree of regeneration
in the protected areas, and even the Major Oak, after tree sur-
gery and with its root area protected from trampling, is put-
ting forth strong new growth. Acceptance of the new policy has
been aided by very active wardening, and full use of the Visitor Centre to provide information and educate the public. An
interesting experiment is taking place this year in the form of
Country subsides to bus services from the surrounding towns to
the Visitor Centre, where connections may be made to Rufford,
Clumber and to Thoresby House /a mansion opened to the public/.
These services, collectively known as "The Sherwood Forester",
will run on Sundays and Bank Holidays in July and August, 1982.

4. Burntstump

If one excepts Cresswell Crags /a Picnic Site on the Derby-shire/Nottinghamshire border run by the two County Councils and attracting about 80,000 visitors a year/ and Newstead /where the house alone had 19,540 visitors in 1981/, neither of which are Country Parks, Burntstump is the one remaining example in Nottinghamshire. It is of markedly different character.[28] Sher-wood Lodge with its grounds was bought by the then Arnold Urban District Council in 1973. The Lodge became the headquarters of the Nottinghamshire County Constabulary, a private house was converted to a public house and subsequently sold, and a pri-vate hospital was being built on another part of the property in 1982, leaving 24 ha for the park. This became a Country Park in 1974. It consists of a shallow dry valley on the Bunter Sand-stone, the lower, western end open and grassy, but merging a-long the sides and to the east into wooded parkland and mixed woodland. Besides carparks with lavatories, and mainly gravel-led walks, amenities include a levelled area at the western end of the Park, with a cricket pitch, and a small artificial pond in the centre of the Park. The pitch is let to Ravenshead Crick-et Club, who have extended and maintain the original small pa-villion, while the Council remains responsible for the mainte-nance of the ground. Management of the Park is kept to a mini-mum. No tree planting has taken place as natural regeneration is ample. Some tree management will be necessary, particularly in the thickest, but large fallen tree trunks are as far as possible left in place for ecological reasons and to provide an element of adventure playground for children. There has been some inconspicuous provision of benches and picnic tables, but most people have their drinks or food near the hotel or car-park. Problemes of management include some difficulties over poorly marked or unfenced boundaries; some damage by rabbits and dogs in the slope beyond the cricket ground; and conflicts with riders.

Burntstump, therefore, may be regarded as a "minimal" Country Park. It lacks facilities beyond the bare minimum, it is relatively small, and it is not easily accessible by public transport. Nonetheless, although precise user data are lacking, it appears to fulfil a useful function as a quiet area of countryside open to the public, which with it "pub" and cricket ground has some mild attractions of a "village green" nature. The carparks and lavatories provide the basic facilities which the motoring public demands, but it is thought that most users are of fairly local origin.

CONCLUSION

Nottinghamshire is increasingly well provided with Country Parks and similar open-air, rural or semi-rural recreational facilities /Fig. 5/. There is a wide range of types, from the simplicity of Burntstump to the complexity of Rufford, but there is a growing tendency to support special features, such as the Sherwood Forest Visitor Centre, or special events, like the Clumber Water Spectacular. These may be linked with major facilities, like the National Water Sport Centre. Organisation may be in the hands of a single authority /e.g. Nottinghamshire County Council at Rufford/ or more complex /e.g. Nottingham City Council and the Severn-Trent Water Authority at Colwick/. Support by the Countryside Commission confers formal Country Park status, but there are parallel facilities elsewhere, as at Newstead. The future is likely to see more development of a similar nature, as with the Leen Valley Country Park. Although there are at present insufficient data to tell how far Country Parks may intercept people who would otherwise visit National Parks or the coast, there can be no doubt that they are immensely popular with the public. Visitors other than for special functions tend to come from within a radius of about 60 kms, which produces rather different hinterlands for the Parks in the north and the south of the county, and a large number of visitors tend to be quite regular in their visits. This is especially true for the urban fringe Parks, where access on foot or by bus is convenient. Although the public appreciates the calm rural surroundings that were the initial aim of Country Park policies, it is also much attracted by the features and events associated with a more promotional type of management.

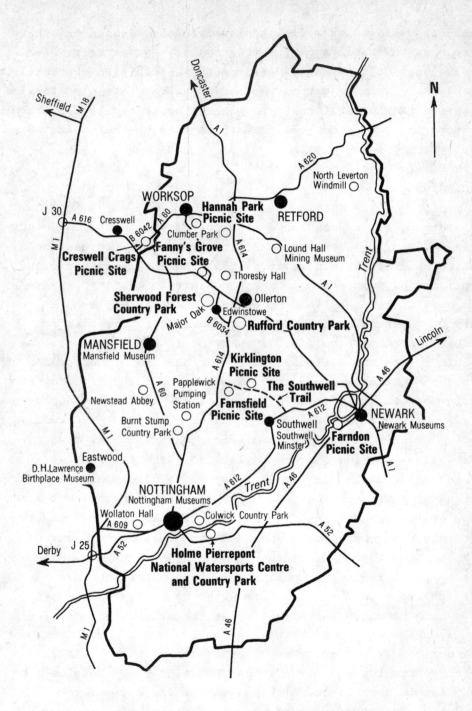

Fig. 5. Countryside sites in Nottinghamshire

The location of Country Parks in Nottinghamshire in the Sherwood Forest area, along the Trent, and in the urban fringe,
fits in well with planning strategies, but is also the result
of historical accident. In any case, the developments clearly
meet a growing public demand, which otherwise would almost certainly be diffused over the countryside to the detriment of agriculture, forestry and the rural landscape as a whole.

NOTES

1. 58 per cent of all households had the use of at least one
   car or van in 1980. Central Statistical Office: Statistical
   trends 12, London /HMSO/ 1982, p. 160.

2. J.T. Coppock and B.S. Duffield: Recreation in the countryside: a spatial analysis. London and Basingstoke /Macmillan/,
   1975, pp. 24-39.

3. "Amenity pressures" denotes all forms of recreational demand,
   ranging from specific sporting requirements to general tour-
   ing, day-visiting and holiday-making activities.

4. Ann and Malcolm MacEwen: National Parks: conservation or
   cosmetics? London /Allen and Unwin/, 1982. Legal divisions
   within the United Kingdom are extremely confusing. Northern
   Ireland and Scotland are frequently the subjects of separate
   legislation to England and Wales, and as much of their administration and most of their statistics are independent,
   attention in this paper is restricted to England and Wales.

5. Ministry of Land and Natural Resources: Leisure in the countryside, England and Wales. Cmnd, 2928, London /HMSO/, 1966.

6. Countryside Act 1968, Section 6/1/, 33, quoted in Countryside Recreation Research Advisory Group /CRRAG/: Countryside
   recreation glossary. London /Countryside Commission/, 1970,
   p. 13.

7. Clive Godron: Financing countryside recreation as part of a
   local authority's responsibilities: a personal view, pp. 71-

76 in CRRAG: Economic aspects of countryside recreation management, Proceedings of the CRRAG conference 1976. Cheltenham /Countryside Commission/ and Perth /Countryside Commission for Scotland/, 1976.

8. N.J. Beynon: The East Midlands in maps: 2 - Country Parks. Trent Geographer 2, 1981, pp. 27-36 /p. 28/.

9. Fourteenth Report of the Countryside Commission for the year ended 30 September 1981. London /HMSO/, 1982.

10. Picnic sites, usually of less than 2 ha, with parking space and perhaps such facilities as lavatories and benches and tables, may be recognised by the Countryside Commission and receive grants. Such sites are for short visits only, and camping is not allowed. There are two recognised picnic sites in Nottinghamshire.

The National Trust was founded in 1895 as a non-profit-making public company to ensure that places and buildings of historic interest and natural beauty are held permanently for the nation. It was converted by Act of Parliament in 1907 to a Trust and given the unique power to declare its properties "inalienable". It is an independent registered charity and is now the third largest landowner in the United Kingdom.

11. Kenneth C. Edwards: Amenity areas in the Nottinghamshire and Derbyshire Sub-regional unit. Geografia Polonica, 36, 1977, pp. 49-55.

12. Andrew Thorburn, Director: Nottinghamshire and Derbyshire Sub-regional Study. Nottinghamshire/Derbyshire Sub-regional Planning Unit, Alfreton, Derbyshire, 1969. pp. 73-76.

13. Information on Holme Pierrepont is largely derived from:

    An undated series of unpublished papers /?1973/ -
       D.G. Controls Ltd: Electronic information board.
       G.S. Dibley: An introduction to the National Water
          Sports Centre.
       Gelsthorpe and Savidge, Architects: The architects'
          brief.

I.M. Jones: The civil engineering works.

M.J. Lowe: The planning issues.

G.S. Dibley: A history of the National Water Sports Centre. Unpublished paper, Holme Pierrepont, 1979.

G.S. Dibley: Holme Pierrepont National Water Sports Centre and Country Park, Director's Report, 1979-1981. Unpublished paper, Holme Pierrepont, 1981.

Private communications from -
Mr. G. Hill, Assistant Director, National Water Sports Centre.
Mr. R. Broadely, Assistant Director, Holme Pierrepont Country Park.

The general strategy of development of the Trent Valley was discussed in H.J. Lowe: The Trent Valley Study. West Bridgford, Nottinghamshire /Nottinghamshire County Council/, 1977.

14. Mr. R. Broadley, ibid. Coarse fishing /i.e. excluding salmon and trout/ in fresh water is said to be the largest participator sport in Britain.

15. Information on Colwick Country Park is largely derived from: Countryside Commission, unpublished report, 1978.

E.S.P. Evans: Colwick Park: proposal for its development as a regional recreation centre. Nottingham /City Planning Department, Nottingham Corporation/, 1967.

Private communications from Mr. T. Wyke, Parks Manager, City of Nottingham Recreation Department.

16. A structure which has been "listed" as having historic importance may not be demolished, repaired, altered or added to without giving three months' notice to the Secretary of State for the Environment /in England/. Department of the Environment: List of Ancient Monuments in England correct to 31st December 1977. London /HMSO/, 1978, p. 3.

17. Private communication based on unpublished survey data by Mr. J.N. Beynon, Department of Town and Country Planning, Trent Polytechnic.

18. Information on the Leen Valley Country Park is based on private communications from Mr. C. Gordon, Assistant Director of Leisure Services /Countryside/, County of Nottingham. There are also modest proposals for urban-rural fringe management or Country Park development in the Erewash Valley from 1983.

19. "Interpretation: The process of developing a visitor's interest, and enjoyment and understandig of, an area, or part of an area, by describing and explaining its characteristics and their inter-relationships. N.B. /1/ interpretation implies more than simply the provision of information; it seeks to encourage direct involvement... and to incorporate a conservation message: /2/ Interpretation normally has a theme... cultural heritage, conservation or archaeology: /3/ A variety of interpretive techniques may be used ... collectively these are often referred to as interpretative services." CRRAG, ibid. /6/ above.

20. Information on Clumber is largely derived from private communications from Mr. P. Browning, Regional Information Officer, National Trust, Clumber Park, and from unpublished Countryside Commission noter of 1978, and from C. Watkins and P.T. Wheeler /eds./ The study and use of British woodlands. Nottingham /Institute of British Geographers, Rural Geography Study Group/, 1981. 118-120.

The Forestry Commission was established in 1919 to encourage forestry and to own and manage state forest lands, and is now the largest land owner in the country. Considerable areas of state woodlands have been opened to the public as "Forest Parks" and the Commission is exercising a growing influence on landscape management. There are no Forest Parks in Nottinghamshire.

21. Sites of Special Scientific Interest are areas which need special protection because of their flora, fauna, geology or physiography. They are declared by the Nature Conservancy Council, and access and development are subject to control. There are 56 SSSIs in Nottinghamshire.

22. Information on Rufford is largely derived from:

> Coopers Lybrand Associates Ltd.: Rufford Country Park
> marketing study: a report to the Countryside Commis-
> sion and Nottinghamshire County. Council, Cheltenham
> /Countryside Commission/ and West Bridgford /Notting-
> hamshire County Council/ 1979.
>
> Countryside Commission, unpublished notes of 1978.
>
> Robert Jenkins:Marketing a country park, Supplement to
> Local Government Chronicle, 28th May, 1982.
>
> Private Communications from -
>   Mr. C. Gordon, ibid. /18/ above.
>   Mr. S. Lamottee, Marketing Officer /Countryside Div./
>   Nottinghamshire County Council.

23. The Department of the Environment is a major department of
central government which is responsible for most environmental and planning matters, including the maintenance of
certain historic buildings.

24. Coopers Lybrand, ibid. /22/ above.

25. Data from a survey carried out by Social and Community
Planning Research for Nottinghamshire County Council and
the Countryside Commission, 1981.

26. Information on Sherwood Forest Park is largely derived from:

> Countryside Commission: unpublished notes of 1978
>
> Nottinghamshire County Council: Sherwood Forest Study.
> West Bridgford /Nottinghamshire County Council/ n.d.
> /?1972/.
>
> Nottinghamshire County Council: The future of Sherwood
> Forest: public consultation copy January 1972. West
> Bridgford /Nottinghamshire County Council/, 1972.
> /These two NCC publications also deal with the wider
> "Regional Park" area./
>
> J.A. Zetter: Planning for informal recreation at the
> local scale: Sherwood Forest study. London /Country-
> side Commission/, 1973.

Private communications from -
    Mr. C. Gordon, ibid. /18/ above.
    Mr. S. Lamottee, ibid. /22/ above.

27. The most recent and most thorough examination of the Robin
    Hood legend is by J.C. Holt: Robin Hood. London /Thames and
    Hudson/, 1982, who says: "It is more likely than not that
    Robert Hood, outlaw, the original of the story, was a real
    person... It is not apparent at what point Sherwood and the
    and the sheriff ot Nottingham came into the tale... the
    nearer Robin gets to Nottingham the less authentic he be-
    comes. It is to Barnsdale and South Yorkshire that the
    greater part of the original tradition of Robin belongs."
    /pp. 187, 188 and 75/.

28. Information on Burntstump Country Park is largely derived
    from unpublished notes by the Countryside Commission, 1978,
    and personal communications form -

        Mr. R. Gibson, Parks Officer, Gedling Borough Council.
        Mr. D.B. Slinger, Planning and Estates Office, Gedling
            Borough Council

    To them, also, I am indebted for information on Bestwood
    Lodge Park.

UTILIZATION OF ALTERNATIVE ENERGY RESOURCES ON THE GREAT HUNGARIAN PLAIN

L. GÖÖZ

INTRODUCTION

As a consequence of the energy problem, increasing tension is apparent in the Hungarian economy, reflected in production costs, in the balance of payments, in investment plans and in other fields.

Between 1970 and 1979 direct energy consumption increased by 60 per cent, a faster rate of growth than in the most developed countries of Europe. In 1978, 35.5 per cent of energy consumption was derived from coal and 63.4 per cent from oil and gas, rising to 65 per cent in 1979. If our oil and gas consumption remains the same, it is forecast that by 1985 we shall have to pay 3 billion dollars for oil and natural gas imports. Expressed in another way, while in 1973 16 kgs of meat would have bought 1 ton of oil, today 280 kgs buys the same amount.

There are four main problems affecting energy. Firstly, compared with our rate of economic development and production efficiency, specific energy use is very high. Taking Hungarian consumption for the period 1975-1979 as 100, energy used per person in Great Britain was 148.1, a much smaller difference than for Gross Domestic Product per capita which was 70 per cent higher in Great Britain. Secondly, because our energy consumption is growing faster than in other countries, we have a much greater demand for hydro-carbons. Thirdly, between 1960 and 1970 our economy grew at a rapid pace. A similar rate of development would now disrupt manufacturing industry, as the

key consideration is the maintenance of a good foreign trade
balance. Fourthly, the possibility of importing power resources
from the USSR and other socialist countries is becoming increasingly restricted and the conditions are now less favourable.

1. HUNGARIAN ENERGY POLICY AND ALTERNATIVE ENERGY RESOURCES

The long term energy programme aims at reducing oil and
natural gas usage through the rationalization of energy consumption and an economy drive /Table I, Figs. 1 and 2/. To meet increasing demands, the use of nuclear, coal and renewable energy
resources is urged. The sole uranium deposit in Hungary is to
be utilised within the framework of COMECON. The reserves are
not exceptionally large but at the present level of technology
are sufficient to support a MW capacity of about 4-5000. A dra-
matic change would occur, however, if there was the possibility
for reusage and the introduction of fast breeder reactors: efficiency of exploitation would be multiplied 40-fold. By 1990
our first atomic power station at Paks, situated on the Danube
in the south of the country, will constitute the basis for future electricity development.

Table I. Fossil fuel reserves in Hungary

Coal:	6,4 thousand million tons		
	from this exploitable		
	hard coal:	450 million tons	
	brown coal:	840	" "
	lignite:	2650	" "
Oil:	85 million tons		
Gas:	80 thousand million m^3		

The development of black coal mining is important from the
point of view of coke production since, as can be seen from the
diagram, the annual calorific value of coke imports is equal to
1 million tons of oil /Fig. 3/. The country's one black coal

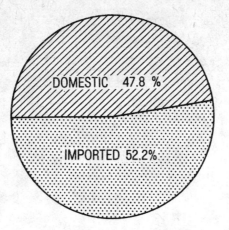

Fig. 1. Power resources

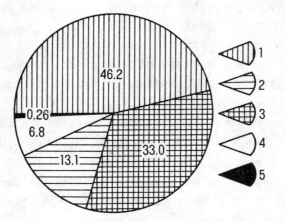

Fig. 2. Structure of domestic power production /in percentages, 1980/

1 = coal and peat; 2 = oil; 3 = natural gas; 4 = water; 5 = other

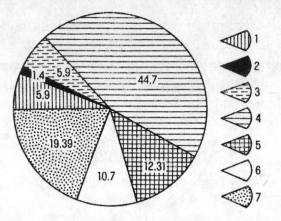

Fig. 3. Structure of imported power /in percentages, 1980/
1 = coal; 2 = briquets; 3 = coke; 4 = oil; 5 = electricity; 6 = oil products; 7 = natural gas

field is situated in the Mecsek region but difficulties arese because of the high geothermal gradient giving a temperature of about 50 °C at the coal face.

In connection with oil and natural gas usage special efforts must be made because of the inefficiency of power stations which in certain cases amounts to only 1.5% for every 8200 calories of gas energy consumed.

Naturally other technologies must be introduced and oil and natural gas should primarily be utilized in the more effective communal sector. The mining and utilization of domestic fuel resources would be the most economical way to improve the energy balance. The cost of producing domestic oil and gas is only one eighth of the world price.

"Renewable" energy resources, i.e. geothermal, solar, biomass and wind energy, from a part of domestic energy research. Of these only geothermal energy has actually reached operational level.

Before we examine the application of alternative energy sources, mention should be made of the main characteristics of Hungarian energy usage. Firstly, a great deal of energy is used

for space heating, only just behind that used by industry. Secondly, in many fields energy is exported in the form of products
where imported energy plays the main role in manufacture. Thirdly, agriculture which amounts for only 8 per cent of all energy
consumption, contributes a considerable proportion of Hungarian
exports to the dollar market. Fourthly, given the structure of
settlement - 46.6 per cent of Hungarians live in villages and
on farms - alternative energy sources may well be the most economical as well as being sufficient to satisfy local demand.

2. THE UTILIZATION OF GEOTHERMAL ENERGY ON THE GREAT HUNGARIAN PLAIN

The Great Plain covers 40 per cent of the country's area
and contains 30 per cent of the total population. This flat area consists of two economic regions and is well endowed for agriculture. For a long time local energy supply was poor but many
new oil and gas fields have recently been discovered in the region, which is fortunate since the Transdanubian fields are now
becoming exhausted. 90 per cent of Hungarian oil and gas reserves are situated in the south and east of the country. 75
per cent of geothermal energy also occurs in the same area, notably in Csongrád county, while the remaining 25 per cent is to
be found in the Little Plain in the north west of Transdanubia.
Utilizable geothermal energy underlies 40% of the country's area and of this 75% is to be found in the Great Plain.

Thermal water research in Hungary has a history going back
100 years. The flow of energy towards the surface of the Pannonian Basin is twice the average heat-flow observed elsewhere
on the surface of the earth. The thickness of the crust beneath
the surrounding Dinaric, Alpine and Carpathian mountain ranges
is at least 35 km, and consists mainly of sediments originating
from the Cretaceous and Neogene periods. The basement forms a
domelike structure which is approximately 19 km high. Since the
MOHO and CONRAD belts are relatively close to each other here
the conclusion can be drawn that the crust must have thinned
out under the basin. This is confirmed by the depth of the CON-

RAD discontinuity which is deeper than normal because of the thickness of sedimentation /3-5 km/. The thinning crust in the basin must have been the result of isostatic sinking and parts of the crust are presumed to have moved more or less freely.

The Carpathians must therefore be seen as a special structural phenomenon, the development of which must have been significantly influenced by plate tectonics. As a result of these circumstances, it can be established that the geothermal anomalies of the Pannonian Basin were not formed near the surface but originated deep within the Basin. The latest research carried out in wells as deep as 3-6 km still show great heat flow gradients.

The geothermal anomaly of the Hungarian Basin was proved by measurements made 40 years ago which were also the first heat-flow observations made on the European continent. Hungarians also carried out the first heat-flow observations in Italy, Czechoslovakia, and in the Viennese Basin in the decades before the Second World War.

The normal heat-flow in Hungary is 2.0×10^{-6} $^{\circ}$C per km^2. The geothermal gradient is higher than the average value for the Earth /30-35 $^{\circ}$C; Figs. 4 and 5/. The technical and economic significance of the Hungarian geothermal anomaly is that water at temperatures of 110-130 $^{\circ}$C can be found relatively close to the surface at a depth of 2 km. This means that in those places where the porosity and permeability of sediments is high the geothermal energy can be utilized in the form of hot water. Research has established the total thermal water reserve of the country to amount to 400 km^3, or 400 billion m^3. Although this is more than the total energy from all other domestic energy sources, more careful estimation places the utilizable quantity at not more than 50 billion m^3.

At present there are 600 thermal wells with a total water output of more than 200 million m^3 per year. 38 per cent of this is used in thermal baths, while only 2.6% is utilized by industry.

Agriculture is the other main consumer, with a percentage utilization nearly equal to that of balneology. The reserve of

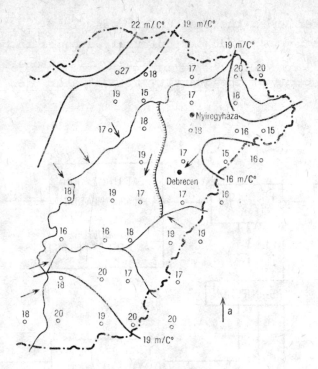

Fig. 4. Average geothermal gradients /m/°C/
a = observed direction of underground waterflow

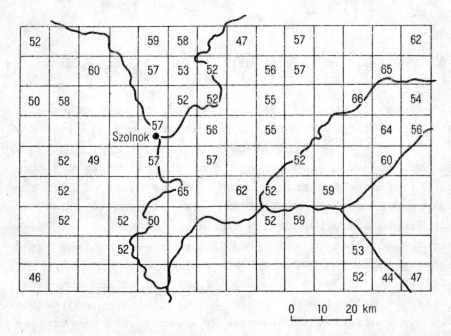

Fig. 5. Mean temperature values at a depth of 1,000 metres

thermal water under the Great Plain was first used for the heating of glass houses and horticultural purposes in general in 1952 to 1954 /Fig. 6/. Indeed, Hungary is now one of the world leaders in terms of the quantity of hot water used in agriculture.

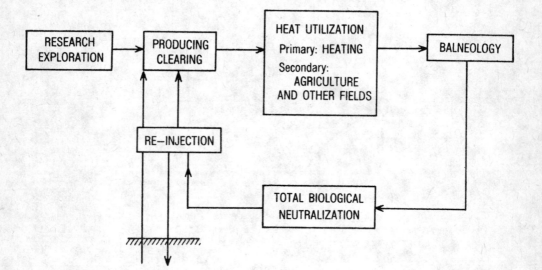

Fig. 6. Model for the complex utilization of geothermal energy

In Szeged 1,000 flats were connected to the geothermal network for heating and domestic hot water supply in 1960 and the system has been working since then without complaint. The output from one well producing 90 m^3 of thermal water per hour at 90 $^{\circ}$C, suffices for this purpose. On the basis of this favourable experiment the Medical University and a textile factory at Szeged and subsequently the hospital at Makó and Hódmezővásárhely and other official buildings have been linked into the same system.

It was the co-operatives that first recognized the possibilities of using thermal energy in agriculture, and utilization is now widespread throughout this sector. 90 per cent of greenhouses and folia coverings in the fields are heated in this way amounting to 2 million m^2 altogether. Other areas of utilization include animal husbandry, poultry-farms, incubators, absorption refrigerators, and dryers for hay, spicepepper, grain and fodder corn. Most of these systems are to be found in the southern part of the Great Plain, where the long hours of sunshine and a horticultural tradition have encouraged their adoption. Because geothermal energy can be used all year round and the community sector requires only 200 days of intensive use, the surplus is being used in the agricultural sector. As a result, we now have much experience of using this energy in fishfarming in winter and in mushroom production under folia coverings in the fields in summer.

According to the new government programme, geothermal energy will supply the heating and hot water requirements of 30,000 flats by 1985. Such installations are economical, since a thermal well with the necessary equipment is roughly equal to the cost of a conventional boiler of the same capacity, while operating costs are only 15-40% of the conventional level. In agriculture geothermal energy of a calorific volume equal to one million tons of oil will be used by 1988, and the government will subsidise large agricultural and other consumers who wish to change from oil to geothermal energy.

The possibilities are therefore great but we are in an analogous situation to the Queen on the glass mountain in the folk tale. Everybody can win the Queen but we tend to forget that we have to climb the mountain for her and that the diamond horseshoe costs a lot of money.

Let us therefore outline briefly some of the problems surrounding production and consumption. Firstly, the deposition of calcium carbonate can harm the equipment although only a few wells have been thus affected so far. There are also wells where the water has special properties and normal technology cannot be used successfully. Dutch and Belgian electro-magnetic and Soviet Ultra Sound equipment have been used in these situations but with poor results.

241

The latest technology reinjects water into the stratum from which it came. This produces a very clean and clear water, the energy is recirculated and no environmental problems are caused. The country has gained considerable experience in the reinjection field from the oil industry and many Hungarian experts are working in Paris in thermal water engineering and in Crete and Greece. Experts from Japan have also visited Hungary to learn about our reinjection technology.

3. THE UTILIZATION OF BIOMASS FOR ENERGY PURPOSES

Biogas equipment was first installed 30 years ago on the Great Plain and possibilities exist for biogas production equal to one million tons of oil in calorific value. Of this amount 75% can be realised in the Great Plain. For this, however, 1,000 plants of 10-20,000 m^3 capacity would be necessary, and the investment cost would be 4-6 times greater than the equivalent development of brown coal production.

In the next few years we cannot therefore expect any rapid development in this field, but tests are being carried out. At the present level of technology, methanol can be produced from many crops, primarily from potatoes and sugar-beet, as cheaply as other fuels. However, economic geographical examination has proved that using the Great Plain for the production of fodder and food crops is more profitable as the export possibilities are good.

Nonetheless the best way to use agricultural and forest waste is as an energy source. For example, about 400,000 tons of wood material is produced on the Great Plain each year and good results from the processing of vine-stems have been achieved. Other agricultural waste can be use more economically with the aid of modern technology for biological processing than by the energy industry. There are many new processes by which much energy can be saved, for example, crops can be stored wet instead of first being dried.

4. TESTS ON THE USE OF SOLAR AND WIND ENERGY

Geographical and meteorological conditions on the Great Plain are favourable for the use of solar energy; for example, in the south of the region insolation per square metre is higher than in Milan. Moreover, during the period from April to September it is equal to the energy gained from 97 kgs of oil. Unfortunately the use of solar energy has only just begun in Hungary. At present only one hospital is equipped with solar collectors for the supply of hot water, although there are plans to use it in agriculture for drying and for heating water /Figs 7, 8 and 9/.

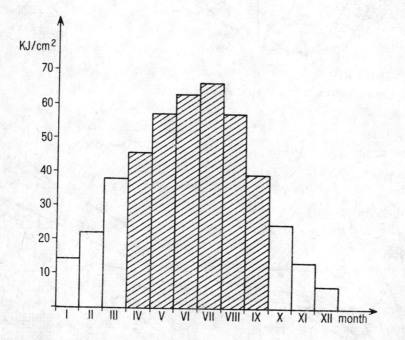

Fig. 7. Total incoming radiation per month

Economic investigations have shown that insolation on the Great Plain could produce energy equivalent to 1 million tons of oil but investment costs are 100 per cent higher than for geothermal energy. The benefit is that it can be used anywhere,

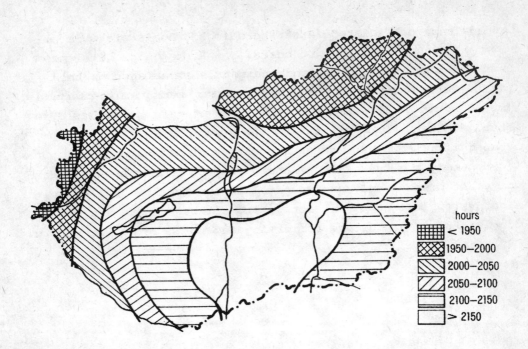

Fig. 8. Mean hours of sunshine per year

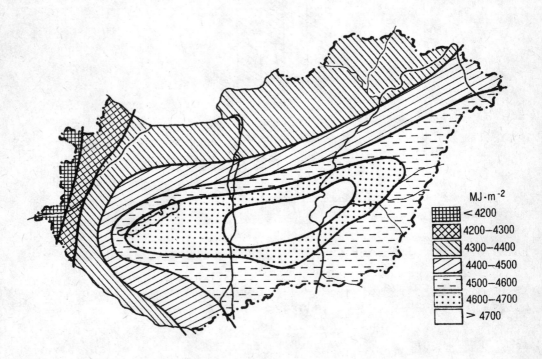

Fig. 9. Mean annual radiation

for instance on isolated farms where fossil fuels are more expensive because of transport costs. The State helps with the development of these tests and one year's experience on the Great Plain has demonstrated that a 15 sq. metre collector provides the calorific equivalent of 1 ton of oil, including the efficiency factor of the collector.

Although we have 100 years experience in the utilization of wind energy on the Great Plain, we are still only at the test stage in this field. According to our measurements of average wind speed, the diameter of wind-mill blades should be less than 15 m and the optimum height for any installation 55 m. For local demand, wind-mills may be used economically but the problems of electricity and hot water storage remain to be solved. Among the imported test wind-mills, an Australian model has provided the best parameters.

5. THE EXAMINATION OF ALTERNATIVE ENERGY COMBINATIONS

Concerning the energy supply of the Great Plain, the most economical solution is to use all local energy sources in combination with each other. The small farms of the region must be taken into special consideration when developing energy structures as settlement is scattered and energy supply is a great problem. Although propane-butane gas cylinders, which provide the farms with hot water for domestic and other uses, have proved a practical solution, the development of alternative energy sources is still important for the future supply of these settlements /Fig. 10/. A new government energy policy proposes that energy should be used in the area where it is found and many tests have been carried out combining different kinds of energy, principally geothermal energy and gas energy, which have produced many interesting models.

Sometimes three or four kinds of energy are used together. In the communal and agricultural sectors an energy benefit can be gained when geothermal energy is utilized, but at certain times of the year we have to switch to other energy types, for instance at times of peak consumption. According to the experience with this energy model the most economical method might be a hydro-carbon and biomass combination. There is no wish to return to the coal age and to old technologies and our aim is to be independent in energy sources and, at the same time, to protect our environment.

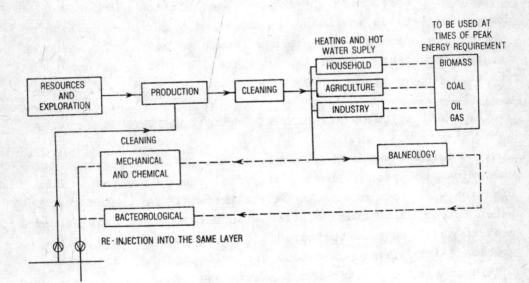

Fig. 10. Model for the utilization of geothermal energy combined with fossil fuels

ALTERNATIVE ENERGIES AND THEIR ENVIRONMENTAL IMPACT WITH SPECIAL REFERENCE TO THE SEVERN BARRAGE

A. HOARE

I. INTRODUCTION

Times readers scanning their newspapers over the toast and marmalade on Wednesday, 17th October, 1973 had much to ponder upon. President Sadat's rockets were aimed at Israel's heart and the latter's tanks were encamped on the Suez Canal. A ghost had been seen in Winchester Great Hall, the correspondence page showed agitation about a planned sewer through a stately home, Brian "I want to stay in football" Clough's departure from Derby county was on page one, while the sports writers were full of England's prospects for beating Poland and qualifying for the World Cup /they drew, and did not/. Easy, then, to miss this 2" piece tucked away on page 8:

SIX NATIONS PUT UP OIL PRICES BY 17%

> Kuwait, Wednesday morning
>
> The 6 largest oil producing countries in the Persian Gulf unilaterally raised the price of crude oil early today. They announced that, henceforth, the cost of crude oil to producing conpanies would not be a matter of negotiation but would be set by market prices which at present are rising sharply. They said that the posted price would be increasing by 17% to $3.65 / £1.40/ a barrel for the standard light Arabian crude.

But the immediate impact of this action /a 2p increase in petrol prices and threatened petrol rationing/ was soon on the front page, as were the wider reverberations in the oil prices and its overturning of the economics and politics of world energy. Some

of the claimed consequences of OPEC action may be hotly disput-
ed /did it really spark off the 1974 inflation in Britain and
other western countries?/ yet others are not. In Britain, the
increased attention on both academic and political levels to
new, "alternative" forms of energy is firmly in the second camp.

Britain's most promising alternative energies /AEs/ include
those drawn from the wind, the waves, the sun, the heat of the
earth's interior /geothermal power/ and the tides /Dept. of Energy 1981c; Hoare 1979/. Many of these are already well established overseas /as in Hungary, for example, where geothermal
fields underlie some 40% of the national territory/, or have enjoyed former glories in Britain as through the medieval tide -
and wind-mill. But all have also enjoyed an upsurge in Britain
since that fateful day in October 1973, undreamed of by their
most ardent supporters. Politically, their seal of approval was
set by the House of Commons Select Committee on Science and
Technology and its massive 500 page report /SCST 1977a/, which
advocated, successfully, more research and development funding
for Britain's AEs. Unfortunately, these "increased" levels of
funding remain paultry compared to the established giants of
the energy field, and the frantic search for a figger slice of
a very small cake has perhaps focussed attention too much on the
rival claims of waves over wind, or sun over tides, rather than
on what they have to offer in common and in partnership.

Which is? Well, first, the supply of almost all AEs are under domestic /United Kingdom/ control /some wave power could be
generated off the Irish coast and transmitted onwards to British
markets/. This is a very real political plus in an era when
OPEC has become a dirty 4-letter word. Second, electricity generations authorities /and electricity is the main energy form
for which wave, wind and tidal power would be destined/ could
obtain their "raw materials" free gratis from the environmnet,
rather than through hard bargaining with other agencies over
coal, gas and oil prices. /Of course, this does not deny that
converting these raw materials into something to work the telly
will not still be very expensive./ Third, all AEs, except geothermal power, are renewable in that their future supply is in-

dependent of past and present levels of use or non-use. In an age when all energy analysts at least agree that oil, gas, coal and nuclear power /in its uranium-derived fission state/ are finite this too is an impelling advantage. Lastly, the most relevant for the rest of this paper, all AEs seem relatively kind to the environment.

II. AEs AND THE ENVIRONMENT

This is not to say that AEs have no effects on the environment. The very fact of their being locked into the active processes of the contemporary environment means that some environmental kick-back is inevitable. It is just that AEs impacts are commonly portrayed as more "benign" that those of conventional energies that ravage the heritage of past environments. Of course, this view might be seen as pitifully naive by the Anglo-Hungarian seminar of 2082. What thought did James Watt give to the greenhouse effect and melting polar ice caps, for example, or Abraham Darby to the devastation of the white pepper moth or acid rain rotting Polish railway lines?

In fact, we can divide the environmental effects of AEs into three:

1. Generation /on-site/ effects: unlike more conventional energies /HEP is the exception/, the garnering of AE raw material and its conversion into usable energy occurs at one and the same place. Thus while coal-fired power stations can be several kilometers from their source coal-field and nuclear ones half a world away from their uranium mines, wave power, for example, is generated out at sea where the waves are captured. Some of the AE's environmental effects here will parallel those of "conventionals": the occupation and sterilisation of sizeable quantities of land, landscape intrusion of large power stations, but there will be differences too. Windmills /or "aerogenerators", to give them their modern title/ can be very noisy, but the emission problems of CO_2 up chimneys, waste heat into rivers, or radiation leaks from every nook and cranny will be a thing of the past.

2. Distribution: assuming most AEs will generate electricity, their environmental effects through the visual intrusiveness of pylons and wirescapes will represent more of what we have already. But as many favourable AE sites are in locations relatively remote from demand centres /like the north west of Scotland/ yet cheek-by-jowl with high amenity landscapes the environmental damage oer unit of electricity generated may be higher that that for conventionals.

3. Downstream effects: AEs both deliberately seek out extreme environmental conditions /high tidal ranges, strong winds and waves, and so on/ and "capture" a proportion of their force for energy generation, leading to some corresponding net loss or change elsewhere. Large ground level solar collectors thus trap solar insolation and leave nearby terrain in unaccustomed shadow. Wave devices could deprive the ecology and geomorphology of off-shore areas in their wake of their major physical control; pressure release following the abstraction of hot water or steam can increase the risk of seismic activity, aerogenerator farms produce unaccustomed turbulence downwind /Dept. of Energy 1979/.

This third case, perhaps, represents the most interesting aspect of the environmental consequences wrought be AEs. Certainly, it is the one to attract the most public attention in the case of tidal power. Here, we have an energy type that must set in train a complex of eonobonmental changes and may set in motion others too, but one that is also sufficiently demanding in its locational needs that these impacts can be debated in a meaty, real-world environment - the Severn Estuary.

III. THE SEVERN BARRAGE/S/

The Severn Barrage /SB/ is really a family of schemes, variously advocated since at least 1910 /SCST 1977a, p. 359/, for generating electricity from the power potential of the tides of the Severn Estuary. Some understanding of the mechanics of tidal power is a prerequisite for grasping the environmental consequences, and Figure 1 represents two of the suite

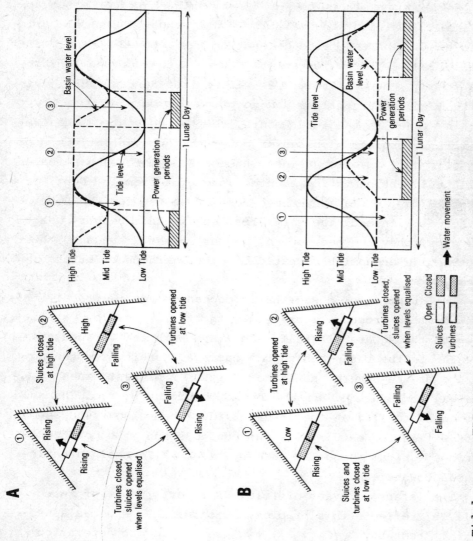

Fig. 1. A: Tidal power: EBB generation; B: Tidal power: flood generation

of generating possibilities most likely /or is it "least unlikely"?/ according to the current state of play. Note how the
electricity generation periods are controlled by the tidal cycle, and how one effect on water behind the barrage is the approximate halving of the existing tidal range. The simple principle behind ebb and flood generation was adopted in the mediaeval tide mill, of which some 170 have been recorded in England /though, surprisingly, few were on the Severn/. But just
as the 12th century miller had to grind his corn at 3 am at
certain stages in the lunar month, so the modern tidal generator will be producing pulses of power at inconvenient times of
the solar day, as often as not, unless some more sophisticated
doublebasin option is implemented /see, for example, Dept. of
Energy 1978c/. While these have been advocated for the Severn
in the past /indeed, the very first scheme this century was of
this type/ they now seem out of favour on the grounds of their
unattractive economics compared to other methods of strong
energy.

The quantity of power, be it mechanical or electrical, that
tidal devices produce, increases with tidal range /or, strict-
ly, with the square of tidal range/ and with the surface area
of water in the basin behind the barrage. Herein lies the advantage of the Severn, as it has Britain's highest tides by
some way /on average, 4 m at the mouth of the Bristol Channel
increasing to 11 m at the Severn Bridge/ but also its dilemma,
since within the estuary the two controls run in opposite directions - tidal range increase upstream while basin area increases downstream.

The latest relevant official SB report /Dept. of Energy
1981a, b/ reflects this problem, by offering 3 schemes as potential "best buys" /Fig. 2/: two are simple ebb generation
schemes in "high" and "low" tidal range areas, and the third
offers an additional, later stage, flood option. Of the two ebb
schemes the downstream one is the more costly to build, but
generates more power, so the costs per unit of power are not
that much different between the two.

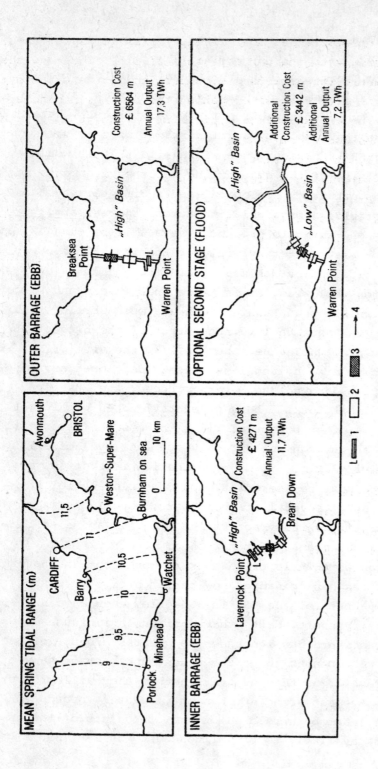

Fig. 2. Three possible Severn Barrage schemes
1 = locks; 2 = sluices; 3 = turbines; 4 = water movement

IV. ENVIRONMENTAL IMPACTS

In physical terms, an estuary is a mixing ground where
fresh and sea water meet. In human terms estuaries have been
barriers across which interaction has been difficult, hazardous
and costly. The inevitability and importance of the "downstream"
effects of any SB is obvious once we realise that it would both
restrict the mixing of the contrasting water environments so
crucial for the estuary's ecological and sedimentary systems,
and probably provide a physical link across the estuary.

But it is one thing to prophecy there will be changes, and
quite another to say what they will be. Looking at the experience of other tidal power schemes is of little help as only two
are in operation worldwide, at La Rance in Brittany and Kislaya
Guba in northern European Russia. Both are much smaller than
projected SBs /La Rance ha 1/35 the output of the biggest SB
scheme in Figure 2, while the other is 1/50 the size of La
Rance!!/ and both are in much less densely developed environments than applies around the Severn /indeed, the Russian
scheme is in almost totally barren country/. When put into a
wider context of other potential tidal schemes the Severn still
stands out as an environment with a very high level of existing
estuarine activity /Fig. 3/. One implication is that "downstream" impacts must be looked at much more closely for the
Severn case than at several of the others, both in terms of the
effects on existing estuary activities /Fig. 4/ and also the
potential that may open up for new ones.

So with no worthwhile precedents to work from the Severn
Barrage Committee has sponsored new research to try to shed
light on this aspect of the SB. To a degree, they have succeeded but their report admits that environmental issues remain   an area where our ignorance is greatest /Dept. of Energy 1981a, p. 43/. Doubts about the extent and cost of many of
the impacts remain, as they do over whether they will produce
a better or worse estuarine environment. However, broad consensus has at least been reached on the components of the estuary's geography likely to be influenced by the SB, and Fig-

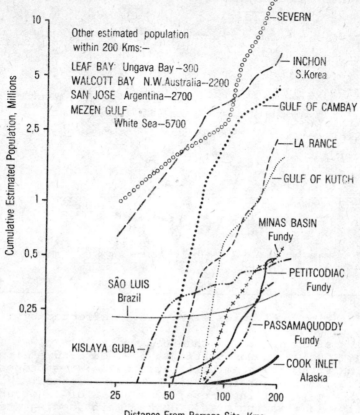

Fig. 3. Population effects of various tidal barrage schemes

ure 5 attempts to represent them, and some of the ways they
are bound together. Clearly, effects in any one component could
set up much under ripples and crosscurrents. Space prevents a
detailed assessment of each and every element in Figure 5 /and
anyway this is available in print already - Dept. of Energy
1981a, b; Shaw 1977; SCST 1977b/. Rather, some attempt will be
made to identify those Severnside groups who might benefit from
the SB, those who might resent its presence, and those for whom
it seems a mixed blessing.

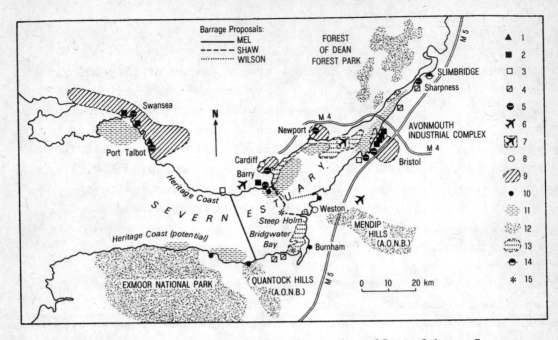

Fig. 4. Existing activities likely to be affected by a Severn
Barrage
1 = steelworks; 2 = chemical works; 3 = power stations;
4 = nuclear power stations; 5 = docks; 6 = airports
/existing/; 7 = airports /proposed/; 8 = proposed M.I.
D.A.; 9 = major industrial areas; 10 = holiday camps;
11 = main sailing areas; 12 = areas of landscape quality; 13 = wading birds, ducks, main feeding areas; 14 =
wildfowl trust; 15 = nature reserves

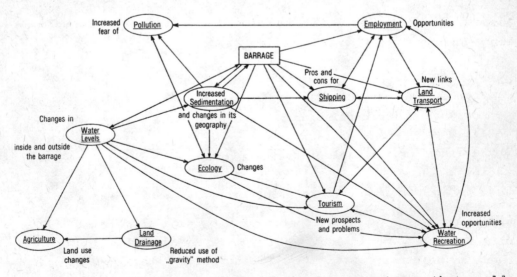

Fig. 5. Model of the geography of the Severn estuary that would
be affected by a barrage scheme

1. The Gainers

a/ The workers

Building a SB will bring work over a period of 15 years or
so. The latest estimate of 21,000 jobs so generated must have
some effect on the local economy and will be especially welcome in
South Wales where unemployment stands at some 3 percentage
points over the Great Britain average of 12.6% /in June 1982/.
Not all these jobs will last for 15 years of course, nor will
they all be for locals. Much of the employment for marine engineering consultants, the yards constructing caissons, turbines and sluice systems, and the quarries supplying embankment
fill will probably be outside Severnside and outside Britain.
Construction companies may bring in their own men for "on site"
work, too, but at least there should be some work for local residents, albeit towards the lower end of the income spectrum,
and further multiplier benefits of local and non-locals working
on site. After the Grand Opening a small /500?/ permanent on-
site staff will be all that can be hoped for directly and it
would be a supreme optimist who would predict a bevy of alumin-
ium companies /just about the only ones closely tied to electricity sources these days/ to boost it much higher. A Severnside international airport behind the Barrage would create much
more work, but this is a pretty long shot at present, and its
association with the SB is something of a marriage of conven-
ience on the part of interested parties.

b/ The crossers

All the barrage schemes in serious contention see it as
providing a new physical link point over the estuary. If so, it
seems a matter of false economics not to top it with a major
road /and railway?/ as well, especially as the need for a broth-
er for the Severn Bridge of 1966, yet already showing its age,
is a live issue in the region. Surprisingly, though, the additional cost of a motorway on top of a barrage broadly equates
with a brand new bridge alone /Dept. of Energy 1981a/, and
there is no guarantee that a crossing point determined on ener-

gy economics would also be optimal on transport economics. A
lower-grade road, such as runs on the embankments of the Dutch
Delta scheme, may prove an acceptable compromise. But a new
crossing of any sort could, depending on its capacity and location, release pent-up trans-estuary business potential for enterprises on the two shores, as did the earlier Bridge /Cleary
and Thomas 1973/, and could also bring another influx of distribution and warehousing units to the region. Neither is likely
to be a major job-spinner, though: the first may merely rob
Cardiff's Peter to pay Bristol's Paul, while the second employ
few workers for the square footage floorspace they occupy.

c/ The recreationists

High "turbidity" /= muckiness/ of its waters and the high
tidal range conspire to limit the range of water-based recreation in the estuary at present. A barrage, by reducing both,
could stimulate a great increase in the variety and quantity of
such activity on an estuary with such excellent motorway connections. The spreading strangulation of harbours on the English Channel as the yachting fraternity goes west is a pointer
in this direction, as is Bristol's plan for using its redundant
city docks partly for yachting marinas and moorings, although
in conception this is an independent venture to a Severn Barrage.

2. The Losers

a/ The fishermen

The estuary supplies catches of eels and a range of other
fish, but it is the salmon that have caught the barrage lime-
light. To the extent that figures of this sort can be believed
/!/ some 35% of England and Wales' salmon rod catch and 20% of
the commercial catch is from the Severn and its near tributar-
ies /the Wye and Usk/. How will those deeply embedded automatic
pilots that bring the salmon unfailingly to their home rivers
to spawn cope with a barrage /albeit one with fish ladders/
and the disorientating calm of the basin beyond, and will the

young not turn to fish fingers in the generator turbines? Many of these fears may be groundless, but neither is there sufficient hard research evidence yet to hand to win over an understandably suspicious fishing fraternity. And whatever else happens, the age-old "putcher" method of salmon fishing, which depends for its success on the same turbidity and tidal range that deters recreationists, would have to go.

b/ The port authorities

The Severn Estuary handles roughly 5% of Britain's shipping traffic. On the wrong side of Britain for the main expanding trade routes to the EEC and with only one modern port at Bristol's Royal Portbury dock /and that lying idle so costing the city's ratepayers some £25 each a year to meet its debt!/, the portents are scarcely rosy, even without a barrage to contend with. The SB brings with it the additional threat of delays and charges at barrage locks, increased estuarine sedimentation and the disruptive chaos of a long barrage construction period, all of which could be enough to persuade footloose shipping companies to take their custom to calmer havens.

c/ The conservationists

Several threats have arisen here. First, decreased estuary currents /the result of the fall in tidal range/ will increase sedimentation in general, and in particular reduce the chances of flushing out of the Estuary waste from domestic and industrial sources currently fed in at an estimated 240 m gallons per day /often in untreated form/. Dangerously high heavy metal levels have been noticed already in shellfish near Avonmouth's industrial complex, and this sort of pollution threat will only increase. Second, the most favoured barrage line /from Lavernock Point to Brean Down - Figure 2/ abuts botanically important sites at either end and passes within a whisker of the Steep Holm nature reserve. Third, a number of sites of particular ecological, geological and geomorphological interest will be threatened by the raised water levels in the basin. While not in the Abu Simbel class, some are nevertheless sufficiently important to be designated as SSSIs. Finally, changes in water levels both up and down-barrage could bring about a lowering of the water table in the fringing lowlands. This would have serious implications for the natural history of the Somerset Levels and hammer another nail in the coffin of Britain's vanishing wetlands.

3. The Don't Knows

a/ The farmers

First, the good news. This same lowering of the ground water table will give the opportunity to improve the income from estuarine farms, turning pasture land into arable and one-crop arable into two-crop. Against this, the drainage improvements consequent upon the raising of low water levels behind an ebb barrage could cost £14-19 m /Dept.of Energy 1981a/, while strengthening the estuary's embankments to protect against increases in average water levels may cost another £10 m. Someone will have to pay, and so far no -one has told the farmers who that someone would be.

b/ The industrialists

Some regional employers may enjoy a windfall from barrage business, and the improved accessibility it supplies on completion. Others may be hit in the pocket if barrage jobs push up wages on Severnside, or if costly adjustments are necessary to the effluent disposal systems of factories dumping waste into the estuary.

c/ The bird watchers

Those with a professional and amateur interest in the estuary's bird life have kept a keen watching brief on barrage proposals. By affecting water levels and sedimentation regimes the SB must affect ecology, so the estuary's rich bird population will find changes in both the location of their feeding groups and the type of feed available. As with the effects on ecology, the outcome for bird life will be one of swings and roundabouts, and individual reactions will turn on issues like one's feelings for waders and shelduck over reed bed warblers.

d/ The tourist entrepreneurs

A barrage in its own right can be an attraction for visitors, while heightened recreational opportunities could also add to the tourist industry's coffers. Set against this, though, the effects on the psyche of traditional seasiders on finding the mecca of their annual pilgrimage is now a strand on an inland lake.

V. THE ENVIRONMENT IN PERSPECTIVE

As should have become clear, it is far easier to ask questions about the environmental impact of a SB than to provide answers. We really know little about how the estuary operates as of now, so how can we know how a barrage will change it? /The Severn Barrage Committee, in admitting this as the weak link in the project assessment to date feels it worthwhile investing public funds further on additional research./ Furthermore, such impacts as it will have are dependent upon the geography of the barrage location and the type of barrage it will be /despite the same Committee's short list of three there are still plenty of other sites in with a shout/. And while some of the impacts must follow from a barrage, as night follows day, others are far from inevitable, but depend on subsequent decisions being taken by the likes of shipping companies, planning committees, water boards, aviation authorities, and thousands of holiday makers.

To keep the debit side of the balance sheet in its place, too, we should remember that many of the "barrage problems" are already with us - pollution in the estuary and its beaches /Edington and Edington 1977/, farming v. conservation battles on the Levels, profitability crises in the ports, declining salmon catches due to "unfair" fishing methods, and the disappearance of the traditional "bucket and braces" holiday market at the resorts. By highlighting these endemic worries the bar-

rage may do a service by hastening a search for successful
solutions.

Down on the Severn it is easy to think that the barrage is
all about the local environment - it isn't, its mostly about
energy as the former Labour government's terms of reference to
the Severn Barrage Committee made clear. All the regional environmental benefits under the sun will be as naught if it looks
like being a bad buy in the national energy market, and as yet
the scheme has not passed this crucial "economic feasibility"
hurdle /Hoare 1979/. Any substantial acceleration in the nuclear programme, or reduction in forecasts of growth in national
energy demand, improvements in energy conversion efficiencies
or in energy conservation, or higher official discount rates
for capital projects would do its chances no good at all, even
without a clear advance in the cost effectiveness of other AEs.

Certainly, the SB will open up many interesting prospects
for estuarine environmental management, just as it does for the
nation's energy balance. Perhaps too interesting, though, if as
one commentator has recently suggested /Williams 1981, p. 14/:

> political decision-making /is/ the art more commonly
> of the convenient than of the possible /because
> "possible" implies at least a degree of adventure/...

But, just suppose a Severn Barrage does somehow become a reality. Its vast and complex ball of intertwined impacts pulls into the debate a correspondingly wide range of public and private bodies whose interests will be directly affected, plus a
maze of inappropriate and conflicting administrative boundaries,
whose status is often unclear, unknown, or simply ignored.
Since so many of these are delimited using tidal levels their
sensitivity to a barrage decision is obvious /Gibson 1980/.
Perhaps all these complications can be handled by ad hoc committees and inter-Departmental circulars. But perhaps instead
the whole problem will lead to the setting up of a new over-
arching administrative body to oversee the post barrage estuary
/SCST 1977a, p. 376; Hoare and Haggett 1979/. Depending on the
powers this in its turn receives a whole new chain of unimag-
inedconsequences may be set in motion. Precedents from the ad-

administrative changes following the Dutch reclamation schemes
and, rather earlier, the Tennessee Valley Authority come readily to mind, the latter in particular being created on a very
narrow pretext, but so extending its interests and influence
that within 5 years of its effective inception in 1933 Lewis
Mumford could write:

> ... the river valley has the advantage of bringing into
> a common regional frame a diversified unit: this is es-
> sential to an effective civic and social life...
> Regional unity is partly an emergent: a cultural pro-
> duct: a result of co-operative political and economic
> action... In the Tennessee Valley and kindred areas a
> basis can be laid, not merely for more efficient in-
> dustrial order, but for a new social order and a new
> type of urban environmnet, provided the requisite polit-
> ical courage and social imagination are collectively
> brought to bear.

/quoted in Friedmann and Weaver 1979, p. 9/.
Perhaps in 30 years time someone will have written something
like that about the Severn Estuary Authority.

REFERENCES

CLEARY, E.J.--THOMAS, R.E. /1973/: The economic consequences of
    the Severn Bridge and its associated motorways. - Bath
    University Press, Bath.
Department of Energy /1978/: Severn barrage seminar. - Energy
    Paper, 27, London, H.M.S.O.
Department of Energy /1979/: Environmental impact of renewable
    energy sources. /Review paper prepared for the Commission
    on Energy and the Environment by the Energy Technology
    Support Unit/. - Department of Energy, London.
Department of Energy /1981a/: Tidal power from the Severn Es-
    tuary: Volume 1. /Report of the Severn Barrage Committee/.
    - Energy Paper, 46, London, H.M.S.O.
Department of Energy /1981b/: Tidal power from the Severn Es-
    tuary: Volume 2. /Report on the Severn Barrage Committee/.
    - Energy Paper, 46, London, H.M.S.O.

Department of Energy /1981c/: Renewable energy sources in the
      United Kingdom. /Paper for the U.N. Conference on New and
      Renewable Sources of Energy, Kenya/. - Department of Ener-
      gy, London.

EDINGTON, J.M.--EDINGTON, M.A. /1977/: Ecology and environment-
      al planning. - Chapman and Hall, London.

FRIEDMANN, J.--WEAVER, C. /1979/: Territory and function: the
      evolution of regional planning. - Edward Arnold, London.

GIBSON, J. /1980/: Coastal zone management law: a case study of
      the Severn Estuary and the Bristol Channel. - Jnl. of Plan-
      ning and Environmental Law, 153-165.

HOARE, A.G. /1979/: Alternative energies: alternative geogra-
      phies? - Progress in Human Geography, 3, 4, 506-537.

HOARE, A.G.--HAGGETT, P. /1979/: Tidal power and estuary manage-
      ment. Being pp. 14-30. In: Severn, R.T., Dineley, D. and
      Hawker, L.E. /Eds./, Tidal power and Estuary management.
      - Scientechnica, Bristol.

SHAW, T.L. /ed./ /1977/: An environmental appraisal of the Se-
      vern Barrage. - Dept. of Civil Engineering, University of
      Bristol, Bristol.

SCST /Select Committee on Science and Technology/ /1977a/: The
      development of alternative sources of energy for the United
      Kingdom volume 2 /minutes of evidence taken before the
      energy resources sub-committee in session 1975-76/. London,
      H.M.S.O.

SCST /Select Committee on Science and Technology/ /1977b/: The
      importance of tidal power in the Severn Estuary. London,
      H.M.S.O.

WILLIAMS, R. /1981/: Britain's energy institutions. Being pp.
      13-26. In: Facing the energy future /Proceedings of an
      RIPA conference/. - Royal Institute of Public Affairs,
      London.